Karl Wilhelm Ludwig Pappe

A Description of South African Forest Trees

Karl Wilhelm Ludwig Pappe

A Description of South African Forest Trees

ISBN/EAN: 9783744646062

Printed in Europe, USA, Canada, Australia, Japan

Cover: Foto ©Andreas Hilbeck / pixelio.de

More available books at **www.hansebooks.com**

SILVA CAPENSIS

OR

A DESCRIPTION

OF

SOUTH AFRICAN FOREST TREES

AND

ARBORESCENT SHRUBS,

USED FOR

TECHNICAL AND ECONOMICAL PURPOSES.

BY

L. PAPPE, M.D.,

COLONIAL BOTANIST AND PROFESSOR OF BOTANY IN THE SOUTH
AFRICAN COLLEGE.

Second, revised, and enlarged Edition.

Trado, quae potui.

LONDON: WARD & CO., 27, PATERNOSTER ROW;
CAPE TOWN: W. BRITTAIN.
1862.

TO HIS EXCELLENCY

PHILIP EDMOND WODEHOUSE, ESQ.,

GOVERNOR AND COMMANDER-IN-CHIEF OF THE COLONY OF THE
CAPE OF GOOD HOPE,

AND

HER MAJESTY'S HIGH COMMISSIONER.

THIS CONTRIBUTION TO SOUTH AFRICAN ECONOMIC BOTANY

IS

WITH HIS EXCELLENCY'S PERMISSION

MOST RESPECTFULLY INSCRIBED

BY

THE AUTHOR.

PREFACE.

The first edition of the Silva Capensis appeared in 1854, as a Commentary to a Collection of South-African indigenous woods, transmitted by the Government to the Paris Universal Exhibition of 1855. Since then, I obtained fresh valuable information on the subject, and made many additions.

Anticipating that the Cape of Good Hope would, like other British Colonies, be represented at the great London International Show of 1862, and wishing to contribute my share towards it, I at an early date repaired to the Eastern Province and British Caffraria, with the intention, of making myself personally acquainted with the many natural resources which these fine and fertile regions afford.

Among them the extensive and hitherto but little appreciated primeval forests, with which that part of the country abounds, attracted my particular attention. I therefore visited many of them, and by procuring specimens from each, succeeded in bringing together the most complete collection of South African woods ever yet made.

This collection, the specimens of which are handsomely prepared and scientifically named, comprises a series of about seventy species, and many of these are serviceable either as timber, or as yielding suitable material for ornamental and common furniture, veneering, the construction of bridges and mills, railway purposes, turnery, wagon making, the manufacture of rural utensils, tools, musical instruments, carving, wood-engraving &c.

The Cape Colony having unhappily remained unrepresented at the present occasion, this collection will now, by His Excellency the Governor's decision, be presented to the Museum of Economic Botany of the Royal Gardens of Kew, and its description forms the contents of the following pages.

In several passages of this little work, the reader will meet with observations on the wanton usage, annually exercised in the Colony, of setting fire to the mountains and bushes,—an injurious practice, which in one sweep destroys large quantities of valuable timber and useful woods. The most awful consequences must necessarily attend such outrageous conduct, it being universally admitted, that forests and woods attract and increase moisture, produce rain, and give rise to springs and running streams, while tracts deprived of vegetation become heated, barren, and dry.

I beg, in conclusion, to tender my most sincere thanks to the numerous Eastern Province friends, who by advice, information, and actual aid, promoted my aim, and enabled me to accomplish the task I had proposed to myself.

L. P.

Cape Town, June 12th, 1862.

AN ENUMERATION

OF

SOUTH AFRICAN TREES

AND

ARBORESCENT SHRUBS.

CAPPARIDEÆ. Juss.

1. *Niebuhria Triphylla.* *Wend.* (*Witbosch-hout.*)—*Branches* divaricating; *twigs* angular. *Leaves* stalked, ternate, leathery; *leaflets* oblong, entire, mucronate, smooth, pale on the lower surface; *stipules* very small, acute. *Flowers* peduncled, terminal, or axillary. *Corolla* none. *Calyx* funnel-shaped, 4 parted, persistent. *Receptacle* cylindrical short. *Stamens* numerous, affixed to the receptacle; *anthers* ovate, 2 locular. *Style* elongated: *stigma* capitate. *Berry* ovate.

Height 20 feet; diameter from 9 to 15 inches. *Bark* greenish-white, almost smooth. *Wood* white, light, tough, resembling *whitebeech.* Well adapted for the inner lining of furniture, follies, agricultural implements, &c.

This handsome tree grows in the Addow Bush, and in the forests of the Uitenhage and Albany districts, Caffraria and Natal. Fl. October.

2. *Capparis Albitrunca.* *Burch.* (*Witgatboom.*)—*Branches* unarmed, spreading. *Leaves* coriaceous, lineari-elliptic, blunt, attenuate at base, entire, smooth; glaucous below. *Flowers* small, racemose. *Racemes* few-flowered, axillary, shorter than the leaves. *Calyx* 4 cleft; *petals* 4; *stamens* numerous. *Fruit,* a berry.

The trunk of this tree appears from a distance as white-washed, and hence its vernacular name. Height of stem from 10 to 12 feet: diameter from 9 to 10 inches. *Bark,* thick, smooth, pure white. *Wood* white, tough, used for yokes, and other œconomical purposes.

Grows in the woods near Sunday River and other parts of the Eastern Province. Fl. October—November.

B

BIXACEÆ. ENDL.

3. *Phoberos Mundtii*. *W. Arnott*. (Eriudaphus Nees. ab. E.) (*Klipdoorn*, *Michell-wood*)—*Branches* spreading, *twigs* compressed; the young shoots from the root, thorny. *Leaves* coriaceous, rhomboid-elliptical, acute, bluntly toothed, veined, glossy above ; *racemes* axillary 4-6 flowered. *Perianth* 10 cleft ; its bottom clothed with dense, cushion-like hairs. *Flowers* small, white ; *stamens* in many rows, numerous; *anthers* beaked ; *style* thick. *Fruit* baccate, roundish.

Height between 20 and 30 feet, diameter 3 feet and more. Bark thin, grey. Wood hard, close, and highly useful for builders, and especially for wagonmakers

Found in the aboriginal forests of the Tzitsikamma, Knysna, and also, but sparingly, on the east side of Table Mountain, in Kirstenbosch. Fl. April—May.

4. *Phoberos Echlonii*. *W. Arnott*. (Eriudaphus Nees. ab. E.) (*Redpear*, *Roodpeer*.)—*Branches* divaricating ; *twigs* compressed. *Leaves* broad, alternate, leathery, rhomboid-lanceolate, acute, indistinctly dentate, smooth, glaucous. *Racemes* axillary, simple, shorter than the leaves. *Perianth*, flowers and fruit, as in the former species.

A forest tree 30 to 35 feet high and 2 to 3 feet in diameter. *Bark* black, chinky. *Wood* hard, heavy, close ; takes a fine polish, and answers well for all kinds of furniture. In the Colony it is mostly used by wheel-wrights for axles, fellies, and spokes, and would suit well in the construction of mills.

This tree is common in the primeval thickets of the Victoria district, and flowers in May.

5. *Phoberos Zeyheri*. *W. Arnott*. (*Wolfs-thorn*; *Hoenderspoor*)—*Branches* ash-coloured, very spiny, *leaves* alternate, short-stalked, leathery, rhomboid-ovate or roundish-ovate, blunt, entire and slightly wavy, netted-veined, smooth, dull green. *Flowers* racemose, small ; *racemes* terminal and axillary 8-12 flowered, clothed with dense short hairs. *Berry* 4 seeded small, crowned with the persistent style.

A tree 15-25 feet high and from 1 to 2 broad. Spines very strong, horizontally diverging, and from one to four inches long. *Bark* thin, grey, smooth. *Wood* hard and heavy, like that of the preceding species, and useful for the same purposes

Grows in the forests of the Van Staden's River and Olifantshoek. Flor. Jun—Jul.

6. *Dovyalis rhamnoides*. *Harv*. (Flacourtia rhamnoides. Burch.)—*Branches* white, armed with patent, axillary, horizontal spines. *Leaves* on short stalks, alternate membranaceous, ovate, entire or slightly dentate, veined, triplinerved at base, smooth. *Flowers* dioecious, axillary; male ones fascicled, female ones solitary. *Perianth* 5 fid, tomentose. *Corolla* none; *stamens* 18-20; *styles* 2; *stigmas* truncate. *Fruit* an ovate berry.

This tree attains a height of from 20 to 30, and a breadth of 2 or 3 feet. *Stem* knotty; *bark* greyish-white. *Wood* citron-yellow, close, hard, and chiefly used for yokes, various wagonwork, and rural implements.

The fruit *Zuurbesje, Cranberries,* which has a sourish taste, is eaten by the natives, and brandy and vinegar have been distilled from it.

Common in the woods of the Krakakamma, Tzitsikamma, Olifantshoek, and Van Stadens Mountains. Fl. May—June.

7. *Kiggelaria Africana. Lin. (Spekhout; Pork-wood.)*— *Branches* erect; *twigs* purplish, more or less downy. *Leaves* stalked, lanceolate, unequally serrate, smooth above, downy beneath. *Flowers* white, dioecious; male ones small, racemose, nodding; female ones much larger, solitary, stalked, erect, axillary. *Calyx* 5 cleft; *stamens* 10-12; *anthers* hairy, perforated at top; *petals* 5, glanduliferous at base; *styles* 5. *Capsule* globose, scabrid, one-celled, many-seeded.

Height of trunk 20 to 25 feet; diameter one foot and a half to two feet. *Wood* soft, spongy. Used occasionally for spars, rafters, rural implements, and fuel.

Common about Cape Town, Wynberg, &c. Fl. November.

TILIACEÆ. JUSS.

8. *Grewia Occidentalis. Lin. (Kruysbesje.)*—Shrubby. *Leaves* alternate, ovate, blunt, smooth; *peduncles* solitary, one-flowered. *Calyx* 5 cleft deciduous, coloured within; *stamens* numerous; *anthers* roundish; *style* 1; *stigma* 4 lobed. *Petals* 5, bright-purple. *Drupe* 4 lobed, fleshy; *lobes* 2 locular, 2 seeded.

This shrub climbs 10 to 12 feet high, but is little more than 3 inches in diameter. *Stem* and *branches* very like those of the small leaved Elm. *Bark* smooth. The wood is very tough and bends extremely well. Being of fine grain, the larger pieces answer for turner's work. From this species, and from the *Grewia Obtusifolia.* Willd. & G *flava* DC., the Bushmen make their bows. The fruit are eaten by them and other savages.

Common near Cape Town and in many parts of the Colony. Fl. January—February.

OLACINEÆ. MIRB.

9) *Apodytes dimediata. E. Meyer—Branches* grey, spreading, *twigs* angular; furrowed. *Leaves* alternate, stalked, ovate or

ovate-oblong, entire, revolute, blunt, penninerved, leathery, wedge-shaped, and often oblique at base, smooth, shining on the upper, and pale on the lower surface. *Flowers* small, white, panicled ; *panicles* terminal, much branched ; *peduncles* and *pedicels* strigose ; *bracts* minute. *Calyx* 4-5 toothed, free. *Petals* 4-5, smooth. *Stamens* 5 ; *style* 1. *Fruit* one celled, kidney-shaped, compressed, unequal-sided, with a lateral fleshy appendage. Linn. Transact. vol. 18. tab. 41.

A tree 30-50 feet high and from one to two or more, in diameter. *Bark* thick, rough, chinky, greyish-white. *Wood* light, yellowish, looks well when polished, and is used for common furniture, and agricultural implements.

Common in the forests of George, Uitenhage, Albany, British Caffraria, and Natal. Fl. Decemb. and Januar.

SAPINDACEÆ. Juss.

10. *Schmidelia decipiens. W. Arnott.* (Rhus spicata. Thbg) —*Branches* smooth, spreading; *branchlets* white, and as well as the leaf and flower-stalks, downy. *Leaves* 3 foliate, alternate, leathery ; *Leaflets* sessile, obovate or lanceolate-oblong, narrowed at base, grossly and bluntly toothed upon the upper half, revolute at the margins, smooth, pale below, bearded in the axils of the veins. *Flowers* spiked, minute, subracemose, pedicellate. *Spikes* as long or somewhat shorter than the leaves ; *flowerstalks* axillary, slender. *Calyx* 4 cleft, concave ; *Petals* 4 white, *filaments* hairy, *style* 2 fid. *Fruit* globose, of the size of a pepper-corn.

A small tree 10 to 15 feet high ; 6 to 10 inches broad. *Bark* thin, white, knotty. *Wood* hard, fine grained, useful for turners and fancy cabinet-makers, and looks very handsome when polished.

Not uncommon in the woods of the Knysna, Uitenhage, Albany, and Caffraria. Fl. Jan.

11. *Sapindus Pappea. Sond.* (*wilde Pruime; wild Plumtree.*) *Branches* and *twigs* spreading. *Leaves* alternate, ovate, or oblong, unequal at base, smooth, blunt, coriaceous, veiny, slightly rolled back at the margin. *Calyx* 5 fid ; *petals* 4-6, bearded inside. *Stamens* 8-10 ; *filaments* shaggy ; *style* 1 ; *stigma* subtrifid. *Flowers* small, racemose with separate sexes by abortion. *Fruit* 3 capsular, drupaceous, fleshy, globose, downy. Hook Jcon. t 325.

A moderate sized tree or shrub Height 15 to 20, diameter 1, to 1½ feet. *Bark*, greyish-white, cracked. *Wood* handsome, hard and tough, and used for furniture, yokes, poles, ploughs, etc. *Fruit* red, of a pleasant taste ; called *wild plum* by the Colonists, and *t' Kaamsbesje* by the Natives. It furnishes a vinous beverage and very good vinegar, and its kernel contains an oil, which, though eatable, is slightly purgative.

The presence of this tree is considered as a criterion of excellent pasturage for wool-bearing flocks.

Abundant in many parts of the eastern districts of the Colony, and in Caffraria. Fl. November.

12. *Hippobromus alata.* *Echl.* & *Zeyh —Branches* grey, smooth, spreading; *twigs* downy. *Leaves* stalked, pari-pinnate 3—5 yoked; *rachis* of the stalk winged, tomentose. *Leaflets* sub-opposite or alternate, sessile, obovate, blunt, reflexed at the margin, unequal-sided and wedge-shaped at base, penninerved, more or less bluntly notched in the upper half, leathery, smooth shining above, pale below. *Flowers* dioico polygamous, panicled. *Panicles* axillary, short-stalked; *stalks* tomentose, much shorter than the leaves. *Calyx* 5 partite, unequal, persistent, silky. *Petals* 5 obovate, smooth. *Stamens* in male flower 8, exserted; *anthers* oblong. *Ovary* in female flower 3 celled; *style* short, thick; *stigma* pin headed, 3 fid. *Drupe* small, fleshy 1—3 seeded.

A middle-sized, resin yielding tree, 15—20 feet high, and from 1, to 1½ wide. *Bark* pale, yellowish-green. *Wood* close and useful for planking, wagon-work, and rural purposes; called *Paardepis* by the Dutch colonists, on account of its peculiar smell.

Common in the forests of the Eastern Province and Caffraria. Fl. Jul.—Aug.

PTÆROXYLEÆ. SOND.

13. *Ptæroxylon Utile. Echl. & Z.* (*Nieshout; Sneezewood.*) —*Stem* smooth; *branches* nodous. *Leaves* impari-pinnate; *leaflets* in 6-7 pairs, coriaceous, entire, irregularly sided. *Flowers* diœcious, axillary, racemose, placed at the extremities of the branches, and between the leaves. *Calyx* 4 parted, *petals* 4, *stamens* 4; *filaments* smooth. *Styles* 2, *stigmas* capitate. *Capsule* 2 celled, 2 seeded, compressed; *seeds* winged, Harv. Thes. Cap. t. 17.

A tree, from 20 to 30 feet in height, and 2-4 feet in diameter. The leaves have some resemblance to those of *Acer pseudoplatanus.* The wood is handsome, takes a fine polish, is strong, durable, and somewhat like Mahogany. It is used for various kinds of furniture and agricultural utensils Being little affected by moisture, it serves as a desirable material in the construction of bridges and mills. From the fact of its producing violent sneezing when sawn or otherwise worked at, it has received the name of *Sneeze-wood.* It is also said to ignite readily, even in its green state, and is the *Omtata* of the Kafirs.

Common in the forests of the eastern districts. Fl. October.

MELIACEÆ. JUSS.

14. *Trichilia Eckebergia. E. Meyer.—Branches* greyish-white; *branchlets* knotty. *Leaves* unequally-pinnate, 3—5 yoked, membranous, crowded at the top of the branches; *leafstalks* flat;

leaflets opposite, except the terminal, stalked-one, nearly sessile, ovate or ovate-oblong, penninerved, acute, oblique at base, perfectly smooth. *Flowers* paniculate, *panicles* slender, axillary; *pedicels* compressed; branches of the panicles loosely cymose. *Calyx* bell-shaped, 4—5 cleft; *sepals* sharp-pointed; *petals* oblong. *Stamens* united into an undivided, cylindrical anther-bearing tube. *Anthers* 8—10. *Style* smooth; *stigma* thick, obscurely lobed. *Fruit*, a capsule, unknown. (*Sonder.*)

A tree 15—25 feet high, 1 or 2 wide. *Bark* reddish-brown. *Wood* soft, white and of little value.

Grows in the forests of the Tzitsikamma, Olifantshoek, and Natal. Fl. November.

15. *Ekebergia Capensis. Sparrm.* (*Essenhout; Cape Ash.*) —*Branches* alternate, scarred, smooth, spreading. *Leaves* placed at the tops of the branches, aggregate, imparipinnate; *leaflets* in 4-5 pairs, oblong, entire, glabrous, pointed at both ends, unequally sided. *Calyx* 4 fid; *petals* 4; *stamens* very short, with *anthers* sessile, within the tube; *stigma* capitate. *Flowers* axillary and terminal, paniculate. *Berry* round, 5 seeded.

A lofty tree, 20 to 30 feet, or more, in height; 2 to 3 feet in diameter. *Bark* grey. *Wood* white, tough, and close. Useful timber for beams, planks, spars, carriage-poles, etc., and employed for all kinds of wagon work, and in the manufacture of many implements, tools, &c.

Found in the primeval forests of the George, Uitenhage, Albany, and Victoria districts. Fl. August.

DIOSMEÆ. R. Br.

16. *Calodendron Capense. Thbg.* (*Wilde Kastanie; wild Chesnut.*)—*Branches* and *twigs* divaricating. *Leaves* stalked, opposite, simple, entire, ovate, obtuse, ribbed, crossed at right angles. *Flowers* terminal on short, shaggy peduncles; paniculated. *Calyx* deciduous, 5 cleft; *petals* glanduliferous. *Stamens* 10; *style* 1. *Capsule* 5 angled, 5 celled; *cells* 2 seeded.

Height 20 to 30 feet, diameter 2 to 3 feet. *Bark* smooth, whitish-grey. *Wood* soft, white, and little used, except for rural utensils, yokes, poles. &c. Its inflorescence somewhat resembles that of the Horse-Chesnut (*Aesculus Hippocastanum*), and hence its colonial name. Like most plants belonging to the family of the *Diosmeæ*, the flowers diffuse a very strong, but pleasant odour

This fine tree grows in the forests of the Swellendam, George, Uitenhage, and Albany districts, Brit. Caffraria, &c. Fl. December—January.

AURANTIACEÆ. CORR.

17. *Myaris inæqualis. Presl. Branches & branchlets* round, greyish-white. *Leaves* impari-pinnate; *leaflets* stalked, alternate,

ovate, unequal-sided, irregularly notched, sprinkled with minute, transparent dots, smooth; *peduncles* and young twigs somewhat downy. *Flowers* paniculate, few-flowered. *Panicles* axillary. *Calyx* minute, 4 cleft. *Petals* 4 concave, white. *Stamens* 8 equally as long as the petals. *Style* deciduous, short. *Berry* fleshy, as large as a pea.

A shrub or small tree 10-20 feet high, and from 6-8 inches broad. *Bark* thin, smooth. *Wood* white, close-grained, heavy, but hitherto little used.

In the forests of George, Uitenhage, Albany and British Caffraria. Fl. Octob.

XANTHOXYLEÆ. Nees ab. E.

18. *Xanthoxylon Capense. Harv.* (Fagara Thbg.) (*Knobwood, Knopjes-doorn*; *Paardepram.*)—*Branches* compressed, flexuose, wrinkled, prickly. *Prickles* flat, sharp pointed. *Leaves* alternate, impari-pinnate; *leaflets* oblique, ovate, blunt, sessile, smooth, slightly crenate, sprinkled with glandular dots. *Calyx* 4 cleft; *petals* 4; *stamens* 6-8, alternately shortened; *filaments* broad at base; *anthers* large; *style* 3 lobed. *Flowers* white, small, paniculated. *Capsule* 2 valved, one seeded, dotted; *seeds* black, shining.

The bark of the trunk of this tree is studded with numerous large, conical, nipple-like protuberances, which afford a very curious aspect. Height from 15 to 20 feet; diameter from 10 inches to one foot and a half. *Wood* yellow, hard, and close, and used in the manufacture of many kinds of domestic utensils, yokes, axles, tools, &c.

The fruit is known to the Colonists as the *wild Cardamom*, and, on account of its aromatic qualities, prescribed for flatulency and paralysis.

Found in the bush near Mossel Bay, in the forests of the district of George and also in those of Uitenhage and Albany. Fl. July—August.

19. *Vepris lanceolata. A. Juss.* (Boscia Thbg.) (*Wit Yzerhout*; *White Ironwood.*)—*Branches* rugose, spreading. *Leaves* alternate, stalked, trifoliate; *leaflets* sessile, elliptical, entire, blunt or pointed, veined, wavy, perfectly smooth. *Flowers* unisexual, small, terminal, panicled. *Calyx* short 4 fid; *corolla* 4 petalous; *petals* narrow, linear; *stamens* 4, shorter than the petals; *styles* 3; *stigmas* 3 persistent; *capsule* dotted, 4 celled, 4 seeded.

Height 20 feet; diameter 2 feet and more. *Bark* thin, whitish-grey, smooth. *Wood* white, hard, very tough. Used chiefly for ploughs, axles, or other wagonwood. Called *Omngumaswile* by the Kafirs. Grows in the primeval woods of the Tzitsikamma, Krakakamma, British Caffraria, &c. Fl. October—November.

OCHNACEÆ. D. C.

20. *Ochna Arborea.* *Burch.* *(Redwood ; Roodhout.)*— *Branches* smooth, spreading. *Leaves* alternate, glossy, penninerved, oval, slightly serrate. *Flowers* subracemose, or often solitary. *Calyx* 5 parted, deciduous ; *petals* 5, yellow; *stamens* numerous, shorter than the petals ; *filaments* slender ; *anthers* linear, opening by pores ; *style* 5-10 fid. *Berry* one-celled, one seeded.

Height of stem 20 to 30 ; diameter 1½ to 2 feet. *Bark* reddish brown, smooth. *Wood* of a red tint, hard, heavy, and tough. Well suited for all kinds of furniture, but chiefly used for wagon poles, tools, triggers, axe-handles, &c.

In the forests of Oliphant's Hoek, Salem, Katriver, Caffraria, Adow (Uitenhage). Fl. September—October.

CELASTRINEÆ. R. Br.

21. *Celastrus Acuminatus.* *Lin.* *(Silkbark ; Zybast.)*— *Branches* unarmed, *twigs* angular, compressed. *Leaves* stalked, oblong, lanceolate, taper-pointed, serrate, veiny, smooth. *Flowers* 2—4, small, nodding, axillary on short pedicels.

A forest tree. Height 12 to 15 feet ; diameter 7 to 12 inches. *Bark* thin, whitish-grey, not thorny. Has this peculiarity along with the leaves, that when broken, they show numerous fine white, silk-like threads, and hence the name of *Zybast*, or *Silk-bark*. *Wood* of a fine grain, heavy, and hard. When polished it displays beautiful shades. To the joiner it furnishes a splendid material for fancy work ; by the turner it will be found very serviceable for wooden screws, &c., as also by the manufacturer of musical instruments. In the colony it has hitherto chiefly been used by wheelwrights. This tree grows best in rocky situations beneath other trees, and is found in many parts of the colony, even in the very vicinity of Cape Town, at Kirstenbosch, on the eastern side of Table Mountain. It is harder and tougher than the Europeon Yoke-elm. Fl. February—March.

22. *Celastrus undatus.* *Thbg.* *(Koko-tree.)*—*Branches* round ; *twigs* flexuose, compressed, angular. *Leaves* alternate, short-stalked, obovate or rhomboid-ovate, wedge-shaped and unequal at base, mostly blunt, wavy, and obtusely sawed at the margins, leathery, netted-veined, shining on the upper, pale on the lower surface. *Flowers* stalked, small, axillary. *Capsule* 3 angular, three celled.

A tree 20-25 feet high and 1, to 1½ in diameter. *Bark* smooth, grey, thin. *Wood* hard, close-grained, very heavy, resembling white-pear, and chiefly used in the construction of wagons or for farming implements.

Common in the forests of the Uitenhage and Albany districts, as well as those in the Amatola mountains. Fl. May.

23. Celastrus Buxifolius. *Lin.* (*Cape-Box*)—*Branches* and *branchlets* compressed or angular, flexuose, usually spiny. *Leaves* alternate, tufted, tapering into a petiole, obovate-oblong, blunt or emarginate, crenate, very veiny, unequal at base, nearly leathery, smooth. *Spines* ash-coloured, patent, strong, mostly naked but occasionally leafy, seldom flower-bearing, and from 1 to 6 inches long. *Flowers* axillary, paniculate, white; *Panicles* many-flowered, cymose, stalked, as long or shorter as the leaves. *Capsule* roundish, of the size of a pea.

A variable shrub or small tree, 8-12 feet high and from 6-8 inches in breadth. *Bark* thin, greyish-white. *Wood* yellowish, very close, hard and heavy, resembling *Boxwood*, and fit for the manufacture of musical instruments, wood-engraving, and all purposes for which Box is commonly used.

Grows in the bushes and woods in many parts of the Colony, from Cape Town to Caffraria. Fl. Octob.—December.

24. Pterocelastrus Tricuspidatus. *Sond.* (*Spekboom.*)—*Branches* erect, rough; *twigs* angular. *Leaves* crowded, obovate, blunt or slightly emarginate at apex, cuneate and narrowed at base, smooth, entire, obscurely veined, often unequal-sided, leathery. *Flowers* cymose, axillary, minute, white. *Capsule* cartilaginous, 3 valved, 3 winged.

Stem 8—10 feet high; 5—10 inches in diameter. *Wood* soft, light. Used for making charcoal; also as fuel.

Common on the sides of Table Mountain, in the Swellendam district, and elsewhere. Fl. Octob.

25. Pterocelastrus Variabilis. *Sond.* (*Cherry-wood; Kersehout*)—*Branches* erect; upper *branchlets* forked. *Leaves* short-stalked, alternate, obovate-oblong or oval, blunt, sometimes emarginate, more or less veined, narrowed at base, quite entire, leathery, smooth. *Flowers* stalked, panicled, axillary, minute, white. *Panicles* cymose, many-flowered, spreading, shorter than the leaves. *Capsule* 3 winged, wings horny, ovate, its lobes either blunt, pointed, or torn.

A tree 20-25 feet high, and from 1, to 1½ or more broad. *Bark* thin, even, dark grey. *Wood* reddish, fine-grained, hard, heavy, and handsomely veined. It would answer well for turnery, cabinet-making and other purposes, and might be fairly tried for railway works.

Common in the forests throughout a great portion of the Colony, from Swellendam to British Caffraria. Fl. October.

26. Pterocelastrus Rostratus. *Walp.* (*White Pear; Witpeer.*)—*Branches* and *twigs* erect, purplish, angular, spreading. *Leaves* stalked, alternate, oblong-lanceolate, obtuse or bluntly pointed, reflexed at the margins, entire, leathery, smooth. *Flowers* white, paniculated. *Panicles* long-stalked, axillary, dichotomously

c

branched, many-flowered. *Capsule* 3 valved, armed with 4 to 6 horn-like wings.

Height from 20 to 25 ; diameter from one to two feet. *Bark* whitish-grey. *Wood* heavy, strong, greatly resembling pear or apple tree. By the colonists it is generally used for wagonwork, and particularly for fellies.

Grows chiefly in the forests of the Swellendam and Uitenhage districts, but is also found on elevated rocky places in the woods on the eastern side of Table Mountain. Fl. September—October.

27. *Hartogia Capensis. Thbg. (Smalblad, Lepelhout ; Ladle-wood.)—Branches* decussate, patent; *twigs* slender, erect. *Leaves* opposite, oblong, coriaceous, crenato serrate, blunt, emarginate, smooth. *Flowers* small, axillary, paniculated, nodding. *Drupe* juiceless, ovate, 2-celled, 2-seeded. Thbg. Prodr. Plant. Cap. 1. tab. 3.

Height from 12 to 15 ; diameter from 1, to 1½ feet. *Bark* thin, greyish-white, more or less wrinkled. *Wood* hard, fine grained, close, and tough. It is adapted for all kinds of fancy furniture, and invaluable to the cabinetmaker for veneering. Turners also and instrument-makers will find it well adapted for the manufacture of the articles of their trade. In the interior it serves for the construction of wagons and rural utensils.

This tree is found in the woods of the districts of Swellendam and Caledon, where it is known by the name of Lepelhout (Ladlewood). and in the bushy ravines on the eastern side of Table Mountain. Fl. January—February.

28. *Maurocenia Capensis. Sond. (Hottentot Cherry ; Aas-vogel-besjes.)—Branches* rigid; twigs purplish, 4 angular. *Leaves* subsessile, opposite, suborbicular or obovate, blunt, somewhat emarginate, revolute, entire, coriaceous, smooth, shining. *Flow-ers* small, white ; *flower-stalks* axillary, short, crowded. *Calyx* fringed; *petals* toothed *Drupe* elliptical, juicy, 3 celled, 1–3 seeded. Hook. Icon. Plantar. t. 552.

Shrubby. Usual height of stem 6 8 feet ; diameter 3 to 4 inches *Bark* grey, very craggy. *Wood* fine, pretty hard, and tough. It looks well when polished, being yellow with brownish veins. It is very fit for the manufacture of musical instruments. The fruit is eaten by the natives.

In the bushy ravines of Table Mountain, Hottentot Holland, and elsewhere. Fl. July.

29. *Cassine Capensis. Lin. (Ladle-wood. Lepelhout)— Branches* and *twigs* angular, erect, patent, purplish. *Leaves* opposite, stalked, ovate, sawed at the margin, entire at base ; obtuse, rigid, smooth. *Flowers* small, white. *Peduncles* axillary, paniculate. *Panicles* dichotomous or trichotomous. *Drupe* nearly round, purple.

Height from 8 to 10 feet; diameter 8 to 12 inches. *Bark* grey, smooth. *Wood* hard, tough, and, when varnished, extremely handsome It furnishes the cabinetmaker with a superior material for all kinds of fancy work, and has proved itself useful to the wheelwright.

This tree grows in the forests along the eastern side of Table and Devil's Mountain, in Hout Bay, also in the districts of Uitenhage, Clanwilliam, and other parts of the colony. Fl. April—May.

30. *Elæodendron Croceum. D. C. (Ilex crocea. Thbg. Crocoxylon excelsum. Echl. & Z.) (Saffronwood; Saffraan-hout.)—Branches* much spreading. *Leaves* opposite, stalked, leathery, rigid, veined, smooth, prickly at the margins. *Flowers* small, paniculated, axillary. *Drupe* juiceless, 4-celled.

Lofty, 20 to 40 feet high, and 2 to 4 feet in diameter. *Bark* whitish, covered all over with a resinous crust of a *gamboge yellow* colour, which makes this tree easily known from all others, and which led probably to its vernacular name of *Saffronwood* This wood, which is fine grained, hard, close, and tough, is very useful to the builder in the shape of beams and planks, and to the cabinet-maker serves extremely well for tables, chairs, wardrobes, and for all kinds of furniture. Butter casks are likewise made of it, and wheelwrights use it for fellies and general wagonwork. The bark also is good for tanning and dyeing.

In the aboriginal forests of the Knysna, Krakakamma, Kat River, and in various parts of Caffraria. Fl. June—July.

31. *Mystroxylon Kubu. Echl. and Zeyh.—Branches* ash-coloured, spreading; *Leaves* alternate, short-stalked, oval, notched at apex, crenate and calloso-serrate at the margins, veined on both sides, leathery, perfectly smooth. *Flowers* small, stalked, axillary, umbellate; *umbels* few-flowered. *Calyx* minute, 5 lobed; *petals* 5 rounded, narrowed at base. *Stamens* 5, shorter than the corolla. *Style* short, *stigma* indistinctly 2 lobed. *Drupe* globose, rose-red of the size of a large pea.

A much branched tree, 20 to 25 feet high, and 1, to 1½ broad. *Bark* grey, rough. *Wood* close-grained, hard, strong, compact, tough; serviceable for fellies, other wagonwork, rural utensils, etc. *Fruit* edible, sweet; known as *Koo-boo-besies.*

Common in the forests of Olifants Hoek, Tzitsikamma, Krakakamma, etc. Fl. Octob—Nov.

32. *Scytophyllum Laurinum. Echl. & Zeyh.—Branches* and *branchlets* angular, erect, purplish. *Leaves* alternate, nearly sessile, narrowed at base, ovate-oblong, blunt or emarginate, subrevolute, obscurely veined, entire, coriaceous, smooth. *Flowers* small, clustered, white, panicled. *Panicles* short-stalked, axillary. *Calyx* 5 cleft; *petals* 5; *stamens* 5, *style* short; *stigma* 2 lobed. *Drupe* obovate, yellow.

A small tree or rather shrub, 10—12 feet high, and from 6—8 inches in diameter. *Bark* black, rent, thin. *Wood* hard, fine-grained, heavy, yellowish brown. Well suited for turners' work, the manufacture of tools, and various other purposes.

Common in mountain ravines near Cape Town, Paarl, Tulbagh, Caledon, Clanwilliam, etc. Fl. Dec—Jan.

AQUIFOLIACEÆ. DC.

33. *Ilex Capensis. Sond. and Harv.*—*Branches* erect, white; *twigs* angular, leafy. *Leaves* alternate, short-stalked, oblong-lanceolate, acute, entire, veined, leathery, pale below, smooth. *Petioles* channelled, purplish. *Flowers* minute, axillary, on short peduncles, crowded, subumbellate, nodding. *Calyx* small, persistent 4-6- toothed: *Corolla* salver-shaped, 4-6 parted; *stamens* 4-6 exserted; *stigmas* 4-6 sessile, obtuse. *Drupe* roundish, crowned with the stigmas. (Sideroxylon mite. Lin.) Bot. Mag. t. 1858.

A shrub or small tree, about 8-12 feet high; diameter 6-8 inches. *Bark* white, rough. *Wood* light, soft, rather spongy, and little used.

Common in the woods of Swellendam, Tulbagh, Uitenhage, Kat River, etc, and also in those on the east side of Table Mountain. Fl. October.

RHAMNEÆ. R. Br.

34. *Zizyphus Mucronata. Willd. (Buffalo-thorn; Buffels-doorn).*—*Branches* and *branchlets* grey, flexuous, smooth or velvety and armed with pairs of sharp-pointed prickles, one of which is recurved. *Leaves* stalked, alternate, often unequal-sided, ovate or subcordate-ovate, crenato-serrate, bluntly acuminate, 3 nerved, veined, smooth, shining above, pale and slightly hairy at the nerves beneath. *Flowers* cymose, axillary, small, yellow; *flower-stalks* channelled. *Calyx* 5 cleft, and as well as the petioles and cymes, downy; *petals* 5 obovate; *stamens* 5 exserted; *styles* 2 diverging. *Drupes* fleshy, globose, red.

A tree 20—25 feet high, and 1 to 2 in diameter. *Bark* rough; *Wood* tough and chiefly used for wagonwork. Common on the banks of the Kat River, likewise in British Caffraria and Natal. Fl. Decemb.

35. *Scutia Commersoni. Brogn. (Katdoorn.)*—*Branches* decussate, spreading, prickly *prickles* recurved. *Leaves* opposite, stalked, ovate or obovate, blunt, pointed or retuse, entire, leathery, smooth. *Flowers* umbellate, axillary, small. *Calyx* pitcher-shaped, 5 cleft; *petals* emarginate. *Stamens* 5, short; *style* single; *stigmas* 2-3 obtuse. *Fruit* roundish, apiculate, 2 celled.

Habit of growth usually shrubby; branches armed with hooked thorns. Height about 4 or 5 feet; diameter from 6 to 8 inches. *Bark* whitish grey, wrinkled. *Wood* fine grained and strong, light-brown; looks well when varnished. Useful to turners.

Common in the woods of Swellendam, Uitenhage, and Albany. Fl. December—January.

TEREBINTACEÆ. Juss.

36. *Rhus Lævigata. Linn. (Taaibosch)*—*Branches* and *twigs* purple, erect. *Leaves* long-stalked, ternate; *leaflets* sessile, ovate, pointed, pale below, ribbed, perfectly smooth. *Flowers* small, yellowish-green, panicled; panicles terminal and axillary, slender. *Drupe* globose, of the size of a pea.

Height 8 to 10 feet; diameter from 8 to 10 inches. *Bark* thin, rough. *Wood* hard, tough, reddish. Sometimes called *Essenhout (Ash-wood)*, in the Western districts, and *Bosganna* by the natives of the East. Used for wagonwork of various kinds, and may be employed with advantage by the turner.

Grows in stony ground, nearly all over the colony. Fl. September-October.

37. *Rhus Viminalis. Vahl. (Karree-wood.)*—*Branches* smooth, slender, flexile. *Leaves* long-stalked, ternate; *leaflets* sessile, linear-lanceolate, mucronate, smooth or fringed, narrowed at both ends. *Flowers* small, panicled; *panicles* axillary and terminal, hairy. *Drupe* 1 celled, 1 seeded, roundish, rather dry.

This little tree, which in its growth and foliage in some measure resembles the *Willow*, grows chiefly on the banks of rivers and rivulets. It attains a height of from 10 to 14 feet, and sometimes measures 8 to 10 inches in breadth. The *Bark* is grey and smooth; the *wood* reddish-brown, hard, and very tough. Its thicker and longer branches are used as spars in thatching houses, and also for wagon tents, as they bend easily without breaking; the younger twigs for bows. The *Karreewood* has the advantage, that it is not infested by noxious insects.

Common on rivers and watercourses in many parts of the Eastern districts. Fl. July.

38. *Rhus Lucida. Linn. (Taaibosch.)*—*Branches* and *branchlets* spreading, downy. *Leaves* short-stalked, ternate; *leaflets* sessile, obovate, wedge-shaped at base, entire, blunt, emarginate, leathery, resinous, glossy. *Flowers* minute, white, panicled, axillary and terminal. *Drupe* as in the preceding species.

Shrubby. Height 4-6 feet, diameter 3-4 inches. *Branches* ash-coloured; wood hard and tough. *Bark* of root and branches used for tanning purposes.

Common on the slopes of the mountains in the Cape, Caledon, and Swellendam districts. Fl. Aug —Sept.

39. *Rhus Tomentosa. Linn.*—*Branches* and twigs purplish, erect, shaggy. *Leaves* stalked, ternate; *leaflets* oval, tapering at

both ends, acute, bluntly sawed towards the apex, smooth above, ribbed and woolly beneath. *Flowers* panicled, small; *panicles* terminal, longer than the leaves. *Drupe* shaggy.

Growth, height, properties, and technical uses like those of the preceding species.

40. *Rhus Thunbergii.* *Hook.* (*Rœmeria argentea.* *Thbg.*) (*Rock-Ash; Klipesse,*)—*Branches* erect, wrinkled. *Leaves* simple, stalked, alternate, obovate-elliptic, retuse, entire, leathery, penninerved, glaucous. *Flowers* panicled, polygamous, white; *panicles* terminal; pedicels, sepals and petals externally shaggy. *Stamens* 5-10; petals 5-6. *Drupe* roundish-oblique, almost dry, 1 celled, 1 seeded. Hook. Icon. Plant. t. 595.

Height 12 to 15 feet; diameter 3 to 4 feet *Bark* rough, craggy. *Wood* resinous, fine grained, hard, close, heavy. Handsome when polished. Valuable in the manufacture of fancy furniture, work boxes, sewing tables, &c., and useful to the turner and maker of musical instruments.
This tree grows in rocky situations in the districts of Stellenbosch, Worcester, and Clanwilliam. Fl. February.

41. *Harpephyllum Caffrum.* *Bernh.*—*Branches* spreading; *twigs* knotty from the fall of old leaves. *Leaves* alternate, impari-pinnate, 6-7 yoked, long-stalked, smooth; *leaflets* sessile, patent, lanceolate, entire, unequal-sided, sickle-shaped, pointed, veiny, wedge-shaped at base. *Flowers* dioico-polygamous, short-stalked, panicled, white; *panicles* terminal, shorter than the leaves. *Calyx* 4-5 cleft, its segments blunt; *petals* 4-5, longer than the calyx. *Stamens* 8-10 free, perigynous; *filaments* short, awl-shaped; *anthers* ovate. *Pistil* columnar, fleshy; *stigmas* 4 recurved. *Drupe* oblong, 2 celled, 1 seeded by abortion, about an inch long.

A handsome tree 20-30 feet high, and from 1 to 2 in diameter, much resembling the *Cape Ash* in habit. *Bark* greyish-brown, rough. *Wood* red, tough, very handsome when polished, and useful for household furniture, planking, and various other purposes. The fruit, known as the *Kafir* or *Wild Plum* (*zuure-pruim*), is edible.
Grows in woody ravines at Howison's Port (Albany), in the forests of the Uitenhage district, and in Caffraria. As an ornamental tree I found it planted at the sides of some of the principal streets in Graham's Town along with *Erythrina caffra.* Fl. April.

LEGUMINOSÆ. Juss.

42. *Millettia Caffra.* *Meisn.* (*Omzambeete; Kafir Ironwood.*) —Upper *branches* and leaf-stalks downy: *leaves* unequally-pinnate, 4-6 yoked; *leaflets* short-petioled, opposite, oblong, penninerved,

fringed at the margins, smooth above, silky beneath; *stipels* bristle-like. *Calyx* bell-shaped, bluntly toothed and as well as the flower-stalks shaggy. *Racemes* terminal, panicled. *Flowers* papilionaceous, purplish-blue, silky; *alæ* and *carina* smooth. *Legume* 4 to 5 inches long, 2 to 2½ broad, acute, leathery, or almost woody, 3 seeded, thickly clothed with brown velvety hairs; *seeds* subovate or oblong, compressed.

A stately tree, 30-40 feet high, and from 2-3 in diameter. *Bark* thin. Furnishes a superior *wood* of great beauty and durability, which when polished, resembles and perhaps surpasses, *Brazilian Rose* or *Jucaranda Wood*.

The Kafirs employ the beans as a vermifuge (particulary for lumbrici) by pounding and taking them in milk, one or two forming a dose. This tree also exudes a kind of resin, resembling *Gwojacum*. Grows in the forests of the colony of Natal, and also in the Manubi forest near Butterworth (Caffraria proper). *J. H. Bowker.*

43. *Erythrina Caffra.* *Thbg.* *(Kafir-tree.)* *Branches* alternate, spreading, prickly; *prickles* solitary, purplish. *Leaves* ternate, stalked; *stalks* unarmed; *leaflets* ovate, broad, pointed, glabrous, entire. *Flowers* papilionaceous, racemose, nodding, scarlet. *Calyx* truncate, 2 lobed, tomentose, rusty; *Vexillum* very large; *Stamens* exserted; *Legume* oblong, constricted between the seeds, many-seeded. *Seeds* scarlet, with a black hilum.

This giant of the forests of Olifantshoek, Albany, and Caffraria, grows 50 to 60 feet high, and 3 to 4 in diameter. Its *bark* is grey, and its wood soft and very light. However it has been turned to advantage by the inhabitants, for, from the tall hollowed trunk they have constructed canoes, made troughs, and employed the wood instead of cork in the construction of their fishing nets. The wood is used likewise for making shingles, which, when tarred, are considered to be very durable and to make very good roofing. Fl. September.

44. *Virgilia Capensis.* *Lamk.* *(Keurboom.)*—*Branches* erect, spreading; *twigs* somewhat shaggy. *Leaves* stalked, imparipinnate, many-yoked; *rachis* channelled; *leaflets* opposite, narrow-oblong; entire, mucronate, glossy above, silky below. *Flowers* papilionaceous, racemose, axillary or terminal. *Calyx* ample, bell-shaped, 2 lipped, 5 toothed, woolly. *Stamens* 10, free. *Corolla* smooth, flesh-coloured, sweet-scented. *Legume* leathery, compressed, oblong, many-seeded, clothed with a rusty wool. Bot. Magaz. t. 1590.

Height 15-20 feet; diameter 1½, to 2 feet. *Bark* black, craggy. *Wood* rather light and soft. Looks well when polished, but is subject to worm-eating. It is occasionally used for yokes, rafters, spars, fuel, etc.

A transparent gum* exudes very freely from the bark, which may be turned to account, the bush-women using the same as a substitute for starch The supply could be rendered unlimited, this gum being easily collected.

This handsome tree, although originally a native of the Eastern districts of the colony, where it is extremely common, is now to be found in moist and shady spots, and especially in mountain ravines in most of the Western provinces, whence it has found its way also into gardens. Fl. April—May.

45. Schotia Speciosa. Iacq. (Hottentot's Boerboon)—

Branches rigid, straitened. Leaves abruptly pinnate, many-yoked; leaflets oblong or elliptical, sessile, unequal at base, entire, mucronate, leathery, smooth. Flowers panicled, terminal, stalked, bright-crimson; panicles many-flowered. Calyx 4 fid, deciduous; petals 5; stamens 10-12; filaments free, exserted, and of unequal length, style filiform. Legume broad, oblong, compressed, leathery, winged; seals few; umbilicus naked. Botan. Magaz. t. 1153.

Height of trunk 8-12; diameter 1 to 1½ feet. Bark brown, rugged. Wood reddish-brown, hard, tough, and durable. Used chiefly for yokes, fellies, triggers, or fuel. The beans, when roasted, are eaten by the natives.

Common on dry, karroo-like places in the Eastern Province and Brit. Caffraria. Fl. Jan.—Febr.

46. Schotia Latifolia. Iacq. (Monkey-Boerboon; Bosch-

Boerboon)—Branches spreading. Leaves equally pinnate, 2-4 yoked; leaflets sessile, obovate, blunt, leathery, smooth. Flowers panicled, terminal or lateral, subsessile, pinkish; panicles branched,

---

* Mr. Schmieterloew has kindly favoured me with the following qualitative analysis of this gum: —" The gum of Virgilia capensis agrees with Cerasin (the gum of the Cherry-tree) more than with either Tragacanthin or Arabin, and contains no Bassorin. It is slowly soluble in cold, but more readily in hot water. One ounce of this gum forms with 12 ounces of water a mucilage of the same thickness and consistency as one ounce of real gum arabic with 2 ounces of water, and of equal transparency. It shows less acidity than gum arabic; and in its chemical characteristics differs from Arabin as follows:

Arabin.	Gum of Virgilia.
Produces a copious precipitate with Oxalate of Ammonia.	Produces, a faint milkiness with Oxalate of Ammonia.
Diacetate of Lead produces a white caseous precipitate.	Diacetate of Lead gelatinizes the mucilage.
Peroxide of Iron forms a brown jelly. Strong Spirits of Wine turns the mucilage white, like curdled milk.	Is miscible with this, without any other effect. Does not throw down any caseous matter, and without impairing its consistency, can be mixed with the half of its bulk, which seems to make the solution more clear.

This gum could be used in medicine like gum Tragacanth, and for many purposes where other gums like gum arabic are applied.

many-flowered. *Stamens* monadelphous. *Legume* much like that of the preceding species, few-seeded; *seeds* with a fleshy yellow *arillus.*

Grows from 20 to 30 feet high, and from 3 to 4 in diameter. *Bark* brownish-grey, smooth. *Wood* white, hard, tough, and heavy, but does not appear to be much used save for triggers, posts, enclosures, &c. The young *beans* are eaten by Hottentots and Kafirs.

Very common in the forests of Uitenhage, Albany, British Caffraria, etc. Fl. January.

47. *Acacia Horrida.* *Willd.* (*Thorn-tree; Doornboom.*)— *Stem* and *branches* smooth, but armed with straight, large white, spiny *stipules; twigs* angular. *Leaves* 2 pinnate; *pinnæ* 2-5 yoked; *leaflets* linear-oblong, blunt, smooth, many-yoked; *leafstalks* glandular at base and apex *Flowers* stalked, bracteate in the middle, axillary, globose, polygamous, yellow, sweet-scented. *Legume* long, narrow, compressed, sickle-shaped, leathery, smooth, many-seeded.

Height 20 to 25 ; diameter 1 to 1½ feet. *Bark* dark grey, contains a large portion of the tanning principle, imparting a reddish dye to leather. *Wood* hard and tough, extensively employed in the interior for building purposes ; looks well when varnished, and therefore adapted for all kinds of common furniture. The colonists generally place the logs for some time in water before using them, in order to render the wood more durable. It furnishes a very good material for wheels, poles, and yokes, and many rural implements, and answers well for turner's work.

The *Gummi Acaciæ,* which exudes spontaneously from the bark both of the trunk and branches, is well known as an article of commerce.

The *Thorn-tree* may be said to be the most common tree met with in the lonely wastes of South Africa. There it inhabits the borders of every stream, and points out at a far distance to the exhausted traveller the cherished spot, where he may quench his burning thirst, and screen himself from the scorching rays of an African sun. Fl. January— February.

SAXIFRAGACEÆ. D.C.

48. *Cunonia Capensis.* *Lin.* (*Red Alder. Rood Els.*)— *Branches* rough, patent. *Leaves* stalked, impari-pinnate ; *leaflets* 4-5 yoked, petiolate, opposite, oblong, acute, sawed, leathery, penninerved, smooth. *Stipules* large, ovate, deciduous ; *petioles* compressed. *Flowers* small, white, racemose, axillary. *Calyx* 5 parted ; *petals* 5 ; *stamens* 10 ; *styles* 2, longer than the corolla. *Capsule* taperpointed, 2-celled, many seeded.

Height 15 to 25 feet ; breadth 1½ to 2. *Bark* black, wrinkled. *Wood* tough, close, somewhat like the *Lime-tree,* and much in request. It is handsome when polished, and the planks are sought after, both by

D

cabinetmakers and wheelwrights It is also useful to turners, and well adapted for screws. As this wood suffers but little from moisture, it may be of service in the construction of mills.

Common in moist, woody places throughout the whole colony. Fl. May—June.

40. *Platylophus Trifoliatus. Don. (White Alder ; Wit-Els.)—Branches* and *twigs* purplish. *Leaves* trifoliate, stalked ; *leaflets* lanceolate, acute, toothed, netted-veined, smooth. *Stipules* deciduous. *Flowers* panicled, small, white; *panicels* axillary, compound, many-flowered; *peduncels* shaggy. *Calyx* 4 cleft, persistent ; *petals* 4, trifid; *stamens* 8-10. *Styles* 2. Capsule cartilaginous, ovate, 2-celled.

Height from 30 to 40 feet ; diameter from 3 to 4 *Bark* whitish grey, rather smooth. *Wood* white, much lighter than that of the preceding species, from which it also differs in colour. It furnishes a good material for common furniture, drawers, boxes, picture-frames, &c., looks well when polished, and is also used for various wagon work.

This stately tree is to be met with in the forests of the Swellendam, Worcester, George, and Uitenhage districts. Fl. January.

HAMAMELIDEÆ. R. Br.

50. *Trichocladus Crinitus. Pers. (Underwood. Onderbosch.)* —*Branches* smooth, greyish-white, spreading. *Leaves* opposite, stalked, ovate or oval, bluntly acuminate, veiny, entire, glossy above. *Twigs*, petioles, calyces and underside of leaves densely coated with brown shag, *Flowers* dioecious, terminal, and axillary, clustered together upon a common receptacle ; *Flower-heads* stalked ; *calyx* 5-lobed; *petals* 5-epigynous, linear, involute ; *stamens 5; styles* 2. *Capsule* hairy, 2-celled, 5-valved ; cells one-seeded.

An arborescent shrub, 10-15 feet high, and from 6-8 inches broad. *Bark* smooth ; *wood* hard, fit for wagon-work, etc. The branches and twigs are used on account of their toughness and elasticity ; they bend well without breaking, and serve as hoops for the manufacture of buckets, etc. This shrub is called *Siduli* by the Kafirs. *Trichocladus ellipticus.* E. & Z does not appear to differ, but by narrower, more elliptical leaves.

Common in the forests of the Knysna and Plettenberg's Bay, Tzitsikamma, Krakakamma, Stockenstrom, Caffraria &c. Flor. Dec—Jan.

OLINIEÆ. W. Arnott.

51. *Olinia Capensis. Klotzsch. (Hardpear.)—Branches* and *twigs* angular, spreading. *Leaves* opposite, oval, leathery, entire, somewhat wavy, tapering into a petiole, emarginate, slighty *pointed*, penninerved, glossy above, pale below. *Calyx* 5-toothed.

Flowers terminal, cymose; *bracts* deciduous; *petals* white, spathulate; *stamens* 5; *filaments* short, inflexed; *stigma* thick, blunt. *Drupe* oblong, dry, 3-4 celled; cells one-seeded by abortion.

Height of stem 25-30 feet; diameter from 2 to 3. *Bark* greyish-white, very rugged. *Wood* yellowish-white, hard, tough and heavy, like the European *white Birch* It is chiefly used by wheelwrights for axles, poles and sundry wagon-work, but may be tried as well for railway purposes.

Konha-wood, which greatly resembles Hardpear, but of which I have been unable to procure branches and leaves for identification, appears to belong to another species of *Olinia*, the wood itself being of finer grain.

Common in the forests and woods throughout a great portion of the Colony. Fl. Jul—Aug.

52. *Olinia Cymosa. Thbg.*—*Branches* 4-angular, very straight. *Leaves* stalked, opposite, obovate, emarginate, or blunt with a point, coriaceous, entire, penninerved, smooth. *Petioles* short, depressed. *Flowers* white, cymose, axillary.

Shrubby. Height of stem 4 to 6 feet; diameter 6-8 inches. *Bark* whitish-grey, cracked. *Wood* hard, close-grained, heavy, well adapted for turner's work.

Delights in rocky spots, and is common on the east side of Table Mountain, and in similar localities of the Western division of the Colony. Fl. July—August.

MYRTACEÆ. Juss.

53. *Eugenia Zeyheri. Harv.* (*Wild Jambos.*)—*Branches* rough. *Leaves* opposite, elliptic-lanceolate, short-stalked, entire, glabrous, slightly revolute. *Flowers* stalked, axillary, small. *Calyx* 4-cleft; *petals* 4; *stamens* numerous; *style* 1. *Berry* subglobose, crowned with the withered calyx.

Height from 15 to 20 feet; breadth from 9 to 12 inches. *Bark* thin, grey, longitudinally rent. *Wood* white, hard, heavy, fine-grained, somewhat resembling *white Maple*. Fit for the manufacture of carpenter's tools, ploughs, axles, &c. *Fruit* edible.

In the forests of the Van Stadensbergen, and near Uitenhage. Fl. December.

CORNEÆ. D.C.

54. *Curtisia Faginea. Ait.* (*Assagay-wood; Assagay-hout.*) —*Branches* decussate, erect; *twigs* purplish, tomentose. *Leaves* opposite, stalked, oblong, acuminate, unequally toothed, glabrous, veined. *Petioles* and *veins* clothed with a dense rusty shag. *Flowers* small, numerous, red, paniculate. *Panicles* trichotomous, shaggy, terminal. *Calyx* 4 parted; *petals* 4; *stamens* 4; *style*

1; *stigmas* 4-5. *Berry* round, fleshy, yellowish, 4-5 seeded. Burm. Plant. African. Decad. t. 82.

Height from 20 to 40 feet, if allowed to grow, for the tree is often felled before it has attained its full size, and commonly measures from 15 to 20 feet high, and from 2 to 3 in circumference. The *bark* is thin, black, and almost smooth. The *wood*, which is highly prized within the Colony, is solid, extremely tough, heavy, close-grained, very durable, and resembles plain mahogany. It answers well for all kinds of superior furniture, tools, &c., but is truly invaluable, and not to be surpassed by any other wood, in the construction of wagons, particularly in this country, where the natural difficulties of the roads, the great distances to go, and the excessive heat of the climate, require strong and sub-stantially-built vehicles for travelling. Called *Omhlebe* by the Kafirs.

The tree grows in the primeval forests throughout the whole Colony, and also in Kafirland. Fl. January—February.

RUBIACEÆ. Juss.

55. *Burchellia Capensis. D. C. (Wild Pomegranate; Buffelshoorn.)*—*Branches* opposite, erect. *Leaves* on short stalks, ovate, acute, subcordate, downy, rigid, entire. *Stipules* deciduous, internally shaggy. *Flowers* of a deep orange hue, capitate, terminal, sessile on a villous receptacle, with minute bracts. *Calyx* tubular, deeply 5 parted ; *corolla* funnel-shaped ; tube hispid. *Anthers* 5, pointed, almost sessile. *Style* 1 filiform ; *stigma* club-shaped, 2 fid. *Berry* 2 locular, turbinato-globose. *Seeds* black, angular.

A small tree 12 to 14 feet high, but sometimes from 1 to 2 in diameter. *Bark* greyish-brown. *Wood* very hard and close, and chiefly used for agricultural implements.

Common in the forests of Swellendam, George, and Uitenhage. Fl. October—November.

56. *Gardenia Thunbergia. Lin. (Wild Katjepiering ; Buffelsbal.)*—*Branches* unarmed, erect, much divided. *Leaves* oblong, attenuate at both ends, stalked, verticillate, entire, veined, glabrous. *Flowers* terminal, solitary, white, scented. *Calyces* tubular, leafy, hispid, cleft at one side with leaflike appendages. *Corolla* tubular, salver-shaped ; *petals* 8, obtuse. *Anthers* 7—9 ; *style* club-shaped, shaggy. *Fruit* baccate-ovate, smooth, white, imperfectly 5-celled, many-seeded, very hard, almost woody. Bot. Magaz. t. 1004.

Height of trunk from 8 to 10 feet ; breadth from 10 to 12 inches. *Bark* smooth, greyish-white. *Wood* hard, heavy, and strong, and used for making tools, clubs, kieries, yokes, axles, fellies, ploughs, and also fit to engrave upon, &c.

In the forests of the Krakakamma and Oliphant's Hock (Uitenhage). Fl. January—February.

57. *Gardenia Rothmannia.* *Lin.*—*Branches* and *twigs* unarmed, brown, angular, rough, erect. *Leaves* on very short stalks, opposite, oblong, acute, veined, entire, smooth, but with hairy glands on the underface of the leaves, situated along the midrib in the axils of the veins. *Flowers* terminal, solitary, sessile, sweet-scented. *Calyces* cylindrical, ribbed, hairy within, 5-cleft, its *segments* filiform, sharp-pointed; *Coro'la* bell-shaped, 5 parted; *petals* 5, pointed, reflexed, buff, sprinkled with purplish dots. *Anthers* 5; *style* one, thickened at top. *Fruit* ovate, fleshy, costate, angular, smooth, 2-valved, 2-celled, many-seeded, black.

Height of stem from 15—20, diameter from 1—1½ feet. *Bark* grey, smooth. *Wood* very hard, strong, and tough. Used chiefly for tools, axles, fellies, and other wagonwork like the preceding.
This fine tree is to be met with in the aboriginal woods of the George and Uitenhage districts. Katberg &c. Fl. January—February.

58. *Plectronia Ventosa.* *Lin.* (*Schapendrolletjes.*)—*Branches* brachiate, patent, spiny; *spines* horizontal; *twigs* quadrangular. *Leaves* stalked, opposite, elliptic, smooth, almost leathery, entire, pale on the lower surface. *Flowers* corymbose, axillary, greenish. *Calyx* tubular, 5-toothed. *Corolla* funnel-shaped, 5 parted, throat hairy. *Stamens* 5, filaments very short; *stigma* capitate· *Drupe* fleshy, didymous, compressed, excised, 2 locular; cells one-seeded. Cruse. Rub. Capens. tab. 2.

Height from 15 to 20 feet; diameter from 6 to 10 inches. *Bark* whitish, smooth. *Wood* hard, close, heavy, and tough; takes varnish well, looks marble-like, and is very handsome. It will suit the joiner for small and fancy furniture, and the wagonmaker for fellies, &c. The *fruit*, though insipid, is eaten by the natives.
Common in mountain ravines and forests throughout a great part of the colony. Fl. October—November.

59*. *Plectronia Mundtiana.* (*Canthium Mundtianum.* *Cham.*) (*Rock-Ash; Klipessse.*)—*Branches* forked, knotty; *branchlets* rather compressed. *Leaves* stalked, oval, smooth or downy, one-coloured, membranous, blunt or slightly pointed; *petioles* somewhat channelled and shaggy on the upper side; *stipules* ovate, mucronate. *Flowers* cymose. *Cymes* axillary, stalked, many-flowered, shorter than the leaves. *Calyx*, flowers and fruit as in the preceding species.

A shrub or middling tree, 12-15 feet high, and from 6-8 inches wide. *Bark* thin, grey, rough; *Wood* yellowish-white, very hard and heavy. Useful to turners for screws, tools, etc; to manufactures of musical instruments, and for other purposes
Grows in the forests of Plettenberg's Bay, the Tzitsikamma, in the woody ravines of the Devil's mountain, &c. Flor. Nov—Dec.

60. *Plectronia Spinosa. Klotzsch.*—*Branches* round, greyish-white, very spiny ; *spines* opposite, strong, horizontally spreading, either naked or leafy. *Leaves* obovate, stalked, narrowed at base, nerved, entire, blunt, pale on the underside ; *stipules* minute, sharp-pointed. *Flowers* cymose, small ; *cymes* axillary, few-flowered. *Corolla* short, ventricose. *Fruit* heart-shaped, compressed, 2-3 celled.

A shrub or small tree, 10-15 feet high, 7-10 inches broad. *Bark* thin, grey. *Wood* fine-grained, heavy, yellowish.

In the Addo-bush between Port Elizabeth and Graham's Town, and in the forests of the Van Staden's Mountains, and Olifant's Hoek. Fl. July.

61. *Canthium Pyrifolium. Klotzsch. Branches* and *twigs* angular or compressed, spreading ; *Leaves* opposite, short-stalked, roundish or oval, blunt, entire, nerved, leathery, smooth, shining above, pale below, glanduliferous in the axils of the veins. *Flowers* cymose ; *cymes* axillary, opposite, many-flowered, branching, longer than the leaves. *Calyx* 4-5 toothed ; *Corolla* cylindrical, 4-5 lobed, *lobes* patent, throat bearded. *Anthers* 4-5, within the throat of the corolla ; *Style* simple filiform ; *stigma* undivided, thick, pin-headed. *Fruit* globose.

A small tree 15-20 feet high, 4-6 inches in diameter. *Bark* thin, black. *Wood* close, heavy, yellowish-white, and looks handsome when polished.

Grows in the forests of the Krakakamma. Fl. Febr.

62. *Grumilea Cymosa. E. Meyer.* (*Lemon-wood.*)—*Branches* angular ; *twigs* compressed. *Leaves* short-stalked, opposite, lanceolate-oblong, acuminate, entire, revolute, narrowed at base, netted-veined, smooth, leathery, glossy above, pale below. *Stipules* large, roundish, pointed, deciduous. *Flowers* terminal, cymose ; *cymes* stalked, 3—forked. *Calyx* 5 toothed, connate with the ovary. *Corolla* monopetalous, 5 lobed, throat shaggy, lobes incurved at apex ; *aestivœtion* valvate. *Stamens* 5, adhering to the tube of the corolla ; *filaments* short, *anthers* oblong, erect, enclosed ; *style* simple ; *stigma* thick, 2—lobed. *Fruit* baccate, globose, crowned with the converging limb of the calyx, 2—celled, as large as a small peppercorn.

A tree about 20-30 feet high, and of considerable width. *Bark* ash-coloured, thin. *Wood* citron-yellow, hard, tough, and useful for many purposes. It is the *Omgokolo* of the Kafirs.

Grows in the primitive forests of Olifant's Hoek, Caffraria, and Natal. Fl. Septemb.

COMPOSITÆ. Juss.

63. *Brachylaena Dentata.* D.C.—*Twigs* angular, tomentose. *Leaves* alternate, short-stalked, wedge-shaped at base, apiculate, entire or more commonly sinuato-tridentate at apex, revolute, leathery, smooth and glossy above, clothed with white shag on the underside. *Flowers* dioecious, racemose; *racemes* spiked, terminal, and axillary; *flower-heads* few-flowered.

A shrub or small crooked tree, 12-14 feet high, and 6-9 inches wide. *Bark* smooth; *Wood* hard: chiefly used for making charcoal.

Grows in shady places in Howisons Poort, (Albany), Olifant's Hoek, Stockenstrom, and Caffraria. Fl. April.

64. *Tarchonanthus Camphoratus.* Lin. (*Sirie-hout.*)—*Branches* and *twigs* erect, angular, clothed with white, short down. *Leaves* stalked, alternate, oblong, blunt, leathery, entire, reticulato-areolate and green on their upper surface; veined, white and shaggy beneath. *Flowers* paniculate. *Panicles* terminal, many headed. *Flower-heads* dioecious; *involucres* scaly; *achænia* woolly.

This arborescent shrub (*Wild Sage; Wilde Salie*) grows from 6 to 8 feet high; its diameter is from 5 to 6 inches. *Bark* brownish-grey, much rugged. *Wood* close, heavy; looking handsome when polished, and useful in the manufacture of musical instruments and joiner's fancy work.

The *leaves* when fresh, have a peculiar smell resembling *camphor;* they are chewed by the Mohammetans, smoked by the Hottentots, and employed in the form of infusion or tea, as antispasmodic, tonic, and resolvent.

Common in the Cape, Swellendam, and Uitenhage districts. Fl. May—June.

ERICACEÆ. Juss.

65. *Philippia Chamissonis.* Klotzsch. (*Kabinet-hout*)—*Stem* erect; *branches* short, flexuose. *Leaves* ternate, linear, blunt, small, smooth. *Flowers* terminal, clustered (3—4), nodding. *Calyx* 4 fid; *corolla* globose, 4—parted; *stamens* 8, connate; *stigma* exserted, peltate. *Capsule* 4—angular, 4—locular, 4—celled.

Height of stem from 2 to 3 feet; breadth from 2 to 3 inches. *Bark* brown, glabrous, fibrous, splitting longitudinally. The *wood*, which is hard and close-grained, looks well when varnished, and will suit both the cabinetmaker and turner for various kinds of fancy work.

Common in rocky localities on the north side of Table Mountain and elsewhere. Fl. June.

MYRSINEÆ. R. Br.

66. *Myrsine Melanophleos. R. Br.* (*Roemeria. Thbg.*) (*Cape Beech*; *Beukenhout.*)—*Branches* rough, spreading. *Leaves* oblong-lanceolate, stalked, leathery, entire, blunt, veined, green above, pale beneath, placed at the extremities of the younger branches. *Flowers* (3-4) small, fasciculate, axillary. *Calyx* 5 fid. *Corolla* 4-5 parted; *anthers* 5; *stigma* 1, capitate. *Drupe* pisiform, one-seeded.

Height from 15 to 20 feet; diameter from 1½ to 2. *Stem* straight. *Bark* grey, warty. *Wood* tough and grained like European Beech. Used chiefly for wagonwork.

To be found in the bushy ravines on the east side of Table Mountain, in the forests of Swellendam, Knysna, &c. Fl. October.

SAPOTEÆ. Juss.

67. *Sideroxylon Inerme. Lin.* (*Milk-wood*; *Melkhout.*)— *Branches* flexuose, erect; *twigs* angular. *Leaves* alternate, stalked, oblong, obtuse, entire, leathery, smooth. *Flowers* small, white, fasciculated, axillary. *Calyx* 5 parted; *stamens* 5, opposite the lobes of the corolla; *style* 1. *Corolla* 5 cleft, rotate. *Fruit* globose, baccate; *ovary* 4—5 celled.

Height from 15 to 20 feet; diameter 1 to 1½. *Bark* grey, craggy. milky, inside. *Wood* whitish, very hard, close, and durable. Being little affected by damp or moisture, it furnishes one of the best materials for boat-building, mill-work, bridges, &c., and is likewise well suited for ploughs and rural implements. The fruit (*Jackalsbesjes*) are edible.

Common in the Cape, Swellendam, George, and Uitenhage districts. Fl. December—June.

68. *Mimusops Obovata. Sond.*—*Branches and branchlets* round, grey, spreading. *Leaves* alternate, stalked, obovate, narrowed at base, entire, blunt, or often retuse, smooth, leathery, glossy, paler below. *Flower-stalks* axillary, shaggy, much longer than the petioles. *Calyx* 6 partite, arranged in a double row, its outer *sepals* rusty-brown, inner ones velvety, white; all lanceolate, taper-pointed. *Corolla* as long as the calyx, white, with linear-lanceolate smooth lobes. *Anthers* arrow shaped, acute, longer than the *filaments; style* subulate, longer then the corolla; *stigma* acute. *Drupe* ovate, apiculate, smooth, orange-coloured, about an inch long. Harv. Thesaur. Cap. t. 44.

A tree 15-25 feet high and 1½-2 in diameter. *Bark* thin, smooth. *Wood* yellowish-white, close-grained, tough, heavy and durable. Used principally for fellies, axles, and various wagonwork.

Grows in the aboriginal forests of Olifant's Hoek, Natal, & Fl. Novemb.

EBENACEÆ. Vent.

69. *Royena Lucida. Thbg. (Black-bark; Zwartbast.)*
—*Branches* and *twigs* erect. *Leaves* on short stalks, alternate, ovate, entire, glossy, fringed. *Pedicels* and middle-nerv shaggy below, the younger leaves silky. *Flowers* axillary, solitary, yellowish. *Calyx* hairy, 5-parted *Corolla* bell-shaped, 5 fid; *limb* revolute. *Stamens* 10; *styles* 2. Berry 4-celled, globose, leathery, covered by the enlargedcalyx. *Seeds* 2—4.

Height of stem from 10 to 12 feet; diameter from 6 to 12 inches. *Bark* black, rather smooth. The *wood*, which is hard and tough, and of a yellow tint with brownish stripes, when polished, is well adapted for furniture, tools, screws, &c., but chiefly used for wagonwork. It is called *Omgugunga* by the Kafirs.

To be found in the woods of the Cape Swellendam and Uitenhage districts. Fl. August—September.

70. *Royena Glabra. Lin.*—*Branches* erect, slender, spreading; *twigs* villose. *Leaves* lanceolate, acute, smooth, entire. *Flowers* stalked, axillary, white; *stalks* shaggy, 1—5 flowered.

Height from 4 to 5 feet; breadth from 5 to 6 inches. *Bark* thin, grey, smooth. *Wood* light, porous. Little used, except for fuel.

Common on the north side of Table Mountain and similar places. Fl. July.

71. *Royena Pubescens. Willd.*—*Branchlets* clothed with adpressed hairs. *Leaves* lanceolate-obovate, blunt, revolute at the margins, attenuated into a short petiole, leathery, smooth, pale, and slightly downy below. *Flowers* solitary, axillary, stalked; *peduncles* pubescent, shorter than the leaves. *Bracts* linear-lanceolate, placed above the middle of the stalk. *Calyx* adnate, deeply 5 cleft, outwardly silky; *sepals* ovate, taper-pointed. *Corolla* bell-shaped, 5 parted, externally hairy; *styles* 5 united at base. *Fruit* leathery, 5, celled, downy, nearly globose.

A large shrub or small tree, 6-8 feet high and 4-5 inches in girth. *Bark* greyish-white, rough. *Wood* very close-grained, heavy and durable; takes a fine polish; resembles *Milkwood* and furnishes a superior material to the turner and wood engraver.

Grows on grassy hills near the Van Staden's River, and in the Krakakamma. Fl. May, June.

72. *Euclea Pseudebenus. E. Meyer. (Cape Ebony.)*—*Branches* spreading, greyish-white, much crooked; *twigs* slender, very leafy. *Leaves* alternate, linear, sharp-pointed, entire, wrinkled, pale, smooth, tapering into a short petiole. *Flowers* dioecious, *male-ones* racemose; racemes few-flowered, their stalks as long as the petioles; *female-ones* solitary, axillary. *Calyx* 5

E

cleft, and as well as the peduncles, downy ; *calyx lobes* ovate, blunt. *Corolla* 5 fid, twice as long as the cup, urccolate-campanulate, externally hoary. *Stamens* 18-20 ; *filaments* short; *styles* 2 ; *stigmas* 4. *Berry* smooth, one-seeded, of the size of a pea.

This valuable tree, though it does not grow very high, attains a diameter of from 10-12 inches and more. It has a very thin *bark*, and the beauty and usefulness of its jet-black, hard, and durable *wood* requires no comment. It grows along the banks of the Orange River, and seems to occur more copiously in the far North, Dr Livingstone having sent large circular specimens of it from the interior to the South African Museum. Fl. Sept.—October.

73. *Euclea Lanceolata. E. Meyer.* (*Bush Guarri.*)— *Branches* purplish-brown, angular, downy. *Leaves* alternate or opposite, erect, short-stalked, lanceolate, blunt, wavy, coriaceous, smooth, glossy, and netted with veins on the upper surface ; pale, rusty and scaly below. *Flowers* dioecious, small, racemose ; *racemes* axillary, 5 flowered, shorter than the leaves. *Calyx* 4 toothed. *Corolla* deeply 4 fid, externally hairy, three times as long as the calyx. *Anthers* 12-22 ; *styles* 2 bifid. *Berry* smooth, pea-like.

A tree 20-25 feet high, and from 10-15 inches wide. *Bark* grey, wrinkled ; *Wood* dark, coloured, heavy. Called *Omgwali* by the Kafirs.
Grows in the forests of George and the Zuurbergen, also in the Addo-bush (Uitenhage), and Brit. Caffraria. Fl. Sept.—Octbr.

74. *Euclea Undulata. Thbg.* (*Guarri-wood.*)— *Branches* erect ; *twigs* spreading. *Leaves* alternate or opposite, obovate, blunt, entire, narrowed at base, wavy, coriaceous. *Flowers* dioecious, racemose ; *racemes* axillary, few-flowered. *Calyx* 4, toothed. *Corolla* 4 fid, bell-shaped, thrice as long as the Calyx. *Stamens* 10—14.

Shrubby ; height 6 to 8 feet ; breadth 5 to 6 inches. *Bark* whitish-grey, rough. *Wood* brown, hard, close grained, and fit for joiner's fancy work, veneering, &c. The *fruit* is well known by the name of *Guarri-besjes*, and eaten by the natives.
Common in karroo-like soil in the Swellendam, George, and Uitenhage districts. Fl. Dec.— January.

75. *Euclea Racemosa. Lin.*— *Branches* erect, rough ; *twigs* much divided. *Leaves* almost sessile, oblong, leathery, blunt, entire, veined, revolute. *Flowers* dioecious, racemose, white. *Racemes* stalked, many-flowered, axillary, pendulous. *Calyx* 4 cleft ; *corolla* bell-shaped, 4 fid ; *stamens* 13—15, connected at base, and hairy at the apices. *Styles* 2. *Berry* one-celled, one seeded, globose, fleshy.

Usual height 6 feet; diameter from 5 to 6 inches. *Bark* grey, smooth, *Wood* hard, heavy; employed by wheelwrights and turners. Answers very well for wooden screws, but is chiefly used as fuel.

Grows on the west side of Devil's Mountain, in Van Camp's Bay, near Wynberg, and in many other localities. Fl. June.

JASMINACEÆ. Juss.

76. *Olea Verrucosa.* *Link.* (*Olive-wood* ; *Olyvenhout.*)— *Branches* and *twigs* erect, tetragonous, rough, with scattered elevated warts. *Leaves* lanceolate, almost sessile, tapering at both extremities, callous at top, leathery, entire, glossy, and green above, yellowish beneath. *Flowers* small, white, paniculated. *Panicles* axillary, trichotomous. *Calyx* 4 cleft; *lobes* sharp-pointed. *Stamens* 2 ; *styles* short, 2 fid. *Corolla* rotate, 4 parted. *Drupe* pisiform, almost dry, one-seeded.

Height from 12 to 15 feet, breadth from 8 to 12 inches. *Bark* thin, grey, chinky. The *wood*, which is very compact and heavy, looks handsome when polished, and is one of the most useful woods in the Colony. On account of its density and extreme hardness, which even wears out iron, it is admirably adapted for furniture, tools, wagonwork, and for the construction of mills and other machinery.

This tree much resembles the European Olive, for which it was formerly mistaken by botanists, and which might be grafted upon it with probable success. Shaded, stony localities are the places where it grows best, while trees exposed to heat and wind remain dwarfish.

Spread over a great portion of South Africa, from Cape Town to beyond the Orange River. Fl. April—May.

77. *Olea Laurifolia.* *Lamk.* (*Ol. undulata Jacq.*) (*Black Ironwood* ; *Zwart Yzerhout.*)—*Branches* spreading, rough, warty. *Leaves* stalked, opposite, oblong, wavy, entire, coriaceous smooth, pale beneath. *Flowers* white, numerous, scented, small, paniculated. *Panicles* terminal, trichotomously branched. *Anthers* yellow ; *stigma* globose. *Drupe* baccate. Botan. Magaz. t. 3089.

Height from 15 to 20 feet; diameter from 1½ to 2. *Bark* grey. *Wood* brownish, hard, close-grained, and heavy. Looks well when varnished, and is used by cabinet-makers for all kinds of furniture, but is chiefly employed for axles, poles, and general wagonwork. Tools, also ploughs and agricultural implements, are manufactured from it.

Grows abundantly in most of the forests of the eastern parts of the Colony. Fl. May—June.

78. *Olea Foveolata.* *E. Meyer.* (*Ironwood* ; *Yzerhout.*)— *Branches* ash-coloured, spreading ; *twigs* forked, young-ones downy. *Leaves* opposite, short-stalked, ovate-oblong, smooth, penninerved, entire with revolute margins, blunt, retuse and recurved at apex, leathery, glossy above, pale and pitted in the

axils of the veins below. *Flowers* cymose; *cymes* short, axillary; *bractlets* and segments of the *calyx* obtuse; lobes of the *corolla* hooded at top. *Drupe* dry, elliptical.

A tree about 20 feet high, and from 8-10 inches broad. *Bark* thin, whitish, smooth. *Wood* white, very close-grained, heavy, and hard, Well adapted for wagonwork of all kinds, and more particularly for poles and the construction of wheels. Grows in the forests of the Krakakamma and Olifantshoek. Fl. Febr.—March.

79. *Olea Capensis. Linn.*—*Branches* and *twigs* quadrangular, rough. *Leaves* short-stalked, opposite, oval or obovate, blunt or sometimes mucronate, entire, leathery, smooth. *Flowers* panicled, minute, crowded, white; *panicles* terminal, three-forked. Drupes ellipsoidal, wrinkled, somewhat smaller than a pea.

A tree 20-25 feet high, and 1-1½ broad. *Bark* white, smooth. *Wood* white, compact, and heavy, like the preceding, and used for similar purposes.
Common in the forests, throughout a great part of the Colony. Fl. Januar.—Febr.

ASCLEPIADEÆ. R. Br.

80. *Secamone Thunbergii. E. Meyer. (Periploca Secamone. Thbg.) (Boschtouw; Melktouw.)*—*Stem* twining. *Branches* alternate, opposite, spreading. *Leaves* stalked, oblong, opposite, obtuse or bluntly pointed, entire, ribbed, smooth, revolute. *Flowers* cymose, white, minute. *Cymes* axillary, dichotomous. *Pedicels* downy, rufous. *Calyx* 5 parted, *coronet* 5 scaled. *Corolla* rotate, 5 fid, villous within. *Follicles* brachiate, acute, glabrous. *Seeds* hairy.

This shrub derives its vernacular name from the milky juice which oozes from it when wounded. The stem, which like that of the wild vine, and other twining shrubs, climbs to the very tops of the tallest forest-trees, serves the baboons instead of ropes, to swing themselves from tree to tree, when in search of food, or in escaping from their enemies *(Baviaanslouw; Baboonsrope).* Bark grey, warty. *Wood* white, hard, and tough; but although the stem often attains a considerable length, its thickness rarely exceeds a few inches. The natives use these twigs as we do those of the willow.
Common in the primeval forests of the Colony. Fl. October—November.

APOCYNEÆ. Juss.

81. *Gonioma Kamassi. E. Meyer. (Kamassi-wood, Kamassi-hout.)*—*Branches* erect, whorled. *Leaves* opposite, or more frequently ternate, oblong-lanceolate, entire coriaceous, ribbed, taper-pointed, dark green and glossy above, paler beneath. *Flowers* small, cymose, leathery, yellowish, sweet-scented. *Cymes*

terminal, many-flowered. *Calyx* 5 cleft; lobes blunt. *Filaments* 5, short; *anthers* inclosed; *style* 1. *Corolla* salver-shaped; tube hairy within, narrowed at the throat. *Follicles* 2, roundish, patent. *Seeds* pendulous, surrounded with an oblong netted wing.

Trunk slender, straight, 16 to 20 feet high, and from 1 to 1½ broad. *Bark* thin, yellowish-grey. *Wood* yellow, very hard, tough, close-grained, and one of the finest in the Colony. It serves the cabinet-maker for furniture and veneering, but is particularly adapted for the manufacture of planes and carpenter's tools, engraving, &c. It is useful also for poles, yokes, ploughs, &c.

This tree, whose flowers fill the surrounding atmosphere with their delightful smell, is pretty common in the aboriginal woods of the Tzitsikamma, Krakakamma, and Addo (Uitenhage). Fl. October.

LOGANIACEÆ. ENDL.

82.* *Atherstonea Decussata.* (*Cape Teak,* or *Kajatenhout.*) —*Branches* and *branchlets* decussate, 2-3 forked; upper twigs compressed, knotty. *Leaves* opposite or fascicled at the top of the branchlets, ovate or ovate-oblong, entire, blunt, triplinerved, revolute, leathery, smooth, glossy, pale and netted-veined below, cuneate and lengthened into a short petiole, 1-2 inches long, ½ to an inch broad. *Interpetiolary stipules* represented by elevated ridges at the bases of the leaf-stalks. *Flowers* hermaphrodite, corymbose, minute, greenish; *corymbs* axillary, few-flowered, *bracts* opposite, amplexicaul, concave, acute. *Calyx* 4-5 partite, free, its *segments* ovate, blunt, and fringed at the margins. *Corolla* monopetalous, regular, campanulate, externally smooth, internally villoso-barbate; *lobes* lanceolate, incurved at top and spreading on expansion; *aestivation* valvate. *Stamens* 4-5 adhering, to the corolla, and alternating with the lobes; *anthers* 2 locular, oval, erect, introrse; *style* simple, thickish, subcapitate, shorter than the stamens; *genitals* enclosed. *Ovary* 2 celled (?) *Drupe* oblong, smooth. *Seeds* unknown.

This tree grows 20-25 feet high, and from 1 to 1½ feet broad. *Bark* brown, rimpled. *Wood* reddish-brown, hard, heavy, tough, and less brittle than Oak. It serves in the manufacture of rural utensils, but is chiefly employed in the form of staves for cooper's work.

Grows in the thickets and forests of Uitenhage, Olifant's Hoek, and elsewhere in the districts of the Eastern Province. Fl. November.

SCROPHULARIACEÆ. JUSS.

83. *Halleria Lucida. Lin.* (*White Olive.*)—Stem trichotomously branched. *Branches* spreading. *Leaves* petiolate, oppo-

---

* Named in honour of Dr. *W. G. Atherstone*, of Graham's Town, a gentleman whose merits rendered to South African Botany and Geology rank high, and to whom I am under great obligations for valuable information towards this work.

site, ovate, acuminate, serrate, smooth. *Flowers* stalked, axillary, aggregate, nodding; *peduncles* one-flowered. *Calyx* persistent, very short, 3 lobed. *Corolla* irregular, curved, funnel-shaped. purple; *limb* bilabiate. *Stamens* 4, exserted; *stigma* acute, *Berry* globose, smooth. Bot. Magaz. t. 1,744.

Usual height of trunk, which is straight, about 12-14 feet; diameter from 6-8 inches. *Bark* very thin, greyish-white, much rent. *Wood* like *Red Beech*, but of a finer grain, hard, tough and well adapted for carpenter's work, planes, screws, joiner's benches, and tools of every description. It also supplies the wagoumaker with a good article for poles, &c.
This small tree is found both in the Western and Eastern districts. Moisty, shady places are most favourable to its vigorous growth. Fl. June—July.

84. *Halleria Elliptica. Thbg. (Oudehout.)*—*Branches* oppo-site; *twigs* erect, quadrangular, patent. *Leaves* oblong, narrowed towards each end, serrate, rigid, smooth. *Flowers* peduncled, axillary, standing in two's. *Corolla* nearly equally lobed, tubular at base, bell-shaped at top, purple, nodding. *Stamens, style,* and *berry* as in *Halleria lucida. Lin.* Burm. Plant. Afric. Dec. t. 89, fig. 1.

Height 6-10 feet; diameter 8-9 inches. *Bark* white, smooth. *Wood* yellowish, soft but tough. Used chiefly for plough-beams, axe handles, &c.
In the woods of the Uitenhage district, and other parts of the Colony. Fl. June.

85. *Nuxia Floribunda. Benth. (Wild Elder.)*—*Branches* greyish, white; *twigs* angular or compressed. *Leaves* opposite, subverticillate, mostly in threes, long-stalked, oblong-elliptical blunt or mucronate, margined, penninerved, entire or faintly toothed, smooth. *Flowers* panicled, white; *panicles* terminal, many-flowered, pyramidal, dichotomously branched. *Calyx* bell-shaped, glossy, 4 toothed; *teeth* short. *Corolla* short, tubular; *limb* patent, 4 lobed. *Stamens* 4, exserted, *style* undivided; *stigma* thick. *Capsule* 2 valved; *Seeds* minute, numerous.

A handsome tree, measuring from 20-30 feet in height and from 1-2 in diameter. *Bark* thin, whitish. *Wood* close, heavy, white, and useful for common furniture, rural implements, wagonwork, &c.
Grows in the forests of George, Uitenhage and Natal. Fl. May—June.

86. *Chilianthus Arboreus. Burch. (Wild Elder.)*—*Bran-ches* and *twigs* alternate, angular, shaggy. *Leaves* opposite, stalked, oblong-lanceolate, acute, veiny, entire, hoary beneath, much resembling those of the common *Olive tree. Flowers* numerous, small, white, paniculated. *Panicles* large, fastigiate,

not unlike those of *Sambucus nigra* (Elder). *Calyx* 4 cleft, bell-shaped, tomentose. *Stamens* 4, exserted; *style* 1, short. *Capsule* ovate, 4 valved, 4 seeded. Jacq. Hort, Schoenbr. t. 29.

A small tree. Height without the branches about 10 feet; diameter 8 to 10 inches. *Wood* hard and tough. Used for common furniture, chairs, table-feet, &c.

To be met with in the Cape, Swellendam, and Uitenhage districts. Fl. November—December.

87. *Buddleia Salviæfolia*. *Lamb.* (*Sage-wood*)—Much branched. *Branches* quadrangular; *twigs* erect, switchy. *Leaves* almost sessile, opposite, lanceolate, crenate, cordate, acute, veined, rugose, dark green above, and covered beneath with a thick rust-coloured shag, along with the twigs, calyces, and flowers. *Flowers* clustered, terminal, numerous, paniculated; *panicles* ovato-pyramidate. *Calyx* bell-shaped, 4 parted. *Corolla* regular, funnel-shaped, 4 fid, yellow. *Stamens* 4; *style* simple. *Capsule* 2 valved, many seeded. Jacq. Hort. Schoenbrun t. 28.

Height 12 to 15 feet; diameter 8 to 10 inches. *Wood* hard, tough, heavy, and well suited for wagonwork, ramrods, yokes, and rural utensils of every kind. Mr. S. J. Hartman, an old experienced resident in the Eastern Province, and an undoubted authority on frontier matters, informs me, that it was this tree chiefly which furnished the Kafir warriors with shafts, for their javelins or assagais.

Common in the districts of George, Uitenhage, Albany and Victoria East. Fl. January – February.

LAURINEÆ. Juss.

88. *Oreodaphne Bullata*. *Nees ab. E.* (*Stinkwood, Stink-hout.*)—Much branched. *Branches* divaricating, smooth. *Leaves* alternate, leathery, elliptical, veiny, netted, glabrous, entire, attenuated into a channelled stalk, and having at the axils of the lower costal veins on the underside deep hollows, ciliated at their edges, and showing on the upper surface corresponding blisterlike protuberances. *Flowers* small, racemose; *racemes* lateral or axillary. *Perianth* 6 parted; lobes obtuse, deciduous. *Corolla* none. *Stamens* 9; glands of the outer-stamens large, capitate. *Style* tapering; stigma peltate. *Berry* surrounded at base by the enlarged, thickened, cup-shaped tube of the perianth. Hooker. Bot. Magz. t. 3,931

Height from 60-70 feet; diameter from 3-5. *Bark* dark-grey, moderately thick. The *Wood* of this beautiful tree (Mr. Barrow's African Oak*) smells very disagreeably when cut or worked at, and owing to the different stages of growth, three distinct varieties, the *white, mottled,* and *dark,* are produced by the same species. Stinkwood is hard and durable, and the mottled and dark take an excellent polish

* The true African Oak of commerce is *Oldfieldia Africana*. Benth. & Hook

and resemble *Walnut*. In the Colony it is extensively used no less for building purposes, than for cabinetmaker's and carpenter's work. It furnishes the finest and most substantial articles of furniture, is superior to every other wood in the manufacture of gunstocks, and serves the wagonmaker also for various purposes. At the river *Knysna*, where this tree attains a considerable size, the *white* variety has been employed even in ship-building.

In consequence, perhaps, of the peculiar odour exhaled by this wood when fresh, furniture made of it is little infested by vermin.

Grows in the primeval forests throughout a great portion of the Colony, and is even found in the bushy ravines of Table Mountain. There however, it is never allowed to become a stately tree, owing to the wanton usage of firing the mountain every year, a practice which not only destroys the most valuable timber, but greatly diminishes the supply of water, the occasional want of which in summer would not be felt so often, if the legislature were either to enact stringent laws against the continuance of this outrage, or to enforce, in a modified form, those in existence. Fl. October.

PROTEACEÆ. R. Br.

89. *Leucadendron Argenteum. B. Br. (Silver-tree; Witteboom.)*—*Branches* and *twigs* round, rough, erect, tomentose *Leaves* crowded, sessile, alternate, lanceolate, glandular at top, entire, silky. *Flowers* dioecious, capitate in both sexes. *Capitula* many-flowered, terminal, solitary, surrounded with imbricated leaves. *Bracts* dilated, imbricated, tomentose. *Calyx* 4 parted, regular. *Stamens* 4; *style* filiform; *stigma* oblique, clavate, emarginate: *cone* of female flowers ovate, large; its scales obtuse, concave, woody. *Nut* black, one seeded, wingless, inclosed within the scales of the *cone*.

Height from 8 to 10 feet; diameter from 8 to 12 inches. *Bark* thick. *Wood* soft, spongy, and liable to be infested by insects. Used occasionally for boxes, &c., but more commonly for fuel.

This handsome tree is, on account of its fine silvery foliage, seen at a great distance, and has a very limited station, being peculiar only to Cape Town and vicinity. Fl. September—October.

90. *Protea Grandiflora. Lin. (Wagon-tree; Wagenboom.)* —Much branched. *Branches* purplish, erect, smooth. *Leaves* alternate, oblong, sessile, glabrous, blunt, leathery, veiny, entire, callous at top. *Flowers* hermaphroditical, capitate, terminal. *Capitula* large, half-round, terminal, involucrated. *Involucres* many-scaled; outer scales ovate, clothed with a rust-coloured shag; inner ones spathulate, smooth. *Perianth* 2 partite, tomentose; *staminiferous laminæ* cohering; *style* awl-shaped, persistent. *Nut* one-seeded, bearded. Bot. Magaz. t. 2,447.

Height about 6-8 feet; breadth 6-8 inches. *Bark* brown, thick, much rent. The *wood* has a reddish tint; its grain is beautifully reticulated, and renders it useful for ornamental furniture, picture frames, &c. It is sometimes employed for fellies, ploughs, &c. The bruised *leaves* mixed with a saturated solution of iron in water, produce a tolerably good, black writing ink. The bark which furnishes a superior article for tanning. is used as an astringent in diarrhœa, and good charcoal is often made of the wood. Abundant in many parts of the Western districts, and particularly common in Hout Bay. Fl April.

91. *Leucospermum Conocarpum. R. Br. (Kreupelboom.)* —*Branches* spreading, very hairy. *Leaves* sessile, oval, rigid, veiny, calloso-dentate towards the top, villose at base. *Flowers* hermaphroditical, capitate, terminal, yellow. *Capitula* many-flowered, involucrated. *Involucres* imbricated, persistent; *scales* ovate, pointed, recurved, villose on the outside, smooth within. *Perianth* irregular, 2 partite, bearded. *Stamens* 4; *style* filiform; *stigma* thick, elongated, unequal-sided, smooth. *Nut* one-seeded, glabrous, white.

Stem from 6 to 8 feet high, and from 4 to 6 inches in diameter; dwarfish, with a flat, broad top. *Bark* brown, thick, cragged. *Wood* reddish, tough but soft; looking well when varnished. In the Colony it is sometimes used for wagon fellies, but oftener for making charcoal, and for fuel. The *bark* furnishes one of the best materials in the tanning of skins, and a decoction of it is recommended as a powerful astringent.

Common near Cape Town and in other parts of the Colony. Fl. September.—October.

92. *Brabeium Stellatifolium. R. Br. (Wild Almond; Wilde Amandelboom.)*—*Branches* purplish, villose at top. *Leaves* whorled, petiolate, lanceolate, acute, serrato dentate, rigid, veiny, smooth, green above, pale and netted beneath. *Petioles* very short. *Flowers* polygamous, fascicled, spiked, white, sweet-scented, supported by *one* common bract. *Spikes* axillary; *peduncles* tomentose. *Perianth* 4 leaved, regular; *stamina* 4; *style* filiform, vertical. *Fruit* dry, one-seeded; *kernel* bony.

Stem from 8 to 10 feet high, and from ½ to 1½ feet broad. *Bark* thick, greyish-brown. *Wood* red, reticulated, looking extremely hand-some when polished, and fit to be used for ornamental joiner's and turner's work. As yet is has been little employed except as firewood. The bark of this proteaceous plant also contains a great deal of the tanning principle. The fruit, a drupe, is clothed in a velvety coat, and has received the vernacular name from its striking similarity to the almond. After having been soaked for some days in water, it is eaten by the natives, being obnoxious* when quite fresh. The *kernel*, when roasted, is used as coffee.

*A fatal case of poisoning caused by the eating of the *Wild Almond* in *its raw state* has just (May, 1862) occurred at Genadendal, where the shrub grows in abundance. A little girl, 6 years, of age having partaken of a quantity of this fruit, shortly afterwards complained of nausea and headache, followed by vomiting, purging, and pains in the stomach and abdomen. Dr. Roser who was sent for three hours after

F

Found in the thickets and woody ravines on the east side of Table Mountain, and in many other localities. Fl. December.

SANTALACEÆ R. Bn.

93. *Osyris Compressa. A. DC.* (*Thesium Colpoon, Thbg.*) (*Pruimbast.*)—*Branches* trichotomous, erect; *twigs* angular, compressed, smooth. *Leaves* on short stalks, opposite, ovate, entire, mucronate, glabrous. *Flowers* monœcious, small, paniculate, terminal. *Corolla* none. *Perianth* turbinate, 4 cleft; *stamens* 4; *style* short; *stigma* 4 lobed. *Drupe* baccate, obovate, one-seeded. Berg. Plant. Cap. Tab 1. Fig 1.

Height of stem from 4 to 5 feet; diameter 4 to 6 inches. *Bark* grey thin. *Wood* heavy, fine grained; useful to the turner and joiner, and very fit for fancy work. The whole of this bush contains a great deal of tanning matter, and is for that reason employed by many colonists for that purpose.

Common in most of the Western parts of the Colony. Fl. May.

MOREÆ. Endl.

94. *Urostigma Natalense. Miq.*—Much branched. *Branches* patent, wrinkled, white, smooth. *Leaves* at the top of the branches stalked, obovate, bluntly-pointed, entire, membranaceous, glabrous, penninerved and netted beneath. *Flowers* monœcious, crowded, enclosed within small, fleshy, globose, pisiform *receptacles*, which are solitary, axillary, almost sessile, and supported at their bases by 3 bracts.

The wild *Fig-tree* (the t'Kaa or Na-touw of the Hottentots and the *Uluzi* of the Kafirs) grows to a considerable height; its diameter being from 8 to 10 inches. *Bark* white, smooth. *Wood* light, spongy, very porous. The *fibres* of the bark serve the natives for the manufacture of very serviceable ropes.

Common in the aboriginal forests of the Uitenhage, Albany, and Victoria East districts; also in Caffraria Proper, and at Port Natal. Fl. July.

95. *Sycomorus Capensis. Miq.* (*Bush-fig, or Malabar-tree*) —*Branches* white, spreading. *Leaves* stalked, ovate or ovate-oblong, entire or sinuato-dentate, apiculate, veined, smooth, membranous, pale on the underside, three or four times as long as the petioles. *Fruit* stalked, scattered on the branches, top-

---

these symptoms had first made their appearance, found the child in spasms and nearly insensible. Emetics and antispasmodics promptly administered proved ineffective, and the poor little sufferer soon expired under convulsions.

At a post-mortem examination made next day, the entire mucous membrane of the stomach and bowels, and particularly that of the colon, was found inflamed; the stomach empty and the other viscera perfectly healthy.

shaped, as large or somewhat larger than a hazelnut. Hook.
Lond. Journ. of Botan. vol 7. tab. 3. B.

A tree of considerable size and width. *Bark* rough, fibrous. *Wood*
white, soft, and of little value.
Common in the primeval forests of the Krakakamma, Tzitsikamma,
Zuurbergen and Natal—Nov.

CELTIDEÆ. Rich.

96. *Celtis rhamnifolia.* *Prsl.* (*Rhamnus celtifolius.* *Thbg.*)
—(*Camdeboo-Stinkwood.*) *Branches and twigs* pimpled, rough.
Leaves short-stalked, alternate, ovate, bluntly-acuminate, serrate,
more or less unequal sided at base, pale with elevated veins below,
leathery, smooth. *Flowers* monœcious, stalked, solitary or
clustered, axillary, greenish, small. *Flower-stalks* pilose. *Perianth*
4 celft, persistent; its segments ovate, concave. *Corolla* none.
Stamens 4, shorter than the perianth and opposite its lobes;
anthers cordate, introrse; *ovary* ovate, hispid, 1 celled; *stigmata*
2 terminal, recurved. *Drupe* fleshy, yellow. Burm. Pl. African.
Decad. t. 88.

Height 20, diameter 2 feet and more. *Bark* grey, even. *Wood*
yellowish-white, tough. Used for planks, yokes, triggers, axehandles,
laths, fences, and cooper's work. The Kafir name for this tree is
Ombabe
Common in the forests both of the Western and Eastern Provinces, and
in British Caffraria. Fl.—Sept.

AMENTACEÆ. Juss.

97. *Salix Gariepina.* *Burch.* (*Willow-tree; Wilgeboom.*)
—*Branches* smooth, pendulous. *Leaves* narrow-lanceolate, acute.
sawed, glabrous, glaucous beneath. *Scales* of the *catkins* downy.
Male catkins cylindrical; *stamens* 5; *female catkins* racemose.
Capsules stalked, ovate, 2 valved. (*Burchell.*)

Height from 15 to 20 feet; breadth from 1½ to 2. *Bark* brown, almost
like cork. *Wood* white, light, soft; liable to attack by insects of the
beetle tribe. The larger twigs are used for spars in house building, the
slender ones in the manufacture of baskets, &c.
This tree much resembles the Weeping-willow, and grows chiefly
along the banks of the river Gariep.

CONIFERÆ. Juss.

98. *Widdringtonia Juniperoides.* *Endl.* (*Cedar-tree; Ceder-boom.*)—*Branches* purplish, squarrose, twiggy. *Leaves* opposite,
minute, decussate, densely imbricated, appressed, ovate, connate,

bluntly pointed, glabrous, glanduliferous. *Flowers* dioecious. *Male cathins* terminal, solitary; female ones, lateral. *Cones* globose, 4 valved; *valves* woody, erect, mucronate.

This valuable tree, if not disturbed, attains a very considerable size. Its usual height, however, is from 15 to 20 feet, and its diameter from 3 to 4. The *wood* resembles fir, has a peculiar smell, and makes valuable timber for ship and housebuilding. It is also useful to the cabinetmaker for various kinds of furniture: chests, drawers, chairs, tables, wardrobes, &c., which are durable on account of the resinous smell of the wood, which keeps them from the aggressions of insects.

Sir JAMES ALEXANDER, in his exploring expedition into the interior of Africa (vol. I., pag. 230, sqq.), in making mention of the *Cedar tree*, remarks, that one of them was cut down in 1836, which was 36 feet in girth, and out of whose giant arms 1,000 feet of planking were sawn. He bitterly complains, that this noble tree is fast disappearing in the Cedar Mountains. Mr. W. VON MEYER,* another South African traveller, says, that in former days the whole of the mountainous chain, to which the Cedar Mountains belong, was studded with these trees, but that of late the *axe* and *conflagrations* have done their *utmost* to *destroy the valuable forests.*

From the branches and cones of this tree exudes a gum, which soon hardens in the air, becomes solid, yellowish, and transparent, and scarcely differs from the *Gummi Olibanum*, an article well known to commerce. This gum is successfully used in the form of fumigations in gout, rheumatism, or œdematous swellings; and is also employed for the purpose of compounding plasters or preparing varnish.

Found only in the Cedar Mountains, in the Clanwilliam district.

99. *Widdringtonia Cupressoides. Endl. (Sapree-wood.)*— *Branches* alternate, erect. *Leaves* quadrifarious, imbricate, sessile, appressed, oblong, blunt, smooth. *Inflorescence* and *fructification* like that of the preceding species.

Attains the height of 12 feet, and measures 6 to 8 inches in diameter. The *wood* is rather light, but said to be of service for cooper's work, especially in the manufacture of pails.

Not uncommon in elevated localities throughout a great portion of the Colony, but seldom allowed to grow to maturity, in consequence of the destructive fires already alluded to.

TAXINEÆ. RICH.

100. *Podocarpus Elongatus. l'Herit. (Outeniqua Yellow-wood.)*—*Branches* whorled, spreading; *twigs* angular, somewhat compressed. *Leaves* almost sessile, alternate, narrow, linear-lanceolate, acutely mucronate, entire, smooth. *Flowers* dioecious; *male cathins* terminal, clustered, spiked, surrounded at base with

---

* Reisen in Süd-Africa, während der Jahre 1840 und 1841. Hamburg, 1843, 8vo. pag. 131.

imbricated bracts. *Stamens* several, short. *Female catkins* stalked, axillary, solitary, destitute of bracts, one-flowered. *Drupe* one-celled, roundish, elliptical, half immersed in the fleshy receptacle.

Height from 50 to 70 feet; diameter from 3 to 7. *Bark* thin, grey, smooth. *Wood* yellowish, not unlike deal, but destitute of resin. It is the *Omcaba* of the Kafirs.

Extensively used in the Colony as timber, in the shape of beams, planks, floors, &c., but also for all kinds of carpenter's and joiner's work, such as bedsteads, tables, presses, chairs; in fact, for common furniture of every description, and looks exceedingly well when polished. The lofty stem of this tree is serviceable for top masts and yards of ships. Common in the primeval forests of the Knysna, where it is found in greatest perfection.

101. *Podocarpus Thunbergii. Hook. (Upright Yellow-wood.)* —*Leaves* broad-oblong, lanceolate, blunt with a callous point, narrowed into a short stalk, one-nerved, leathery, smooth. *Male catkins* short, axillary; *female one* solitary, stalked; *stalk* as long as the 2 teethed receptacle. *Branches* and fruit as in *P. elongatus.* Hook. Lond. Journ. of Botany. vol. 1. tab. 22.

Stem very straight. Height 40-60 feet; diameter 3 to 4. *Bark* thin, whitish-grey. *Wood* bright-yellow, very handsome when polished, of finer grain, and greatly superior to the former. It is particularly fit for furniture, but not less so for a variety of other purposes. The leaves are the broadest of any of the South African species of the genus.

Grows in the forests both of the Western and Eastern districts. Fl. September.

102. *Podocarpus Pruinosus. E. M. (Bastard Yellow-wood.)*—*Branches* grey, much spreading; *twigs* angular. *Leaves* distichous, subsessile, linear-lanceolate, subfalcate, acute, leathery, glaucous, 10 lines to an inch, long, 1½ to 2 lines broad. *Male catkins* cylindrical, 3-4 lines long, crowded in the axils of the leaves; *female flowers* and *drupes* unknown to me.

Attains a very considerable height and circumference. *Wood* pale-yellow, tough, but in all respects inferior to the two preceding species, though extensively used for building purposes throughout the Colony and British Caffraria. Among the Kafirs it goes by the name of *Omtemseba.*

Common in the forests of the Colony and beyond it.

LIST OF SOUTH AFRICAN FOREST TREES AND ARBORESCENT SHRUBS.

BOTANICAL NAMES.	GENERAL HEIGHT.	SIZE OF DIAMETER.	QUALITY.	USES.	VERNACULAR NAMES.
Acacia horrida, Willd...	20-25 feet.	1-1½ feet.	Tough, hard.	Wagonmaking, rural implements; gum; bark for tanning.	Thorntree, doornboom.
Apodytes dimidiata, E. M...	30-50 "	1-2 "	Light.	Common furniture, yokes, &c.	No vernacular name
*Atherstonea decussata...	20-25 "	1-1½ "	Hard, tough, less brittle than oak.	Cooper's works, farming utensils.	Cape teak, or kajatenhout.
Brabeium stellatifolium, R. Br...	8-10 "	1-1½ "	Rather soft.	Tanning, fuel.	Wild almond.
Brachylaena dentata, D. C...	12-14 "	6-9 inches	Hard.	Charcoal.	No colonial name.
Buddleia salviaefolia, Lamk...	12-15 "	8-10 "	Hard, tough.	Wagonwork, yokes, &c.	Sagewood.
Burchellia capensis, D. C...	12-14 "	1-2 feet.	Hard, close.	Agricultural implements, &c.	Wild pomegranate, buffelshoorn.
Calodendron capense, Thbg...	20-30 "	2-3 "	Soft.	Yokes, poles, &c.	Wild chesnut.
Canthium pyrifolium, Kl...	15-20 "	4-6 inches	Close, heavy.	Turner's work.	No colonial name.
Capparis albitrunca, Burch ...	10-12 "	9-10 "	Tough, white.	Yokes, rural implements.	Witgatboom.
Cassine capensis, Lin...	8-10 "	8-12 "	Hard, tough.	Joiner's fancy work.	Ladlewood, lepelhout.
Celastrus acuminatus, Lin...	12-15 "	7-12 "	Fine-grained, heavy.	Joiner's and turner's work.	Silkbark, zybast.
" buxifolius, Lin...	8-12 "	6-8 "	Very hard, close.	Musical instruments, engraving, &c.	Cape box.
" undatus, Thbg...	20-25 "	1-1½ feet	Close-grained, heavy.	Wagonwork and farming utensils.	Kokotree.
Celtis rhamnifolia, Prsl...	20 ft. & more	2 "	Tough.	Planks, yokes, triggers, &c.	Camdeboo stinkwood
Chilianthus arboreus, D C...	10 feet.	8-10 inch.	Hard and tough.	Common furniture, &c.	Wild elder.
Cunonia capensis, Lin...	15-25 "	1½-2 feet.	Tough, close.	Joiner's & turner's work, &c.	Red alder, rood els.

	Height	Thickness	Quality	Uses	Common name
Curtisia faginea, Ait............	20-40 feet	2-3 feet.	Tough, close-grained.	Furniture, tools, turner's work, wagon making.	Assagaywood.
Dovyalis rhamnoides, Harv......	20-30 "	2-3 "	Hard, close.	Wagonwork, ploughs, &c.	Zuurbesje.
Eckebergia capensis, Sparrm...	20-30 "	2-3 "	Close, tough.	Beams, planks, &c.	Cape ash, essenhout.
Elaeodendron croceum, D. C.....	20-40 "	2-4 "	Fine-grained, hard, tough.	Beams, planks, furniture, &c.	Saffronwood, safraanhout.
Erythrina caffra, Thbg..........	50-60 "	3-4 "	Soft, spongy.	Shingles, canoes, &c.	Kafir tree.
Euclea lanceolata, E. M.........	20-25 "	10-15 inch.	Heavy.	Yokes, triggers, &c.	Bush guarri.
" pseudebenus, E. M.........	12-15 ft. & more	10-12 "	Very hard and heavy.	Fancy furniture, turner's work, &c.	Cape ebony.
" racemosa, Lin.............	6 feet.	5-6 "	Hard, heavy.	Wooden screws, and sundry turner's work.	Guarriwood.
" undulata, Thbg............	6-8 "	5-6 "	Close-grained.	Joiner's fancy work, veneering, &c.	Ditto.
Eugenia Zeyheri, Harv..........	15-20 "	9-12 "	Fine-grained, hard.	Carpenter's tools, ploughs, axles, &c.	Wild jambos.
Gardenia Rothmannia, Lin fil ...	15-20 "	1-1½ feet.	Very hard and tough.	Tools, axles, fellies, engraving, &c.	Unknown.
" Thunbergia Lin. fil......	8-10 "	10-12 inch.	Very hard and tough.	Like the preceding.	Wild katjepiering, buffelsbal.
Gonioma kamassi, E. M..........	16-20 "	1-1½ feet.	Hard, close, tough.	Tools, veneering, engraving.	Kamassiwood.
Grewia occidentalis, Lin	10-12 "	3 inches	Very tough.	Turner's work, bows, &c.	Kruysbesje.
Grumilea cymosa, E. M..........	20-30 "	2-2½ feet	Hard, tough.	Rural utensils, &c.	Lemonwood.
Halleria elliptica, Thbg..........	15-20 "	8-10 inches	Tough.	Yokes, axe-handles, plough beams, &c.	Oudehout.
" incida, Lin...............	12-14 "	6-8 "	Hard, tough.	Tools, screws, &c.	White olive.
Harpephyllum caffrum, Bernh...	20-30 "	1-2 feet	Red, tough.	Furniture, planking, &c.	Wild or Kafir plum.
Hartogia capensis, Thbg.........	12-15 "	1-1½ "	Fine-grained, hard, tough.	Furniture, veneering.	Smalblad.
Hippobromus alata, E. & Z.....	15-20 "	1-1½ "	Close.	Planking, wagonwork, agricultural implements.	Paardepis.
Ilex capensis. Sond. & Harv......	8-12 "	6-8 inch.	Soft, spongy.	Little used.	Unknown.
Kiggelaria africana, Lin..........	20-25 "	1-1½ feet.	Soft, spongy.	Spars, rafters, fuel.	Porkwood, speckhout.

List of South African Forest Trees and Arborescent Shrubs – *continued.*

Botanical Names.	General Height.	Size of Diameter.	Quality.	Uses.	Vernacular Names.
Leucadendron argenteum, R. Br..	8-10 feet.	8-12 inch.	Soft, spongy.	Fuel.	Silvertree, witteboom.
Leucospermum conocarpon, R Br.	5-8 „	5-6 „	Tough, but spongy.	Tanning, fuel.	Kreupelboom.
Maurocenia capensis, Sond......	6-8 „	3-4 „	Hard, tough.	Musical instruments.	Hottentot cherry.
Millettia caffra, Meisn..........	30-10 „	2-3 feet.	Hard & durable.	Furniture, &c.	Kafir ironwood, omzambetee.
Mimusops obovata, Sond..........	15-25 „	1½-2 „	Close-grained, tough, heavy.	Fellies, axles, and other wagonwork.	Red milkwood.
Myaris inæqualis, Prsl..........	10-12 „	6-8 inch.	Heavy, close-grained.	Little used.	Unknown.
Myrsine melanophleos, R. Br.....	15-20 „	1½-2 feet.	Tough.	Wagonwork.	Cape beech, beukenhont.
Mystroxilon Kubu, E. & Z.........	20-25 „.	1-1½ „	Hard, tough.	Fellies and other wagonwork, rural utensils, &c.	Kooboo.
Nichuhria triphylla, Wendl.....	20 „	9-15 inch.	Light, but tough.	Furniture, fellies, &c.	Withoschhout.
Nuxia floribunda, Bth............	20-30 „	1-2 feet.	Close, heavy.	Common furniture, rural implements, wagonwork.	Wild elder.
Ochna arborea, Burch............	20-30 „	1½-2 „	Heavy, tough.	Tools, triggers, poles, &c.	Redwood, roodhout.
Olea capensis, Lin..............	20-25 „	1-1½ „	Very hard and heavy.	Axles, poles, tools. &c.	Ironwood, Yzerhout.
„ foveolata, E. M...............	20 „	8-10 inch.	Very hard and heavy.	Wagonwork of all kinds, &c.	Ditto.
„ laurifolia, Lamk.............	15-20 „	1½-2 feet.	Close-grained, heavy.	Cabinet or Wagonmaker's work, &c.	Black ironwood.
„ verrucosa, Link..............	12-15 „	8-12 inch.	Compact, heavy, hard.	Furniture, millwork, wagon making, &c.	Olivewood, olyvenhout.

Olinia capensis, Kl......	25-30 feet	2-3 feet	Hard, heavy and tough	Axles, poles, railway sleepers, &c.	Hardpear.
" cymosa, Thbg..........	4-6 "	6-8 inch.	Close-grained, heavy.	Turner's work	No particular name.
Oreodaphne bullata, Nees. ab. E.	60-70 "	3-5 feet	Hard, like walnut.	Beams, planks, furniture, &c.	Stinkwood
Osyris compressa, A. D. C........	4-5 "	4-6 inch.	Heavy, fine-grained.	Turner's work, tanning	Pruinbast.
Philippia Chamissonis, Kl........	2-3 "	2-3 "	Hard, fine grained.	Joiner's fancywork	Kabinethout
Phoberos Ecklonii, W. Arn........	30-35 "	2-3 feet.	Hard, heavy, close.	Furniture, wagonwork, &c.	Redpear, roodpeer.
" Mundtii, W. Arn	20-30 "	2-3 "	Hard, heavy, close.	Ditto ditto	Michellwood, klipdoorn.
" Zeyheri, W. Arn........	15-25 "	1-2 "	Hard, heavy, close.	Ditto ditto	Wolfsthorn, hoenderspoor.
Platylophus trifoliatus, Don	20-30 "	3-4 "	Soft, but tough.	Cabinet and wagonmakers-work.	White alder, wit els,
Plectronia Mundtiana..........	12-15 "	6-8 inch.	Hard, heavy.	Turner's work, screws, tools, &c.	Rock alder, klip els
" spinosa, Kl........	10-15 "	7-10 "	Fine-grained, heavy.	Ditto ditto	Unknown.
" ventosa, Lin........	15-20 "	6-10 "	Heavy, tough.	Fellies and other wagon-work.	Schapendrolletje.
Podocarpus elongatus, l'Herit....	50-70 "	3-7 feet.	Close-grained, not unlike deal.	Beams, planks, &c.	Outeniqua yellow-wood.
" pruinosus, E. M......	50-70 "	3-7 "	Tough.	Ditto ditto.	Bastard yellow-wood.
" Thunbergi, Hook....	40-60 "	3-4 "	Fine-grained.	Furniture, planks, &c.	Upright yellow-wool.
Protea grandiflora, Lin........	6-8 "	6-8 inch.	Light but tough.	Fellies, ploughs, fancy furniture, picture frames.	Wagontree, wagenboom.
Ptaeroxylon utile, E. & Z......	20-30 "	2-4 feet.	Very strong, hard close.	Furniture, building, and waterworks.	Sneezewood, nieshout
Pterocelastrus rostratus, Walp...	20-25 "	1½-2 "	Heavy, strong	Wagonwork, fellies, &c., railroad works.	Whitepear, witpeer.
" tricuspidatus, Sond.	8-10 "	5-10 inch.	Soft and light.	Charcoal, fuel.	Spekboom.
" variabilis, Sond......	20-25 "	1-1½ feet.	Fine-grained, heavy.	Turner's work, agricultural implements.	Cherrywood, kersenhout.

G

List of South African Forest Trees and Arborescent Shrubs —*continued.*

Botanical Names.	General Height.	Size of Diameter.	Quality.	Uses.	Vernacular Names.
Rhus laevigata, Lin	8-10 feet.	8-10 inch.	Heavy, close.	Wagonmaker's and turner's work.	Bosganna.
„ lucida, Lin	4-6 „	3-4 „	Hard, tough.	Bark used for tanning	Taaibosch.
„ tomentosa, Lin	4-6 „	3-4 „	Hard, tough.	Ditto	Ditto.
„ Thunbergii, Hook	12-15 „	3-4 feet.	Hard, close, heavy.	Fancy furniture, turner's work, musical instruments, &c.	Rock ash, klipesse.
„ viminalis, Vahl	10-14 „	8-10 inch.	Hard, very tough.	Thatching, wagon tents, &c.	Karreewood.
Royena glabra, Lin	4-5 „	5-6 „	Wood light, porous	Fuel.	Unknown.
„ lucida, Thbg	10-12 „	6-12 „	Hard, tough.	Screws, tools, wagonwork, &c	Blackbark, zwartbast.
„ pubescens, Willd	6-8 „	4-5 „	Close grained, heavy.	Turner's work, wool engraving.	No colonial name.
Salix gariepina, Burch	15-20 „	1½-2 feet.	Light.	Spars, basketmaking, &c	Willowtree, wilgeboom.
Sapindus Pappea, Soud	15-20 „	1-1½ „	Hard, tough.	Yokes, poles, ploughs, &c.	Wild plum.
Schmidelia decipiens, W. Arn	10-15 „	6-10 inch.	Fine-grained, hard.	Turner's and fancy cabinetmaker's work	Unknown.
Schotia latifolia, Jacq	20-30 „	3-4 feet.	Hard, tough, heavy.	Triggers, posts, enclosures, &c.	Monkey boerboon; bosch boerboon.
„ speciosa, Jacq	8-12 „	1-1½ „	Hard, tough.	Yokes, fellies, triggers, &c.	Hottentot's boerboon.
Scutia Commersoni, Brogn	4-5 „	6-8 inch.	Strong, fine-grained.	Turner's work.	Katdoorn.
Scytophyllum laurinum, E. & Z.	10-12 „	6-8 „	Hard, heavy.	Tools, turner's work, &c.	No particular name.

	Height	Diameter	Quality	Uses	Common name
Secamone Thunbergii, E. M.	8-10 feet.	1-1½ inch.	Hard, tough.	Bows, basket making, &c.	Melktouw.
Sideroxylon inerme, Lin............	15-20 "	1-1½ feet.	Close, hard, heavy.	Boat building, millwork, &c.	Milkwood.
Sycomorus capensis, Miq..........	15-18 "	1-1½ "	Soft, spongy.	No particular use.	Bush-fig, malabar tree.
Tarchonanthus comphoratus, Lin.	6-8 "	3-6 inch.	Close, heavy.	Joiner's fancy work, &c.	Sirfewood.
Trichilia Eckebergia, E. M........	15-25 "	1-2 feet.	Soft	Little used	Unknown.
Trichocladus crinitus Pers.........	10-15 "	6-8 inch.	Tough, elastic.	Hoops, ribs for wagon tents, &c.	Underwood, onderbosch.
Urostigma natalense, Miq..........	10-15 "	8-10 "	Spongy, fibrous.	Bark used for ropes.	Wild figtree, natouw.
Vepris lanceolata, A. Juss.........	20 ft. & more	2 ft. & more	Hard, very tough.	Axles, ploughs, poles, carpenter's tools.	White ironwood.
Virgilia capensis, Lamk..........	15-20 feet.	1½-2 feet.	Light, soft.	Yokes, rafters, spars, &c.	Keurboom.
Widdringtonia cupressoides, Endl.	12 "	6-8 inch.	Light, resinous.	Cooper's work.	Sapreewood.
" juniperoides, Endl.	15-20 "	1-2 feet.	Hard, resinous.	Timber.	Cape cedar, cederboom.
Xanthoxylon capense, Harv.......	15-20 "	1-1½ "	Heavy, close, hard.	Axles, yokes, tools, &c.	Knobwood, paardepram.
Zizyphus mucronata, Willd.......	20-25 "	1-2 "	Tough	Wagonwork, agricultural implements.	Buffalothorn, buffelsdoorn.

APPENDIX I.

MYRICA CORDIFOLIA, LIN,—THE CAPE WAX-BERRY MYRTLE.

ABOUT a century ago it was the opinion of Naturalists, and believed by most people, that *wax* was a mere vegetable substance, a primary constituent of plants, and especially found in the *pollen* or dustlike powder which fills the cells in the *anthers* of flowers. From these it was supposed, that the wax was extracted by the labouring bee, then transformed and modified by animal digestion, and ultimately used for the purpose of making the combs of the bee-hive. Recent researches however, and particularly the acute observations and sagacious experiments of HUBER, have proved this theory to be erroneous, showing that bees' wax is really the peculiar secretion of the working bee.

Yet wax is likewise a vegetable production, frequently seen, not only on the upper surface of the leaves of many plants, but also on the epidermis of various fruits, viz: the plum, grape, fig, &c., forming what is called the bloom, and serving apparently as a kind of varnish against moisture.

There are, besides, plants which produce vegetable wax in great abundance, and amongst them the genus *Myrica* has long been known for its fecundity in yielding this substance. Wax obtained from the *Myrica Cerifera* (the candles' berry myrtle), an American shrub, which grows plentifully in the swamps and marshes of Carolina, Virginia, and Pennsylvania, was an article of commerce more than a century ago, and appears to have been exported in the form of cakes from these American colonies to England long before their struggle for independence commenced.

At the Cape seven* species of *Myrica* have been discovered, named, and botanically described. All of them are ceriferous, but particularly the following three, of which a somewhat detailed diagnosis is here given:—

I. MYRICA CORDIFOLIA. LIN.

Shrubby. *Height* 2 to 6 feet above ground; *stem* erect, smooth, ash-grey, very branchy. *Branches* curved and ranged in whorls; the upper leafy-ones pubescent. *Leaves* crowded at

---

* Myrica Cordifolia, Aethiopica, Serrata, Quercifolia, Brevifolia, Kraussiana, and Burmanni.

top, small, sessile, smooth, rather stiff, nearly cordate, toothed, bluntly pointed, and covered on the under surface with impressed resinous dots. *Flowers* forming *catkins* in the axils of the branches and on the stem; *male catkins* spiked; *scales* ovate, concave, fringed; *female catkins* ovate, solitary. *Fruit* berry or drupe round, of the size of a 5 gr. pill, and covered with a white waxy crust.

II. MYRICA SERRATA. LAMK.

Shrubby. 2 to 3 feet high. *Branches* striped, pubescent. *Leaves* alternate, oblong-lanceolate, attenuated into leaf-stalks, downy, unequally jagged on the margins, green above, and covered beneath with numerous yellow dots. *Catkins* axillary; *scales* ovate, pointed. *Drupe* smaller as in the preceding species.

III. MYRICA QUERCIFOLIA.* LIN.

Shrubby. *Stem* 2—4 feet high, erect. *Branches* spreading in whorls, curved, downy. *Leaves* alternate, obovate-oblong, blunt, attenuated at base, smooth, slashed, about one inch long, bearing resinous dots on the lower surface. *Inflorescence* as in the former species. *Fruit* rather small.

Myrica Cordifolia and *Myrica Serrata* have been figured and imperfectly described by J. BURMANN, † from drawings made by order of Governor S. VAN DER STELL, but not the slightest mention is made of their utility, or peculiarity in yielding wax. The first and principle information with regard to the usefulness of the waxberry myrtle in the Cape colony, is contained in a letter addressed to the Revd. Mr. A. BUURT, at Amsterdam, by the Revd. J. F. BODE, then minister of the Dutch Reformed Church in Cape Town, and of which the following is a faithful translation :—

"Cabo, March 1, 1777.

"REVEREND SIR,—By this opportunity I send you a small box containing three sea-plants, with which, I hope, you will be pleased, and a small branch covered with white berries. This is a shrub that grows on the sandy hills or downs, between the *Cape and Stellenbosch*, and whose fruit, when boiled in water, furnishes a beautiful wax.

"I have, I believe, transmitted to you some years ago a specimen of this wax, which however, has turned out to be of greenish tint.

"This shrub has been taken little notice of hitherto, or rather neglected, but in October and November last, some persons commenced

* *Myrica Laciniata*, Willd. is nothing but a variety of this species.

† Rariorum Africanarum plantarum decades 10. Amsterd. 1739. 4to, pag. 262—263. Tab. 98, fig. 1 and 3.

collecting the berries, preparing from them a kind of wax, which is useful for all purposes where wax is needed. A muid of the berries yields 15—20 lbs. of wax. In course of time this may become an article of commerce, for the plant grows in the dry sands, where nothing else will thrive, and of that description of soil we have over-abundance. Who can tell what more may be discovered.

"Speaking of the fruits or berries, I must observe, that the *sparrow hawk** is extremely fond of them, and that they should be gathered before the great heat of the summer sets in, in order to prevent their melting on the bush, as is already visible on some of them. There are several farmers here that have collected some hundreds of pounds. I do not exactly know the size of the shrub, but I presume it cannot be less than 5 or 6 feet in height. All this I hope to ascertain myself, &c.

"J. F. BODE.†

"The Revd. A. Bourt, Amsterdam."

The wax-bush referred to in this document is the *Myrica Cordifolia,* a shrub not only common in the locality named, but also in the sandy tracts which gird the shores of the Colony. It is as abundant at Cape L'Agulhas and in the downs of Algoa Bay, as in the vicinity of Cape Town, and will probably be found likewise on the Western Coast. Few plants are better calculated to keep down the loose shifting sand than this, and for that reason alone, it would be of infinite service, were it not for the additional benefit derived from the waxy coat of its drupes. When the intelligent wanderer drags his weary steps through the deep sands of these inhospitable wastes, he will meet with a bush, which at first sight appears to be low and insignificant. On closer inspection the delusion will vanish; for what seemed at a distance a middle-sized shrub, is now discovered to be branches only of a subterraneous, creeping trunk of considerable length. ‡ It should be remarked, that the male plant attains a larger size than the female.

Wax obtained from plants of the Myrica tribe exudes from the surface of the fruits, chiefly towards the time of their maturity. It is exhaled in a liquid state, but soon hardens when exposed to the atmosphere, and forms a white powder, which under the microscope displays the shape of minute scales.

This *vegetable-wax,* and that prepared *by bees,* must be regarded as a concrete fixed oil. Both kinds are indifferent to the action

---

* The bird alluded to in this letter, is *Colius Capensis,* the muisvogel of the colonists.

† Neue kurzgefasste Beschreibung des Vorgebirges der guten Hoffnung. Leipz. 1779. 8 pag. 217 and 218.

‡ The wood of this shrub is very brittle; hence its vernacular name of Glashout (Glasswood).

of acids, and contain a large proportion of *Oxygen*. Vegetable wax differs however in the following points:

Myrica-Wax before it is bleached has a greenish hue; its specific gravity exceeds that of animal wax; it is harder, more brittle, easily powdered, and melts more readily. It contains besides a good deal of a peculiar substance, which is analogous to *Stearine* or *Stearic-acid*, and which, for that reason is called *Myricine*. *Bees-wax* contains a smaller quantity of this ingredient, but a much larger one of *Cerine*, another constituent of wax. *Vegetable-wax* dissolves in boiling turpentine, and combined with Alkalis forms a compound possessing the properties of *Soap*. In manufacturing candles, an equal proportion of tallow ought to be added to it, in order to make them burn brightly, for candles prepared from the wax alone, give a rather dim and insufficient light.

The proper time for collecting the fruit of Myrica are the months from May to November, when they are found to have arrived at maturity. At all events, the bush and its branches should be preserved in the process, and the rude manner in which the berries have generally been gathered hitherto, ought to be abandoned. The ripe fruit being but loosely attached to the branches, may be stripped off with ease, or be obtained by placing a piece of canvas underneath. By striking the bush gently with a stick or shaking it, the fruit will drop off on the canvas.

The Candle Berry Myrtle is best propagated by sowing its seeds, which ought to be done in autumn, after the first rains have steadied the sand, which is its principal location, although it thrives as well and as vigorously in richer soil, nay even ascends mountainous regions, removed for many miles from the sea-shore. *Lichtenstein* found the *Myrica Cordifolia* abundently on the Zwarteberg, near Caledon, but the bush did not exceed two feet in height, an observation which has since been corroborated by subsequent Botanists. These shrubs may also be multiplied by cuttings and layers, a practice generally adopted for their propagation in the gardens of Europe.

Of late a method for purifying the Myrica Wax has been discovered, and some little energy displayed by the farmers would make this production a valuable article of export. The bark of the stem and root being astringent is used for tanning skins.

APPENDIX II.

CONTRIBUTIONS TO THE SOUTH-AFRICAN ECONOMIC FLORA.

1. *Aberia caffra. Harv. Mss. (Bixaceæ)*—*Branches* flexuose, greyish-white, spiny. *Leaves* exstipulate, short stalked, lower-ones fascicled, upper alternate, entire, ovate, blunt, veined, glossy, perfectly smooth, reflexed. *Flowers* dioecious, axillary, small. *Petals* none. *Male* flowers cymose, *female* solitary. *Calyx* of male flower 5 cleft; *sepals* oblong, fimbriato-ciliate. *Stamens* 12, erect, exserted. *Calyx* of female flower 7-8 partite, persistent; *styles* 7, pilose. *Fruit* fleshy, 4 celled, 3-4 seeded, crowned with the withered styles ; *placentæ* 7, parietal ; *seeds* shaggy.

A shrub or middling tree, and native of Caffraria Proper. The fruit *(Kei-apple)* having the size and appearance of a large plum or small apricot, is of a sourish taste but edible, and makes good preserve.

2. *Adenogramma galioides. Fenzl. (Caryophylleæ.)* Annual. *Stems* herbaceous, procumbent, spreading, branched from above the root. *Branches* slender, alternate. *Leaves* narrow-linear, whorled, glaucous, acute, smooth. *Flowers* minute, crowded, axillary, umbellate. *Calyx* 5 partite ; *sepals* oblong, blunt. *Petals* none; *stamens* 5; *style* simple; *stigma* capitate; *capsule* obliquely acuminate, brown.

This little herb, the *Mugge-grass (Gnat-grass)* of the colonists, which during the wet season occurs abundantly, is regarded as superior fodder for cattle, which fatten when feeding upon it.

3. *Asparagus laricinus. Burch. (Smilaceæ)*—Perennial. *Stem* twining, smooth. *Branches* alternate, bent backward, armed at base and at the axils of the leaves with solitary, short, straight, reflexed prickles. *Leaves* subverticillate, clustered, awl-shaped, sharp-pointed, stipulate, longer than the internodes. *Peduncles* 2, very slender, one flowered, pendulous, nodulose above the base. *Flowers* bell-shaped, patent, white, small.

The young succulent shoots of this and several other wild species of *Asparagus* furnish a most excellent dish ; they have an aromatic taste, and are preferred by many to the European kind cultivated occasionally in Cape gardens. The diuretic property of asparagus is well known.

4. *Aponogeton distachyon. Lin. (Saururæ.)*—*Root* tuberous, fleshy, submerged. *Leaves* radical long stalked, oval or lanceolate,

entire, smooth, floating. *Flowers* disposed in a double spike on the top of the common *peduncle*, and placed within an ovate *bract*.

The root of this water-plant (*Wateruintjes*; Water-onions) when roasted, is very palatable, and somewhat resembles the chesnut in taste. Its flowers, which are lightly scented, are eaten as spinage, and used as pickles.

5. *Andropogon Ivarancusa. Nees ab. E. (Graminea.)*— *Culm* simple, knotty, smooth. *Leaves* linear, rough at the margins. *Spikes* 2, few-flowered, fascicled, bracteate ; *rachis* and *pedicels* of the male hairy ; inferior *glume* oval, oblong, blunt; the fertile flower awned.

The creeping fibrous roots of this grass have a peculiar and rather ferulaceous smell. By the name of *Akirwanie* they are known to most colonists, and serve as a preventative against the destruction of wearing apparel, &c., by moths and other noxious vermin. This grass is also very healthy and nutritious food for all kinds of livestock.

6. *Annesorhiza capensis. Ch. and Schltdl. (Umbelliferæ.)* —*Root* spindle-shaped. Radical *leaves* prostrate, 2 pinnatisected, smooth, soon withering. *Stem* leafless, streaked; *branches* erect; *umbels* terminal, with only a few rays; *involucre* few-leaved ; *involucels* ovate, acute, as long as the flowers. *Fruit* straw-coloured, winged.

The turnip-like root of this umbelliferous plant is very nutritious, and has been used for many years past as food by the natives and colonists, who call it *Anise-root* (Anys-wortel). It is much improved by cultivation, loses its acrid taste, and becomes a very good vegetable.

7. *Cucumis Africanus. Lin. fil. (Cucurbitaceæ.)—Stem* angular, smooth, decumbent. *Leaves* alternate, stalked, 3-5 lobed, shaggy, hispid underneath. *Flowers* peduncled, single, opposite the leaves. *Fruit* an oblong, bristly pepo.

This species of cucumber *(Thorn-cucumber)*, which is easily recognized by its prickly coat, inhabits the more remote northern portion of the Colony. It supplies horses and cattle with a welcome cooling food in those dry and dreary regions, and has found its way into the gardens of the colonists, who use it in the form of pickles.

8. *Cyperus textilis. Thbg. (Cyperaceæ.)—Culm* round, smooth, erect, leafless, sheathed at base. *Umbel* decompound ; *leaves* of the *involucre* numerous, stiff, rough, twice or three times longer than the umbel. *Spikelets* compressed, 10-15 flowered, sharp-pointed.

A rush, 2 or 3 feet high, which grows in marshy localities and in the beds of rivulets. From it baskets and mats are manufactured by the natives, who call it *Mat-rush* (matjesgoed).

H

9. *Elegia nuda.* *Endl.* (*Restiaceæ.*)—*Rootstock* scaly, creeping. *Stems* simple ; *leaflets* erect, round, articulated, sheathed at intervals, smooth. *Sheaths* cylindrical, awned, persistent below, deciduous above. *Flowers* dioecious, panicled, clustered, sessile, supported by a small, obovate, acute scale or bract. *Panicles* terminal, forming a spike.

This useful reed (*Thatching-reed*; Dakriet) covers the sandy tracts of a great portion of the Colony. Not only does it fix the otherwise shifting sand, but supplies the farmers with a most excellent material for roofing their houses.

10. *Emex spinosus.* *Campd.* (*Polygoneæ*)—Herbaceous. *Leaves* ovate, cordate at base. *Flowers* polygamous, standing in whorls. *Perianth* 6 parted, spiny, covering the oblong nut.

The young leaves of this herb, which belongs to the sorrel tribe, are used as spinage. They make a tolerably good dish, and are slightly aperient The colonial name is *Dubbeltjes-blâren.*

11. *Ficinia filiformis.* *Schrad.* (*Cyperaceæ*)—Root fibrous. *Culm* and *leaves* very slender; *spikelets* 3 to 5, lateral, ovate, compressed. *Involucre* formed by two leaves, the upper one of which is very long. *Fruit* obovate, rough.

On account of its elasticity, this sedge is extensively used for stuffing beds, matresses, &c. It grows in dense tufts, and is common in many parts of the Colony.

12. *Gnidia oppositifolia.* *Lin.* (*Thymeleæ*)—*Stem* shrubby, erect, branchy; *branches* and twigs slender, purplish, forked, leafy. *Leaves* alternately opposite, sessile, erect, ovate, acute, keeled, smooth, often glaucous on the upper surface. *Flowers* sessile, terminal, capitate; *flower-heads* 4-5 flowered. *Calyx* none. *Perianth* funnel-shaped, clothed externally with greyish-white down ; *limb* 4 partite ; *lobes* ovate, blunt, patent, internally smooth ; *throat* crowned with 4 oblong, brown, petal-like scales. *Anthers* 8 ; *filaments* short ; *style* filiform ; *stigma* pin headed.

The bark of the stem and larger branches of this as of all other Thymeleæ, being exceedingly tenacious, is converted by the natives into a kind of very strong cordage or rope. It is the *Kanna-bast* of Hottentots.

13. *Grubbia stricta.* *A. DC.* *Taxus Tomentosa Thbg.* (*Grubbiaceæ.*)—Shrubby. *Branches* 4 angular, smooth; *branchlets* appressedly hairy, streaked. *Leaves* stalked, alternately-opposite, linear-lanceolate, apiculate, entire, revolute at the margins, glossy, and papillated above, woolly below. *Flowers* hermaphrodite, connate into a cone. *Cone* axillary, many flowered,

sessile, ovate, globose when mature. *Stamens* 8, of unequal length ; *ovary* inferior ; *style* short.

The big bulky roots of this shrub, which grows on the mountains of the Stellenbosch, Tulbagh, Caledon, and Swellendam districts, furnishes superior charcoal. Its fruit, which has the size of a pepper-corn, is exceedingly hard and almost bony.

15. *Hermas gigantea. Lin. (Umbelliferæ)—Stem* round, leafless, erect, branchy. *Branches* alternate, spreading. *Radical leaves* on long stalks, oblong, blunt, toothed, very woolly. *Umbel* terminal, smooth. *Involucre* many-leaved, shorter than the umbel. *Flowers* purple.

The thick, white, woolly integument of the leaves of this plant, serves the natives for tinder, and the women prepare from it very curious little fancy articles. The plant which grows on the mountains near Tulbagh, in Du Toitskloof and on the Kandeberg (Clanwilliam), is known as the *Tinder-bush* (Tondel-blad).

15. *Hibiscus Ludwigii. E & Z. (Malvaceæ)*—Shrubby, often 8-12 feet high, slightly branched. *Branches* and *leafstalks* clothed with starlike, yellowish down. *Leaves* stalked, deeply cordate at base, 5 lobed, notched, rough with scattered hairs on both surfaces. *Flowers* monadelphous, axillary, stalked, large, yellow; *stalks* covered with stiff hairs and shorter than the petioles. *Involucre* 5 partite, its *leaflets* ovate, many-nerved; *sepals* lanceolate-ovate, pointed, 5 nerved ; *capsule* ovate, acuminate, bristly.

The stems of this Hibiscus furnish superior fibres of great toughness and strength, resembling *Jute* or Manilla Hemp, and well adapted for the manufacture of cords, ropes, and similar articles. This plant, which is common in the George, Uitenhage, and Katriver districts, and known there as *Rose-touw*, deserves cultivation.

16 *Hydnora Africana. Thbg. (Cytineæ)—Rootstock* succulent, creeping, purple inside. *Stem* simple. *Branches* and *leaves* none. *Flower* solitary, hermaphroditical. *Perianth* fleshy, tubular, swollen at base and divided at top into three segments. *Stamens* 3; *style* one, short, thick; *stigma* nearly capitate. *Fruit* a coated, round berry.

This interesting and extraordinary plant, which grows parasitically on the roots of *Euphorbia Tirucalli* and other succulent shrubs, is one of the numerous discoveries made by THUNBERG, who mistook it at first for a *Fungus*. Its fruit, which like that of the Earth-nut, is subterraneous, has the form, size, and taste of a potato.

It is of a reddish-brown tint, thoroughly mealy ; and when frijed under the embers, very palatable. Some wild animals, and particularly the porcupine (Hystrix cristata), are fond of this fruit, which is called *Kannip* or *Kauimp* by Hottentots, and *Jackals-kost* by the Dutch Colonists.

17. *Moraea edulis.* *Lin.* (*Irideæ.*)—*Root* a corm or bulbous root. *Scape* round, sheathed by a radical leaf, which is three times its length; upper leaf short. *Flowers* yellow or blue; their stalks waving. *Spathe* scarious at top and awned. *Capsule* columnar, trigonal.

The mealy bulbs, commonly known as *Uintjes* (bulbs), are nourishing and somewhat approach chesnuts in taste. In collecting them, it is necessary to have them dug up by persons sufficiently acquainted with the plant, and I have had an opportunity of cautioning the public elsewhere (Prodromus. fl. med. Cap. p. 37), against the obnoxious properties of *Homeria collina* (the cape tulip.), the bulbs of which had in one fatal case been eaten by mistake for those of this plant.

18. *Moraea polystachya.* *Ker.* (*Irideæ.*)—*Scape* round, articulated, divided into many spikes. *Leaves* plane, ribbed, linear, tapering towards the apex. *Spathe* scarious at top. *Flowers* large, showy blue.

In the Eastern districts this species serves the same purpose as the preceding. Its young leaves, however, are said to be unwholesome to horned cattle.

19. *Mesembryanthemum edule.* *Lin.* (*Mesembryaceæ.*)— Succulent. *Stem* erect; branches two-edged, prostrate, branching. *Leaves* opposite, connate, scimitar-shaped, fleshy, serrulate at their edges, perfectly smooth. *Flowers* solitary terminal, large, yellow.

The antiseptic virtues of this valuable plant are too well known to require comment. The *fruit* (Hottentots, Fig) has a pleasant, sourish taste and is eaten either raw or preserved, and used as sweetmeats.

20. *Osteospermum pisiferum.* *Lin.* (*Compositæ*).—Shrubby, unarmed. *Branches* erect, angular, spreading. *Leaves* on short stalks, alternate, obovate, smooth, entire or grossly toothed. *Flower-heads* terminal and solitary on shaggy peduncles. External scales of the *involucre* lanceolate, internal ones broad-ovate, fringed, sharp pointed. *Pappus* none. *Fruit* of the ray baccate; *kernel* bony.

The bony kernels or seeds are enclosed within an oblong berry-like fruit, which, though small, is eaten by the natives and called by them *Biedouw-besjes.* They are of a sweet taste and palatable.

21. *Oxalis cernua.* *Lin.* (*Oxalideæ*)—*Root* bulbous. *Leaves* radical, stalked, ternate; *leaflets* obcordate, 2 lobed, often blotched, smooth. *Scape* erect, umbelliferous. *Flowers* peduncled, the open-ones erect, the closed-ones drooping. *Stamens* 10; *styles* 5, very short.

A weed, common throughout a great portion of the Colony, where it is known as the *Wild Sorrell* (Wilde Zuring.) On account of their acidity, the leaves, mixed with other vegetables, are used for culinary purposes. The bulbs, eaten raw, are pronounced to be a good vermifuge.

22. *Pelargonium peltatum. Ait. (Geraniaceæ)—Stem* shrublike; *branches* angular somewhat downy. *Leaves* fleshy, 5 lobed, nearly peltate, glandularly notched; *umbels* 7-8 flowered; *petals* spreading.

The juice of the petals produces a blue colour of the tint of indigo, and may be advantageously used for painting; while the sap of the leaves is astringent and antiseptic, and of good service in ulcerated sore throat. The vernacular name of this plant is *Kafir Sorrel* (Kaffer Zuring.)

23. *Penicillaria Plukenetii. Link. (Gramineæ)—Inflorescence* racemose-oblong, cylindrical; *spikelets* 2 flowered; *pedicels* villose, as long as the spikelets. *Bristles* of the *involucre* rough or hairy, sometimes shorter than the spikelets. *Glumes* 2, short, membranous. *Lower flower* either male or neuter; *upper* hermaphrodite or sometimes female; *paleæ* small, thin, blunt. *Stamens* 3; *anthers* bearded at top; *styles* 2; *stigmata* tufted with pencil-like hairs. Knots of the *culm* shaggy. *Leaves* rough. (Nees ab. E.)

The *Poco-grass* of Caffraria and Natal, from the grains of which the natives prepare an intoxicating liquor or beer.

24. *Physalis pubescens. Lin. (Solanaceæ)—*Herbaceous, hairy. *Stem* erect, branchy. *Leaves* stalked, cordate, wrinkled, acute, entire or unequally toothed. *Peduncles* solitary, drooping. *Corolla* rotate, yellow, marked with purple dots. *Berry* globose, smooth, 2 celled, many-seeded, covered by the large, angular, inflated *calyx.*

Although this plant, the *Cape Gooseberry* (Appel der Liefde), cannot in the strict meaning of the word, be called indigenous, being a native of South America, yet it has become so common in this country, that it is found now in most shady localities, where it grows perfectly wild. The round fruit, a fragrant, smooth, yellow berry, of the size of a gooseberry or cherry, is agreeably acid and sweet, and very palatable. It is eaten either raw, or made into a delicious marmalade.

25. *Polygala myrtifolia. Lin. (Polygaleæ.)—Stem* shrubby, much branched. *Branches* alternate, erect, shaggy. *Leaves* oblong, leathery, blunt, entire, smooth. *Flowers* racemose, axillary, crested.

The grey bark of this shrub is used by the Mahommedans (who call it *Langelier*) for a particular purpose. It is scraped off when fresh with a knife or piece of broken glass, mixed with water, and stirred about until it scums. With this saponaceous preparation they are in the habit of washing their dead before interment.

26. *Prionium palmita. E. M. (Iuncaceæ.)*—*Stem* partly submersed, black, tough, spongy, as thick as a man's arm; its rising portion tall, often 8-12 feet high. *Leaves* broad-ensiform, sheathed, serrate, channelled, smooth. *Flowers* panicled. *Panicles* much branched, terminal. *Perianth* scaly, double; external-one 3 leaved; internal 3 partite. *Stamens* 6. *Ovary* 3 angular; *style* 1; *stigmata* 3 sessile, feathery. *Capsule* 3 valved, 3 celled, many-seeded. Hook. Journ. of Botan. and Kew Garden Miscellany. vol. 9. tab. 4.

The bases of the macerated old leaves yield an abundant supply of strong, coarse fibre, fit for the manufacture of brushes and brooms. The rest of the leaves abounds in a more elongated and finer thready substance available for a variety of economic purposes. The young rootlets of the *Palmiet* furnish a good dish for the dinner table.

27. *Rubus pinnatus. Willd. (Rosaceæ.)*—Shrubby. *Branches, stalks,* and *nerves* of the leaves, clothed with short down, and armed with hooked prickles *Leaves* alternate, petioled, ovate, acuminate, double-sawed, veiny, smooth. *Stipules* narrow, taper-pointed. *Calyx* tomentose; its segments longer than the petals. *Flowers* racemose; *fruit* black.

The fruit of the *Bramble* or *Blackberry* bush (Braambosch) ripens in the month of January. It is equal in flavour and taste to that of Europe. The roots are astringent, and used in the form of decoction against chronic diarrhœa, &c.

28. *Sorghum saccharatum. Pers. (Gramineæ.)*—*Culm* 8-10 feet high, tinged with purple; *sheaths* bearded. *Leaves* broad, ensiform, acute, rough at the edges. *Panicle* close or branching, erect; branches whorled, flexuose, smooth or shaggy; *rachis* angular somewhat hairy; *spikelets* ovate, mucronate; *pales* of fertile flowers unarmed; *glumes* longer than the fruit, white-reddish at base, fringed at the margin, slightly pubescent at both ends, but smooth and glossy at the back. *Seeds* roundish compressed, mucronate, white, dotted with purple.

This hardy grass, the *African Sugar-cane,* which abounds more or less in saccharine juice, is extensively cultivated by the Kafirs and Fingoes, who call it *Imphee.* The young shoots in particular are very sweet, and therefore chewn by these natives, while the mature grains serve them for the preparation of flour. Amongst the colonial farmers this plant goes by the name of *Zoet Stronk* or *Suiker riet.*

29. *Stapelia pilifera Lin. (Asclepiadeæ.)*—*Root* fibrous. *Stem* simple or branchy, leafless, succulent, round, furrowed tubercled; *tubercles* hair-pointed. *Flowers* stalked, solitary. *Calyx* 5 cleft; its segments ovate, acuminate, patent.

The stem of this plant, which grows in the dreary wastes of the Karroo, is fleshy and of the size and form of a cucumber. It has an insipid, yet cool and watery taste, and is eaten by the natives who call it *Guaap*, for the purpose of quenching their thirst. Infused with spirits, this plant is said to be a useful remedy in piles.

30. *Suhria vittata. I. Ag. (Algæ.)*—*Base* callous, fixed parasitically on the stems of larger Algæ. *Frond* leaf-like, linear-lanceolate, branchy, mid-ribbed at base, prolificating. *Prolifications* issuing chiefly from the margins of the frond as fringes, or in the form of small obovate leaves, which contain the fructifictions. *Substance* cartilaginous ; *colour* deep purple.

The whole of his handsome sea-weed is soluble in boiling water, and transformed into a gelatinous mass. In the shape of *jelly* or *blanc-mange* it is usefully employed in pulmonary complaints, as a demulcent and nutritive.

31. *Trachyandra revoluta Kth. (Asphodeleæ.)*—*Root* growing in clusters. *Scape* erect, compressed, divaricately branched. *Leaves* radical, strap-shaped, fleshy, rough, erect. *Flowers* racemose, stalked, bracteate; *sepals* spreading, revolute. *Capsule* ovate, furrowed ; *seeds* small, globose.

The flower heads of this plant, which thrives abundantly in the deep sands near the sea-shore, furnish a kind of culinary vegetable, which somewhat resembles asparagus, and is known as *Hottentot's Cabbage* (Hottentot's Kohl). When stewed and properly prepared, they make no contemptible dish.

Abortive and *abortion*, terms used where the symmetry of the flower is not complete, or imperfectly developed

Achenium, the fruit of the family of the *Compositæ,* which is one-seeded and does not open, but the *pericarp* of which is separable.

Acuminate, tapering at top, sharp-pointed.

Acute, pointed, not tapering.

Aestivation, the arrangement of the petals in the unexpanded bud.

Alæ, (wings), the lateral petals of papilionaceous flowers.

Alternate, placed one above another.

Amplexicaul, stem clasping.

Angular, having angles on the margin.

Anther, a membranaceous body, borne by the filament, containing a dust-like powder.

Apiculate, tipped with a little point.

Areolate, divided into distinct angular spaces.

Arillus, a fleshy coat surrounding the seed.

Attenuate, gradually diminishing in breadth.

Axillary, growing in the axil.

Baccate, berried, covered with a soft flesh.

Beaked, terminating gradually in a straight point.

Bilabiate, two-lipped.

Bipinnate, if a compound leaf is divided twice in a pinnate manner.

Brachiate, when branches issue nearly at right angles.

Bract, a floral-leaf, a leaf from which flowers proceed.

Callous, hardened, indurated.

Calyx, flower cup, the exterior covering of a flower.

Campanulate, bell-shaped.

Capitate, formed into a head.

Capitulum, a head of flowers in *Compositæ:*

Capsule, a membranaceous seed-vessel, opening by valves.

Carina (or keel), the two anterior boat-shaped petals of a papilionaceous flower.

Cartilaginous, hard and toughs.

Catkin, a deciduous unisexual spike, whose flowers are destitute of calyx and corolla, but supplied with bracts.

Channelled, concave, so as to resemble a gutter.

Ciliated, fringed with short, stiff, marginal hairs.

Clavate, club-shaped, gradually thickening upwards.

Compound, composed of several parts.

Compressed, flattened.

Cone, a dry fruit formed by scales covering naked seeds.

Connate, united at base.

Cordate, heart-shaped.

Coriaceous, leathery.

Corolla, the inner envelope of the flower, constituting what is commonly called the *flower.*

Corona or *coronet*, scaly or petal-like bodies, intervening between the petals and the stamens.

Corymb, a raceme in which the lower stalks are longest, and the upper ones so shortened that the flowers are placed in one horizontal plane.

Costate, provided with ribs.

Crenate, having rounded marginal teeth.

Cuneate, wedge-shaped.

Cyme, a branched inflorescence resembling an *umbel*, where the flowers seem to lie in one plane, the successive central flowers expanding first.

Cylindrical, having a cylindrical shape.

Deciduous, falling off after having performed its functions, as the calyx of *Grewia occidentalis*.

Decussate, crossing at right angles.

Dichotomous, divided by two's; forked.

Didymous, growing in pairs.

Diœcious, a plant is called diœcious, when male and female organs appear upon different individuals.

Distichous, regularly arranged one above another in two opposite rows, one on each side of the stem.

Divaricating, issuing at an obtuse angle.

Drupe, a fleshy fruit enclosing a hard nut.

Dry, not fleshy.

Ellipsoidal, a solid with an elliptical figure.

Elliptical, pointed at both ends.

Emarginate, having a notch at the point.

Entire, without marginal teeth or incisions.

Epigynous, placed above the the ovary.

Fasciculate, standing in bundles.

Fastigiate, having a pyramidal shape, from the *branches* being parallel and erect.

Ferrugineous, rust-coloured.

Filament, stalk, bearing the anther.

Filiform, thread-like, slender.

Flexuous, waving, bent in a zig-zag manner.

Foliaceous, leafy, having the appearance and structure of a leaf.

Follicle, a fruit formed by a single carpel and opening by one suture.

Glabrous, smooth, bald.

Glanduliferous, bearing glands.

Glaucous, covered with a pale-green bloom.

Globose, round, spherical.

Hermaphroditical, a flower is so called when both sexual parts are contained in the same cover.

Hirsute, rough-haired, covered with long stiff hairs.

Hispid, covered with long rigid hairs.

Imbricated, sessile parts covering or overlapping each other like tiles.

Impari-pinnate, unequally yoked; pinnate leaves ending in an odd leaflet.

Inflorescence, a term applied to the way in which flowers are arranged on a stalk or branch.

Introrse, turned inwards towards the centre of the part of attachment.

Involucre, bracts surrounding a head of flowers in a whorl.

Involute, rolled inwards.

Lanceolate, tapering gradually to each end.

Leaflet, the division in a compound leaf.

Legume, a seed-pod with two valves, the seeds of which are fixed on one and the same suture, but alternately upon the 2 valves.

Linear, very narrow; when the length much exceeds the breadth.

Limb, the broad part of a petal, or a leaflet forming part of the calyx.

Lobed, divided into segments.

Loculi, cavities in an anther or fruit.

Membranaceous, having the appearance and structure of a membrane.

Monadelphous, having the stamens united into one bundle.

Monoecious, when male and female flowers are separated from each other, but grow upon the same individual plant.

Monopetalous corolla, a flower in which the petals are united at their edges into a cup or tube, either entirely or at the base only.

Mucronate, abruptly terminating in a hard, sharp point.

Oblong, elliptical, obtuse at each end.

Obovate, inversely ovate, viz: the broadest part being above the middle.

Obtuse, blunt, not pointed.

Ovate, egg-shaped, broadest at base, narrowed upwards.

Panicle, an inflorescence where subordinate stalks are again divided.

Papilionaceous Flower, butterfly-shaped, consisting of 4 petals, the vexillum, two alæ, and the carina.

Patent, spreading horizontally.

Pedicel, the stalk supporting a single flower.

Peduncle, the general flower-stalk.

Peltate, shield-like, flattened and expanded at top.

Pendulous, hanging down.

Penni-nerved (leaf), whose ribs are disposed like the parts of a feather.

Perianth, a term used where the calyx and corolla are combined, partaking of the nature of both.

Perigynous, growing round the ovary.

Persistent, remaining attached.

Petals, flower-leaves, leaves forming the corolline whorl.

Petiole, the leaf-stalk.

Pinnate (leaf), a compound leaf, having leaflets arranged on each side of the central rib

Pinna, a leaflet.

Pisiform, having the shape and size of a pea.

Polygamous, plants bearing hermaphroditical, as well as distinct male and female flowers.

Pubescent, covered with short and soft hairs.

Quadrangular, four-sided, four-angled.

Quadrifarious, in four rows.

Raceme, a cluster of flowers, where from one common stalk undivided flower-stalks arise.

Rachis, the common stalk upon which the leaflets of a compound leaf are inserted.

Receptacle, the expanded part of the fruit-stalks, which bears the parts of fructification.

Reflexed, bent backwards.

Reticulated, netted.

Retuse, blunt and slightly indented.

Revolute, rolled-backwards.

Rigid, stiff, inflexible, not easily bent.

Rotate (corolla), whose limbs spread out at right angles.

Rufous, brown inclining to red.

Rugose, wrinkled.

Rhomboid, oval, somewhat angular in the middle.

Scabrid, rough, covered with short, stiff hairs.

Serrate, toothed, like the indentations of a saw.

Sessile, stalkless.

Spathulate, shaped like a spattle.

Spike, an inflorescence where stalkless flowers are arranged on a common axis.

Squarrose, when parts spread at right angles from one common axis.

Stamen, the male organ of a flower, formed by the filament or stalk, and the anther.

Stigma, that upper part of the female organ of a flower, which has a soft spongy structure, and is destined to the reception of the impregnating principle.

Stipels, secondary stipules.

Stipule, a leaf-like appendage, situated at the base of real leaves, or of leaf-stalks.

Style, the columnar or filiform elongation of the pistil, which supports the stigma, and proceeds upwards from the ovary.

Ternate, composed of three leaflets.

Terminal, on the summit.

Tetragonous, having four angles.

Trifid, divided into three segments.

Tomentose, covered with dense, entangled, rigid short hairs.

Trichotomous, having the division of three's.

Trifoliate, consisting of three leaflets.

Triplinerved (leaf), when 3 ribs or nerves proceed from the base, but where the two lateral-ones diverge from the midrib above the base.

Truncate, lopped off, terminating abruptly.

Turbinate, formed like a top.

Umbel, an inflorescence in which numerous stalked flowers arise from one point.

Umbilicus, the hilum or base of a seed.

Urceolate (corolla), when the tube is swollen or nearly globose, and contracted at the orifice with a small limb.

Valve, the portions which separate self-opening capsules.

Ventricose, big-bellied, swelling out on one side.

Verticillate, ranged in whorls.

Vexillum, standard, the upper petal of a papilionaceous **flower**.

Villose, shaggy, covered with long, weak hairs.

Whorl, a kind of inflorescence in which the flowers are placed around the stem or branch on a common axis.

INDEX.

FLORÆ CAPENSIS MEDICÆ

PRODROMUS;

OR,

AN ENUMERATION OF SOUTH AFRICAN
PLANTS USED AS REMEDIES

BY

THE COLONISTS OF THE CAPE OF GOOD HOPE:

BY

L. PAPPE, M.D.

Second Edition :
WITH CORRECTIONS AND NUMEROUS ADDITIONS.

Multum adhuc restat operis, multumque restabit.—SENECA. Epist. 64.

CAPE TOWN :
W. BRITTAIN, 44, ST. GEORGE'S-STREET

1857.

CAPE TOWN:
SAUL SOLOMON AND CO., STEAM PRINTING OFFICE,
LONGMARKET-STREET.

PREFACE.

THE first edition of this little work appeared towards the close of 1850. It was intended as a commentary to a choice collection of Cape medical drugs, sent by Messrs. S H. SCHEUBLE & Co. to the great London Exhibition of 1851, and for which they obtained a well-merited prize.

In the meantime, my pamphlet met with a reception which surpassed my most sanguine expectations, and as it soon became scarce, on account of the very limited number of copies printed at the time, I was urged by different parties, to prepare and issue a second impression.

Thus emboldened by repeated applications, I yield with pleasure to the call, the more so, as I have since been enabled to correct, improve, and make numerous additions.

Having been left entirely to my own resources, I greatly regret the total want of co-operation on the part of the country practitioners, who have daily and ample opportunities of making themselves acquainted with the various domestic remedies commonly used.

The contents, therefore, of the present publication can be considered only as preliminary, or as mere contributions to a more complete Cape Pharmacopœia. There can, indeed, be no doubt amongst reasonable men that, judging from the vast extent of the South African Territory, and from the richness of its almost inexhaustible Flora, many highly useful officinal drugs will still be discovered. However, the greater part of our information on this point, we owe, not so much to scientific research, as to the experience of the colonial farmer, residing in the more remote parts of the interior, to occasional travellers, or to the wandering native.

In reviewing the first edition, I have found it advisable to deviate to some extent from the original plan, by inserting in the list several plants, which, though not strictly indigenous, have yet become fully naturalized, and are much used in the Colony.

There are, on the other hand, Cape plants of unquestionable worth, which I have not enumerated, because they are not actually employed by the inhabitants. The different kinds of *Sebæa* (Gentianeæ), for instance, possess a pleasant, bitter taste ; they could replace the *Summitates Centaurei minoris* of the Pharmacopœias, and even serve as a good substitute for Gentian. The large tuberous roots of many of our beautiful and common *Orchideæ*, such as *Satyrium* erectum, cucullatum, candidum, carneum, *Disa* barbata, lacera, etc., contain a great quantity of a sweet mucilaginous, nutritious juice, and might easily be transformed into *Salep*. The dried and powdered leaves of our wild *Olive* trees (Olea verrucosa and laurifolia) have the reputation of a styptic, when applied to fresh bleeding wounds, and the herb of *Chironia baccifera* to be of good service in syphilis. A decoction of the gamboge-yellow, crusty epidermis of the bark of *Elæodendron croceum* (Saffron-wood), is said by some to counteract the deadly effects of the bites from venomous snakes, when taken internally, and the bark of *Protea grandiflora*, to act as an astringent in diarrhœa and other complaints.

For the purpose of rendering this publication accessible to persons more familiar with the sexual than the natural system, I have added the *Linnean* classes and orders to which the plants belong, as well as a glossary of technical terms, which, in works on Natural History, are indispensable.

L. P.

Cape Town, 10th October, 1856.

SOUTH AFRICAN MEDICAL PLANTS.

KNOWLTONIA. SALISB.

(*Ranunculaceæ.*)

XIII.—6. POLYANDRIA POLYGYNIA. LIN. SYST.

1. *Knowltonia vesicatoria. Sims.* Herbaceous. *Leaves* triternate, leathery, smooth ; segments oval or sub-cordate, sawed ; lateral ones obliquely truncate at base. *Flowers* umbellate ; *umbel* nearly unbranched, few-flowered ; *flowers* yellowish ; *petals* linear.

Every part of this acrid plant is used as an Epispastic. The bruised herb, when applied to a painful part, raises a blister. It is therefore recommended in rheumatism, ischias, lumbago, and similar affections caused by sudden atmospheric changes. The root, when cut in slices, is a good substitute for Emplastrum Janini. The plant is found in almost every part of the Colony, and from its effects is well known by the name of *Brandblâren.*

RANUNCULUS. LIN.

(*Ranunculaceæ.*)

XIII.—6. POLYANDRIA POLYGYNIA. LIN. SYST.

2. *Ranunculus pubescens. Thbg. Root* fibrous. *Stem* herbaceous, erect, downy ; all the *leaves* hairy ; the radical ones petiolate, ternate, their leaflets inciso-dentate. *Leaves* of the *stem* either trifid or subpin-natifid, toothed ; the uppermost sessile. *Flowers* stalked, single, terminal, yellow. *Calyx* reflexed ; *carpels* smooth, slightly mucronate, tuberculated.

This herb grows in ditches and marshes, etc., and is peculiar to the Cape and Uitenhage districts. The expressed juice, when fresh, is recommended in carcinomatous ulcers, and therefore has received the Dutch name of *Kankerblâren.*

CISSAMPELOS. Lin.

(*Menispermaceæ.*)

XXII.—10. DIOECIA MONADELPHIA. LIN. SYST.

3. *Cissampelos capensis. Lin. Stem* shrubby, twining.
Leaves ovate, petiolate, blunt, entire, glabrous ; *leaf-stalks*, short, downy. *Flower bunches* branchy, hardly
longer than the leaf-stalks. *Flowers* diœcious, axillary,
minute, whitish, tomentose.

This shrub is found in almost every mountainous part of
the Colony. The roots are used as an emetic and purgative by the Boers, and go by the name of *Davidjes.* Its
foliage is poisonous to cattle.

POLYGALA. Tourn.

(*Polygaleæ.*)

XVII.—5. DIADELPHIA OCTO-DECANDRIA. LIN. SYST.

4. *Polygala Serpentaria. Eckl. and Z. Root* thick,
woody. *Stem* almost herbaceous, branchy, procumbent. *Leaves* alternate, obovate, smooth, entire, glaucous beneath, mucronate. *Flowers* on short pedicels,
axillary, subcristate.

A shrub found in Kaffraria. Though small, yet the root
is comparatively thick and long, and is considered by the
natives as a sure antidote against the bites of venomous
snakes, whence its colonial name of *Kaffer Slangenwortel.*
It belongs to the same section of the genus as the *Polygala
Senega,* and may probably possess similar properties.

MUNDTIA. Kunth.

(*Polygaleæ.*)

XVII.—5. DIADELPHIA OCTANDRIA. LIN. SYST.

5. *Mundtia spinosa. D. C.* Shrubby, erect, smooth,
divaricating. *Branches* spiny at their apices. *Leaves*
on short stalks, oblong, glabrous, veiny, blunt,
mucronate. *Flowers* crested, sessile, axillary. *Fruit*
a red, juicy berry.

A decoction of the tops of the branches of this shrub,
which is very common in the Downs, is used in atrophy,
phthisis, &c., apparently with some effect, while the fruit,
which is somewhat astringent in taste, is eaten by children
and Hottentots, who call them *Skildpatbesjes.*

MALVA. Lin.

(*Malvaceæ.*)

6. *Malva rotundifolia. Lin. Stem* prostrate ; *leaves* stalked, cordate, nearly obicular, serrate-crenate, five-lobed, smooth. *Flowers* small, axillary. *Fruit-stalks* downy, bent downwards.

The whole of this plant is mucilaginous and emollient. Although a native of Europe, it has now become perfectly naturalized, and grows everywhere near towns and villages. The colonists know it by the name of *Keesjes-blåren* (mallow leaves), and frequently use its leaves in the forms of decoction, fomentation, or poultice in sore throat, opthalmia, or for the purpose of maturing abscesses.

PAPPEA. Eck. and Zeyh.

(*Sapindaceæ.*)

7. *Pappea capensis. E. and Z.* A small tree. *Leaves* alternate, ovate, oblong, unequal at base, glabrous, blunt, coriaceous, veiny, slightly rolled back at the margin. *Flowers* small, racemose, with separate sexes by abortion. *Fruit* tricapsular, drupaceous, fleshy, globose, downy.

This tree is pretty common in Kaffirland, and in the districts of Uitenhage and Albany, where its fruit is known as *wilde pruimen* or *t'Kaamsbesjes* (wild plums). It has some resemblance to the plum, is savoury, and furnishes a vinous beverage and excellent vinegar. Its kernel contains an oil, which, though edible, is somewhat purgative, and is recommended as an external remedy in tinea capitis, alopecia, or similar diseases, and may serve as a substitute for Macassar oil.

DODONÆA. Lin.

(*Sapindaceæ.*)

8. *Dodonæa Thunbergiana. E. and Z. Stem* shrubby, with angular branches. *Leaves* at the top of the twigs, sessile, alternate, narrow, lanceolate, attenuate at both ends, acute, entire, smooth. *Flowers*

terminal, erect, stalked, small, greenish. *Fruit* a winged three-celled capsule.

A small tree or shrub, common about Piquetberg, Worcester and Clanwilliam, where it is called *Zand Olyf.* A decoction of the root is used as a slight purgative in fevers.

MONSONIA. LIN. FIL.

(*Geraniaceæ.*)

XVI.—7. MONADELPHIA DECANDRIA. LIN. SYST.

9. *Monsonia ovata Cav.* *Root* annual, spindle-shaped. *Stem* herbaceous, simple, erect, shaggy. *Leaves* stalked, alternate, oblongo-ovate, subcordate at base, veiny, crenate, wavy, pubescent, *Stipules* and *bractlets* awl-shaped, rigid. *Peduncles* one-flowered, bracteate in the middle, villose. *Flowers* white, with purplish veins.

The *Keita* of the Hottentots. The root and herb of this plant are very astringent, and used with great success in dysentery. It grows abundantly in the district of Uitenhage.

PELARGONIUM. L'HER.

(*Geraniaceæ.*)

XVI.—4. MONADELPHIA HEPTANDRIA. LIN. SYST.

10. *Pelargonium* (Polyactium) *triste.* *Ait.* *Root* tuberous. *Leaves* alternate, tripinnatifid, hispid; their *segments* bipinnatifid, and their *pinnules* wedge-shaped, incised. *Umbel* many-flowered. *Flowers* scented, yellow, with a dark purple spot at base.

The scarlet-coloured root of this Pelargonium is somewhat astringent. If dried and pulverised, it is useful in diarrhœa and certain forms of dysentery, where purgatives have been previously given. It has also been recommended as a vermifuge, and is commonly found on the sides of Table Mountain.

11. *Pelargonium* (Jenkinsonia) *antidysentericum.* *E. and Z.* *Stem* tuberous, fleshy. *Branches* lateral, erect, furrowed, angular. *Leaves* smooth, alternate, stalked, subcordate, lobed. *Lobes* incised. *Petioles* curved, longer than the leaves. *Stipules* prickly. *Flowers*

purplish, and the nectariferous tube twice as long as the calyx.

This plant, which is indigenous in Namaqualand, has tuberous roots, which often attain the size of a man's head, and are called *t'Namie* by the aborigines, who boil them with milk, and make use of them in dysentery.

12. *Pelargonium* (Peristera) *anceps.* *Ait.* Herbaceous, smooth. *Stems* decumbent, three-sided, two-edged. *Leaves* petiolate, roundish, cordate, lobed, toothed. *Stipules* oblong, two-parted. *Peduncles* axillary, elongated, umbellate. *Umbels* many-flowered. *Flowers* subcapitate, small, crimson.

This species, which grows plentifully along the watercourses in the Cape and Swellendam districts, is a great favourite with the Malays, who call it *roode Rabassam*, and pretend that a decoction of the herb cures suppression of the catamenia, and promotes parturition and *abortion*.

13. *Pelargonium cucullatum.* *Ait.* *Stem* shrubby, the whole plant viscid, hairy. *Leaves* alternate, kidney-shaped, hooded, waved, dentato-crenate. *Petioles* patent, channelled, longer than the leaves. *Flowers* terminal, umbellate, purple. *Umbels* many-flowered.

This fine species, which is very common along the side of Table Mountain, has been recommended in the form of decoction, or as an enema, in colic, nephritis, and suppression of urine, and is also an excellent emollient. It appears, that formerly this herb has been exported to Holland, under the name of *Herba Altheæ.* *Cf. N. L. Burmanni* Specimen Botanicum de Geraniis. Lugd. Bat. 1759, 4to pag. 35.

14. *Pelargonium.* (Dibrachya.) *scutatum Sweet.* *Stem* shrub-like. *Branches* angular, somewhat downy. *Leaves* fleshy, five-lobed, nearly peltate, glandularly notched. *Umbels* 7-8 flowered. *Petals* patent.

The *Kafir-sorrel* (Kaffir zuring.) of the colonists The *sap* of its leaves is astringent and antiseptic, and of good service in aphthæ, sore-throat, etc. The juice of its petals produces a blue colour of the tint of indigo, and may, according to *Burchell*, be advantageously used for painting. Very common in many parts of the Eastern districts.

OXALIS. Lin.

(*Oxalideæ.*)

15. *Oxalis cernua.* Lin. *Root* bulbous. *Leaves* radical, stalked, ternate. *Leaflets* obcordate, two-lobed, often blotched, smooth. *Scape* erect, umbelliferous. *Flowers* peduncled, the open ones erect, the closed ones drooping.

A weed, common throughout a great portion of the colony, where it is known as the *wild sorrel* (wilde zuring). On account of their acidity, the leaves, mixed with other vegetables, are used for culinary purposes. They contain, indeed, a good deal of *oxalic acid,* and Thunberg relates that, at his time, this salt in its crystallized form was easily obtained from the juice of this plant. The *bulbs,* moreover, eaten raw, are said to be a good vermifuge.

MELIANTHUS. Lin.

(*Zygophylleæ.*)

16. *Melianthus major. Lin.* Shrubby. *Leaves* alternate, smooth, unequally pinnate, glaucous beneath. *Leaflets* sharply-toothed. *Stipules* large, solitary, foliaceous, adnate with the leaf-stalk. *Flowers* racemose, reddish brown. *Peduncles* twisted, downy.

Every part of this plant has a nauseous smell, whence it has received the Dutch name of *Truytje roer my niet* (Gertrude, don't touch me). A decoction of the leaves is an excellent external remedy in tinea capitis, crusta serpiginosa,* necrosis, and foul ulcers. It is also useful as a gargle and lotion in sore throat and in diseases of the gums, and the bruised leaves, applied to ulcers, pro-

---

* A shoemaker, about 25 years of age, had laboured for some time under a most obstinate attack of *crusta serpiginosa.* All the usual remedies having failed, his medical attendant at last advised him to try a decoction of this plant, to be applied in a tepid state. With this treatment, and occasional aperients and spare diet, he was perfectly cured within a month.

mote granulation.* It is common in the Cape Flats, and other parts of the colony, and deserves a trial in cases of plica polonica.

DIOSMA. Lin.

(*Diosmeæ.*)

17. *Diosma* (Barosma) *crenata. D. C.* A glabrous branchy shrub. *Branches* round, purplish, the upper and smaller ones angular. *Leaves* stalked, smooth, oblongo-ovate, blunt, dotted beneath, and notched with transparent, resinous glands on their margin. *Flowers* peduncled, solitary, axillary ; *petals* white, oblong, subsessile.

The *Bucchu leaves* have, as is well known, become an article of export lately. Their principal medical effects are owing to their possessing a considerable quantity of an aromatic volatile oil, and to a particular very tenacious principle, called *Diosmin*, as also to a semi-resinous substance. They have a peculiar smell, and a slightly astringent, bitter, taste. When used in the form of infusion, they promote perspiration. Hence their utility in chronic rheumatism, gout, and other diseases, caused by the sudden suppression of cutaneous action. They have been prescribed also in cholera morbus, and are very beneficial in diseases of the bladder, especially in chronic inflammation of the mucous membrane of that organ (catarrh of the

---

* I am indebted to my friend, Dr. A. Brown, for the following practical remarks on the medical properties of this plant :—" For many years past, I have found the *Melianthus major* very serviceable in necrosis and foul ulcers, and its effect in promoting granulation is very remarkable. After cleaning the sores with the decoction, some of the boiled leaves are applied to the parts, and found to answer well. I have not only used it with decided benefit, but in many cases where the *materia medica* has failed me, or the degree of healing was not satisfactory, it has almost invariably succeeded. In carcinoma I have seen it applied with effect in cleaning the ulcers, and rendering their otherwise highly disagreeable odour less offensive. In indolent leprous sores it can also vie with the other applications that we use in that intractable disease. I have tried it in tinea capitis with great effect, but in other affections of the skin it has as yet failed to satisfy me decidedly whether it did good or not. In cases where tinctura myrrhæ is recommended, I have found it a better remedy. In fact, I may say that in my practice it is almost daily used."

bladder); also in hæmaturia, calculus, and in suppuration of the vesica, urethra, and prostrate gland. By increasing the secretion of urine, they impart to it their peculiar smell. They have also been given in dropsy;—in fine, in all those cachectic and hydropical complaints, arising from suppression of the perspiration or urine. As a stimulant to the stomach, some practitioners have used the bucchu leaves in indigestion ; a sensation of warmth has accordingly been produced in that organ, and the appetite increased.

A bath of the bucchu leaves is of service in rheumatism, and the *Bucchu vinegar*, as also the *Bucchu brandy*, are excellent embrocations in rheumatic pains, luxations, sugillations, sprains, and contusions.

In trade, this valuable drug is often adulterated by the substitution of less powerful sorts of the same family of plants, which, although of a similar smell, are by no means equal to it in their therapeutical effects. One of these plants is the *Diosma* (Barosma) *serratifolia. Lodd.*, a species common in the district of Swellendam, and another, the *Empleurum serrulatum. Sol.*, easily distinguished by its linear-lanceolate, serrated leaves.

The true *Diosma crenata* is a native of the mountains of Hottentot's Holland, Stellenbosch, Drakenstein, Tulbagh, and Worcester.

FAGARASTRUM. Don.

(*Xanthoxyleæ.*)

VIII.—1. OCTANDRIA MONOGYNIA. LIN. SYST.

18. *Fagarastrum capense. Don.* A shrub, about 6 feet high. *Branches* compressed, flexuous, wrinkled, prickly. *Prickles* flat, sharp-pointed. *Leaves* alternate, impari-pinnate ; *pinnæ* ovate, blunt, erect, sessile, smooth, slightly crenate. *Flowers* small, paniculated. *Capsule* dotted ; *seeds* black, shining.

Found in the bush near Mossel Bay, and in the forests of the district of George, as also in those of Uitenhage and Albany. The fruit is known to the colonists as the *wild Cardamom*, and, on account of its aromatic qualities, prescribed for flatulency and paralysis.

METHYSCOPHYLLUM. Eckl. and Zeyh.

(*Amyridaceæ.*)

v.—1. PENTANDRIA MONOGYNIA. LIN. SYST.

19. *Methyscophyllum glaucum. E. and Z.* A resinous shrub. *Branches* erect, alternate. *Leaves* opposite, lanceolate, pointed at both ends, veiny, glabrous, glaucous, repando-dentate, bent back at the margin. *Flowers* paniculated. *Panicles* axillary, opposite, forked, few-flowered.

An infusion of the leaves of this shrub is pleasant to the taste, and used in cough, asthma, and other diseases of the chest. It grows about the Zwarte Kei River, where it is a favourite beverage with the Bushmen and others, who also chew it, and call it *Boschjesmansthee.*

CYCLOPIA. Vent.

(*Leguminosæ.*)

X.—1. DECANDRIA MONOGYNIA. LIN. SYST.

20. *Cyclopia genistoides. Vent.* A glabrous shrub. *Stem* and *branches* erect, twiggy. *Leaves* alternate, sessile, trifoliate ; *leaflets* linear, bluntly mucronate, revolute at the margin. *Flowers* axillary, bracteate, stalked, yellow. *Peduncles* one-flowered. *Bracts* two, oblongo-ovate, pointed.

This plant is common in moist places on the Cape Flats, near Wynberg, Houtbay, and elsewhere. In the form of decoction or infusion, it is often made use of for the purpose of promoting expectoration in chronic catarrh, and even in consumption. It has a sweet, astringent taste, and is generally considered as a restorative. Its vernacular name is *Honigthee.*

BORBONIA. Lin.

(*Leguminosæ.*)

XVII.—6. DIADELPHIA DECANDRIA. LIN. SYST.

21. *Borbonia parviflora. Lamk.* A small, glabrous shrub. *Branches* compressed, angular, winged. *Leaves* alternate, amplexicaul, cordate, many-nerved, mucronate, ciliato-dentate. *Calyx* and *corolla* nearly smooth. *Flowers* yellow.

Common on the Lion's Head and on Table Mountain,

and used, under the significant name of *Stekelthee*, apparently with good effect in asthma and hydrothorax. It is commonly given as a diuretic, in the form of decoction.

VASCOA. D. C.
(*Leguminosæ.*)
XVII.—6. DIADELPHIA DECANDRIA. LIN. SYST.

22. *Vascoa amplexicaulis. D. C.* A glabrous undershrub. *Stem* erect, branchy. *Leaves* simple, amplexicaul, suborbicular, cordate at base, reticulated, quite entire, blunt; those of the stem alternate; the floral ones opposite, coloured. *Flowers* in the upper axils, glabrous, solitary, without bracts, shortly pedicellate, yellow.

The roots of this pretty bush taste like liquorice, whence its name of *Zoethout-boschje*. They are used in the form of decoction, as a demulcent in catarrh and phthisis, and are a good substitute for the liquorice itself. This useful plant inhabits the mountains of Worcester and Tulbagh.

23. *Vascoa perfoliata. D. C.* A small shrub. *Stem* glabrous, erect. *Leaves* amplexicaul, cordate, suborbicular, entire, bluntly mucronate, rigid, netted. *Flowers* yellow.

A strong decoction of the leaves of this species acts as a powerful diuretic, and is of great service in the various forms of dropsy. It grows on the mountains of Hottentot's Holland.

MELILOTUS. TOURN.
(*Leguminosæ.*)
XVII.—6. DIADELPHIA DECANDRIA. LIN. SYST.

24. *Melilotus parviflorus. Desf.* *Stem* erect, branchy. *Leaves* trifoliate, upper ones oblong, toothed; lower ones obovate, entire. *Flowers* laxely racemose, small, yellow; *stipules* linear; *legumes* ovate, wrinkled, one-seeded.

This herb (*Melilot, Steenklaver*), a native also of the north of Africa, diffuses the same sweet, fragrant scent which we observe in the *Melilotus officinalis* of Europe. In its medical effects it is discutient and emollient, and used externally in the form of fomentation, poultice, and plaster, in indurations, glandular tumours, etc. Its powder is one of the ingredients in the manufacture of snuff. Abundant in sandy soil in many parts of the colony, where it flowers from September to November.

SUTHERLANDIA. R. Br.

(*Leguminosæ.*)

XVII.—6. DIADELPHIA DECANDRIA. LIN. SYST.

25. *Sutherlandia frutescens. R. Br.* Shrubby. *Stem* erect, twiggy. *Leaves* stalked, alternate, impari-pinnate, many-yoked; *pinnules* on short petioles, oblong, obtuse, emarginate, silky. *Flowers* racemose, peduncled, axillary, scarlet. *Legume* ovate, scarious, inflated.

A fine showy shrub, which, on account of its beautiful scarlet flowers, is a horticultural ornament, and cultivated as such in our gardens. It grows wild in hilly parts all over the colony. According to *Thunberg* (Travels, vol. I., pag. 160), the roots and leaves of this plant, when dried and pulverised, are of use in diseases of the eye.

ACACIA. Neck.

(*Leguminosæ.*)

XVI.—9. MONADELPHIA POLYANDRIA. LIN. SYST.

26. *Acacia horrida. Willd.* A large tree. *Stem* and *branches* glabrous, but armed with large white spinous stipules. *Leaves* bipinnate; *pinnæ* 2–3 yoked; *pinnules* many-yoked, oblong, blunt. *Leafstalks* glandulous at base and on the apex. *Flowers* stalked, axillary, globose, polygamous, yellow, scented.

The demulcent derived from the *Doornboom* is well known as an article of commerce. It exudes spontaneously from the bark of the trunk and branches, and hardens in the sun, without losing its transparency. Although the *Cape gum* is inferior in appearance, and in intrinsic value, to that of Northern Africa, it may yet be improved by care and attention. The bark of this useful tree is highly astringent, hence its effect, in the form of decoction, in inveterate *fluor albus*, in diarrhœa, dysentery, and as a substitute for the Peruvian bark in fevers. The *Acacia giraffæ. Willd.* (Kameeldoorn), growing beyond the limits of the Cape Colony, is said to yield a superior gum, and is eaten by the natives.

RUBUS. Lin.
(*Rosaceæ.*)

27. *Rubus pinnatus. Willd.* Shrubby. *Branches, stalks,* and *nerves* of the leaves clothed with short down, and armed with hooked prickles. *Leaves* alternate, petioled, ovate, acuminate, double-sawed, veiny, smooth. *Stipules* narrow, taper-pointed. *Calyx* tomentose, its segments longer than the petals. *Flowers* racemose. *Fruit* black.

The roots are astringent, and used as decoction for chronic diarrhœa, etc. The fruit of this species of *Bramble* or *Blackberry-bush* (Braambosch) is equal in flavour and taste to that of Europe. Abundant in mountain ravines in the Cape and Stellenbosch districts. Flowers, October, November. Fruit, January.

CLIFFORTIA. Lin.
(*Sanguisorbeæ.*)

28. *Cliffortia ilicifolia. Lin.* Shrubby. *Stem* brown, scaly, branched. *Leaves* cordato-ovate, elliptical, 3–5 toothed, spiny, many-nerved, amplexicaul, rigid, imbricated, smooth. *Flowers* dioecious, small, axillary, subsessile.

A plant pretty common in the district of Uitenhage, where the Boers recommend it as an emollient and expectorant in coughs. This species, whose leaves are sharp-pointed and spiny, is called *Doornthee.*

PUNICA. Tourn.
(*Granateæ.*)

29. *Punica granatum. Lin.* A shrubby tree. *Branches* often thorny. *Leaves* opposite, entire, lance-shaped, pointed at each end, smooth. *Flowers* at the top of the branches; *petals* scarlet, wrinkled. *Fruit* round, with a coriaceous rind; *pulp* acidulous; *seeds* oblong, angular.

·The rind of the *Pomegranate* (Granaat-appel) and its roots are astringent, and contain tannin and gallic-acid. They are used in diarrhœa, accompanying general debility, in the form of decoction, while infusions are known to be of service as injections in obstinate leucorrhœa. From the pulp surrounding the seeds, a refrigerating syrup is prepared. The efficacy of the fresh bark of the root was known to the Ancients, who praised it as a sure remedy for the expulsion of the tape-worm. This effect has been tested in our days with decided success. The best way of using the remedy is in the form of a decoction of two ounces of the bark in two pints of water, boiled down to *one* pint. A wine-glassful taken every hour early in the morning is the dose generally administered.

Though a native of the north of Africa, the Pomegranate tree is extensively cultivated within the colony, especially for the purpose of forming hedges.

EPILOBIUM. LIN.

(*Onagrariæ.*)

VIII.—1. OCTANDRIA MONOGYNIA. LIN. SYST.

30. *Epilobium villosum. Thbg. Stem* herbaceous, erect, round, branched, shaggy. *Leaves* sessile, alternate, lanceolate, sawed, acute, hairy. *Flowers* terminal, axillary, purple. •

As a house-medicine, this herb, inhabiting the mountains of several districts, is renowned for its usefulness in cleansing foul ulcers.

PILOGYNE. SCHRAD.

(*Cucurbitaceæ.*)

XXII.—3. DIOECIA TRIANDRIA. LIN. SYST.

31. *Pilogyne Ecklonii. Schrad.* Dioecious. *Root* tuberous ; *stem* climbing. *Branches* striped, nearly quadrangular. *Leaves* stalked, triangular, cordate, 3-lobed, sharp-pointed, toothed, green and rough above ; white, downy beneath. *Flowers* stalked, axillary ; male ones small, white, racemose ; female ones solitary.

The porous resinous root of this old Hottentot remedy is nauseous in taste. In the form of decoction, it acts simultaneously as an emetic, cathartic, and diuretic. The natives call it *Davidjes-wortel*, and use it in cutaneous affections, dropsy, and syphilis. The tincture, or infusion of the root in wine or brandy, is, according to *Thunberg*

(Travels, I., pag. 128), a powerful emetic and purgative. This plant, the *Bryonia Africana* of former botanists, grows upon the slopes of Table Mountain, amongst bushes; also in the Eastern districts, near Port Elizabeth, etc., and flowers in the month of October.

CITRULLUS. Schr.

(*Cucurbitaceæ.*)

XVI.—10. MONOECIA MONADELPHIA. LIN. SYST.

32. *Citrullus amarus. Schrad. Stem* angular, furrowed, hispid, decumbent. *Leaves* alternate, stalked; the upper ones 3-parted ; middle segment sinuated, pinnatifid ; lateral ones 2 fid ; lobes blunt, scabrid, pimpled ; radical leaves 5-parted. *Tendrils* axillary. *Flowers* dioecious. *Fruit* glabrous, elliptico-globose.

This annual plant resembles a water-melon in foliage. Its fruit, a round pepo of the size of a child's head, is filled with a spongy pulp. By the farmer, this fruit, which is bitter and loathsome, is called *Bitter-appel* or *Wild Water-melon,** and is common in the sands of the Cape Downs, near Tygerberg and Rietvalley, and in similar localities. The pulp of the pepo, like that of *Colocynth,* is a very strong, drastic purgative, and serves the same purpose, and is used as a cathartic in dropsy and other complaints. An extract can easily be prepared from it, equal in its effects to the extract of Colocynth.

PHARNACEUM. Lin.

(*Paronychiaceæ.*)

V.—3. PENTANDRIA TRIGYNIA. LIN. SYST.

33. *Pharnaceum lineare. Thbg.* Suffruticose. *Root* fibrous, stemless. *Branches* radical, diffused, smooth, repeatedly forked. *Leaves* sessile, whorled, linear, unequal, entire, patent, blunt. *Stipules* scarious, torn.

---

* Thunberg (Trav. II., p. 171) relates, that at the Cape the Colocynth-fruit is eaten, when pickled, both by the natives and colonists, although it is very bitter.—This is a mistake : the fruit alluded to by that author, is that of *Citrullus caffer. Schrad.*, called by the colonists, *Kaffir-watermeloen.*

Peduncles axillary, elongated, terminal. *Flowers* paniculated or umbellate, white and purplish.

This little plant, which thrives best in a sandy soil, and abounds in the Cape Flats and Downs, is employed in pulmonary affections. It is generally used in the form of infusion, which is of a rather pleasant, aromatic, bitter taste, and is also somewhat mucilaginous and slightly diuretic. By the name of *Droedas kruiden*, it is known to many colonists, who make use of it in coughs, and especially in those that threaten consumption.

CRASSULA. LIN.
(*Crassulaceæ.*)
V.—5. PENTANDRIA PENTAGYNIA. LIN. SYST.

34. *Crassula tetragona. Lin.* *Stem* suffruticose, succulent, round, branchy, procumbent, smooth. *Branches* alternate, erect. *Leaves* connate, decussate, three-sided, incurved, acute, entire. *Flowers* terminal, corymbose, small, white.

A succulent plant, rather astringent, and a native of the district of Uitenhage. If boiled in milk, the leaves of this species are used as a tonic in diarrhœa. The *Crassula portulacacea Lam.*, which is called *t'Karkey* by the Hottentots, is said to be used in similar cases.

TETRAPHYLE. ECK. AND ZEYH.
(*Crassulaceæ.*)
V.—5. PENTANDRIA PENTAGYNIA. LIN. SYST.

35. *Tetraphyle furcata. E. and Z.* *Root* fleshy, scaly, spreading. *Stem* erect. *Branches* quadrangular, fastigiate. *Leaves* standing in fours, small, ovato-lanceolate, imbricated, smooth. *Flowers* 5–10, terminal.

This plant becomes very brittle when dried. It is bitter and astringent, and used in the form of decoction for diarrhœa and dysentery. During one of the late Kafir wars, when the latter disease prevailed amongst the troops, this remedy appears to have been tried with marked success.

COTYLEDON. LIN.
(*Crassulaceæ.*)
X.—5. DECANDRIA PENTAGYNIA. LIN. SYST.

36. *Cotyledon orbiculata. Lin.* *Stem* fleshy, leafless, elongated, branchy. *Leaves* opposite, flat, obovate,

spatulate, blunt, acuminate, (often) farinaceously glaucous, with a red border. *Flowers* paniculate, nodding.

This succulent shrub is common in mountainous parts. The leaves are thick, and from their shape called *Varkens-ooren* (pig's ears). The fresh juice is of service in epilepsy, and has been prescribed by me in the case of a young man, subject to this frightful disease. Not only were the symptoms evidently diminished, but subsequent attacks were less violent. The leaves form an excellent application to hard corns. On removal of the epidermis of the upper side of the leaf, it is left on the part for 8 or 10 hours, when it will be found that the juicy portion of the leaf is gone, and the corn feels soft, and may be removed with ease. It should be remarked here, that *Crassula arborescens. Willd.*, has the same properties.

MESEMBRYANTHEMUM. Lin.

(*Ficoideæ.*)

XII.—2. ICOSANDRIA PENTAGYNIA. LIN. SYST.

37. *Mesembryanthemum edule. Lin.* Suffruticose ; succulent. *Stem* erect. *Branches* two-edged, prostrate, spreading. *Leaves* opposite, connate, scimitar-shaped, three-edged, fleshy, serrulate at their edge, perfectly smooth. *Flowers* solitary, terminal, large, yellow or purple. *Fruit* eatable.

Few South-African plants are so much in domestic use than this species and *Mesembryanthemum acinaciforme. Lin.*, both of which are common in the sandy tracts of the colony. They are astringent and sourish in taste, on account of the acidulated alkaline salt with which they seem to be impregnated. The expressed juice of the succulent leaves, taken internally, checks dysentery, and acts as a mild diuretic ; while it is also for its antiseptic property, used as an excellent gargle in malignant sore throat, violent salivation and aphthæ, or in the form of a lotion in burns and scalds. At the Cape these plants are called *Hottentots vygen* (Hottentot-figs).

38. *Mesembryanthemum crystallinum. Lin. Root* annual. *Stem* herbaceous, angular, procumbent, fleshy, covered all over with large pustules. *Leaves* broad, amplexicaul, waved at the margin, ovate, entire. *Flowers* axillary, nearly sessile, small white.

The *Iceplant* contains a good deal of malic acid and lime. The expressed juice of the herb, when fresh and rendered limpid, has been recommended as a specific in incontinence of urine, proceeding from spasm (Enuresis spastica), and is given in doses of a tablespoonful at intervals. The Iceplant is common in the neighbourhood of Cape Town, especially in the sandy flat near Riet-valley, where it flowers in the midst of summer.

39. *Mesembryanthemum tortuosum. Lin. Stem* short. *Branches* procumbent, elongated, divaricating, twisted. *Leaves* connate, pointed, entire, oblongo-ovate, concave, somewhat pustular, keeled, crowded. Lobes of the *calyx* unequal.

This species, a native of the Karroo, appears to possess narcotic properties. The Hottentots, who know it by the name of *Kauw-goed*, are in the habit of chewing it, and become intoxicated, while the farmers use it in the form of decoction or tincture, as a good sedative.

HYDROCOTYLE. Lin.
(*Umbelliferæ.*)
V.—2. PENTANDRIA DIGYNIA. LIN. SYST.

40. *Hydrocotyle Centella. Cham.* Suffruticose. *Stems* filiform, decumbent, geniculate, flexuose. *Leaves* stalked, oblongo-lanceolate, 3-nerved, subfalcate, pubescent, acuminate, entire. *Flowers* 3-5 polygamous, umbellate, whorled, axillary. *Involucral bracts* 4-5, ovato-lanceolate, acute. *Petals* glabrous.

The roots and stalks of this plant are astringent, and a decoction of them is used with effect by many colonists in violent diarrhœa. They are also said to be of great service in cases of dysentery, after the necessary evacuations have been previously procured, and where the disease has assumed a chronic form. Among the farmers, the plant is known under the name of *Persgras*; it inhabits the Cape and Stellenbosch districts, and grows abundantly about Vlaggeberg.

41. *Hydrocotyle asiatica. Lin. Stems* slender, prostrate, creeping. *Leaves* stalked, reniform, crenato-dentate, ribbed, smooth. *Flowers* small, axillary. *Umbels* simple, few-flowered. *Leaf* and *flower*-stalks slightly tomentose.

Found in moist, shady localities, at watercourses, and in the beds of empty rivers, throughout a great portion of

C

the colony. This small plant has of late been recommended in India as a remedy for leprosy, and the Madras *United Service Gazette* states, that the local Government had authorised its use at the Leper Hospital. The use of this plant was discovered by Mr. Jules Lepine, of Pondicherry, and instantly communicated to the Madras authorities and the public. He was guided to his discovery by Dr. Boileau of the Mauritius, who himself suffering from this fearful disease, had devoted himself to experiments with it. Of 40 adult patients, to whom it had been administered, all were in a fair way for recovery in 1853. How far the real efficacy of this new remedy can be proved by experience, remains to be seen.

SIUM. Lin.

(*Umbelliferæ.*)

V.—2. PENTANDRIA DYGYNIA. LIN. SYST.

42. *Sium Thunbergii. D. C.* Herbaceous. *Root* fibrous, stoloniferous. *Stem* erect. *Branches* angular. *Leaves* pinnate ; *leaflets* ovate, pointed, regularly sawed. *Umbels* stalked, lateral or terminal ; segments of the *involucre* (3-5) linear, entire. *Flowers* white.

In marshy spots near Zeekoe-valley, in the bed of the Zwartkops-river, and in similar localities. Flowers February and March.

The root of this umbelliferous plant, called *Tandpyn-wortel* (Toothache-root) by the colonists, is renowned for its allaying toothache when held in the mouth or chewed.

BUBON. Lin.

(*Umbelliferæ.*)

V.—2. PENTANDRIA DIGYNIA. LIN. SYST.

43. *Bubon Galbanum. Lin.* A smooth, resinous shrub. *Stem* erect, round, geniculated, branchy. *Leaves* alternate, pinnate, triternate, rigid, glaucous ; *segments* rhomboidal, toothed, or pinnatifid; terminal ones 3-lobed. *Petioles* sheating. *Umbels* compound, many-rayed. *Involucres* many-leaved. *Leaflets* linear. *Flowers* yellowish-green.

This umbelliferous plant, which attains a height of from six to eight feet, and is found all over the colony in moist places, or in the ravines of mountains, is reputed amongst the inhabitants as an excellent diuretic, under the name of *Wild Celery*. A decoction of its leaves proves salutary in cases of dropsy, and has been even administered successfully in gravel. At times some resinous matter exudes from the stem, which however, in its appearance, smell, and in every respect, greatly differs from the *Gummi galbanum*, the well-known drug of our dispensaries. Linnæus, in giving the name to this species, seems to have been led astray by mistake, the real drug being derived from a different plant, a native of the north of Africa, and probably from a kind of Ferula.

ARCTOPUS. LIN.
(*Umbelliferæ.*)
V.—2. PENTANDRIA DIGYNIA. LIN. SYST.

44. *Arctopus echinatus. Lin. Root* spindle-shaped, resinous, stemless. *Radical leaves,* pressed to the ground, stellate, hispid ; their expanded lobes nearly round, incisid, 3 fid ; single lobes dentate, ciliated, spiny. *Flowers* dioecious, umbellate ; male umbel stalked, female sessile. *Petals* white.

This plant, the *Platdoorn* or *Ziehte-troost* of the Boers, is one of those few indigenous remedies, which, from the very establishment of the colony, have been constantly used by its inhabitants. At that early period, the European settlers, being often without their necessary stock of medicines, had to learn from their Hottentot neighbours, who held this plant in great esteem. It is demulcent and diuretic, and somewhat approaches the *Sarsaparilla*. The decoction of the root is the general form under which it is prescribed in lues, lepra, or cutaneous chronic eruptions of all kinds. It also furnishes a sort of resin, which is easily procurable by making incisions into the root while it is fresh. It has been shown from chemical experiments, that the root of this plant contains an alcaloid, which, combined with acids, assumes the form of neutral salts. Thus the *Arctopium sulphuricum* consists of small scaly white crystals, which are astringent in taste, and which in half grain doses, produce coagulation of the saliva within the mouth.

VISCUM. LIN.
(*Loranthaceæ.*)
XXII.—4. DIOECIA TETRANDRIA. LIN. SYST.

45. *Viscum capense. Lin. f.* A parasitical leafless shrub. *Stem* blunt, square, erect, articulated, smooth.

Branches decussate. *Flowers* dioecious, whorled, sessile. *Fruit* a globose white berry.

A parasitical shrub (called *Vogeleend*), growing on the stems of several species of *Rhus* and *Euclea*, in most parts of the colony. In its appearance and properties it is nearly allied to the European *Mistletoe*. Its stems are mucilaginous, and a little astringent. These are employed as an antispasmodic in cases of epilepsy in children and young females, where the bowels are loose, and where the disease is just commencing. It has also been recommended in St. Vitus' dance, asthma, and similar complaints, and is prescribed in the form of powder or decoction.

VALERIANA. Lin.

(*Valerianeæ.*)

III.—1. TRIANDRIA MONOGYNIA. LIN. SYST.

46. *Valeriana capensis. Thbg. Root* tuberous. *Stem* herbaceous, erect, smooth. *Leaves* opposite, petiolate, 3-yoked, pinnatifid ; lobes alternate, ovato-dentate, pointed ; the uppermost largest. *Petioles* amplexicaul. *Flowers* corymbose, red. *Bracts* 2 opposite, setaceous.

This species is very closely allied to the European *Valeriana officinalis*. Although it may not be quite so powerful in its effects, yet it resembles the same, not only in its appearance, but also in its medical virtues. Its roots are a favourite remedy in morbid susceptibility of the nervous system, and in the form of infusion are successfully given in typhoid fevers, epilepsy, hysteria, and similar maladies. They are at the same time sudoriferous, and have a salutary effect on intestinal worms. This plant grows in moist places in many parts of the colony, and is particularly common in the George district.

MATRICARIA. Lin.

(*Compositæ.*)

XIX.—SYNGENESIA. LIN. SYST.

47. *Matricaria glabrata. D. C. Root* annual, fibrous. *Stem* herbaceous, erect, branchy, angular. *Leaves* alternate, pinnatifid ; lobes linear, entire, pointed ; the upper ones toothed. *Flower-heads* terminal, solitary. Scales of the *involucre* blunt, with

a broad scarious border. *Ray* white, reflexed. *Recep-tacle* ovate, conical.

The *Wild Chamomile*, which, in the months of November and December, so plentifully covers the Cape Downs, is one of those plants which deserve the peculiar attention of our apothecaries. It is a *true Matricaria*, and in many respects not only equals, but even surpasses, the European species. Large sums of money are yearly expended in importing this useful and popular drug, while we can gather a plant of the same order, the same genus, and the same properties at our doors. In the more remote parts of the country, where dispensaries are not so abun-dantly found as in the vicinity of our metropolis, the farmers and the coloured people employ the Wild Chamo-mile as often, and with the same good effect, as we do the *Matricaria Chamomilla*, or the *Anthemis nobilis*. In short, this herb, which contains a superfluity of volatile oil, is an excellent antispasmodic, and most useful in colic and other spasmodic complaints, while, on account of its aromatic bitter taste, it is recommended as a stomachic in dyspepsia and in derangements of the digestive organs generally. Its local application as a resolvent is suffi-ciently known.

GARULEUM. Cass.

(*Compositæ*.)

XIX.—SYNGENESIA. LIN. SYST.

48. *Garuleum bipinnatum. Less.* Suffruticose. *Roots* long, woody. *Stem* erect, striated, branchy. *Leaves* alternate, bipinnatifid; pinnæ nearly opposite, linear-lanceolate, acute. *Flower-heads* terminal, solitary; *ray* blue, *disk* yellow.

Amongst the medical indigenous plants of the Cape, the present deserves particular notice. It is well known to almost every resident as the *Snake-root*, having acquired its vernacular name from its effects as an antidote against the bites of venomous snakes,* with which the country abounds. The root of this plant, which is a native of the Eastern districts, where it grows in the deserts of the Karroo, has a great similarity to the *Radix Senegæ* of the

* The most formidable of these reptiles are the *Naja Haje Merrem.* (Cobra Capella) and the *Vipera Brachyura. Cuv.* (Poffadder).

Pharmacopœa. It is bitter and acrid, and contains a good deal of a resinous substance, almost homogeneous to that which we observe in the root of the *Polygala Senega*. In the form of decoction or tincture, this root is a great favourite with the colonial farmer, in various diseases of the chest, asthma, and such affections where a free secretion of the mucous membrane of the lungs and bronchiæ is desirable. It also promotes perspiration, and acts as a diuretic in gout and dropsy. This valuable root ought to have a place in the Materia medica.

TARCHONANTHUS. Lin.
(*Compositæ*.)
XIX.—SYNGENESIA. LIN. SYST.

49. *Tarchonanthus camphoratus. Lin.* A shrub 4-5 feet high. *Stem* erect, striated ; branches angular, shaggy. *Leaves* stalked, oblong, entire, rugose, blunt, coriaceous, smooth above and tomentose beneath. *Flowers* paniculate, terminal, many-headed ; *flower-stalks* short, downy.

The whole of this shrub has a camphorated odour. Its leaves, when dried, are smoked by the Hottentots and Bushmen instead of tobacco, and, like the *Dagga*, exhibit slight narcotic symptoms. In the form of infusion, they promote perspiration, and are said to be useful in spasmodic asthma.

COTULA. Lin.
(*Compositæ*.)
XIX.—SYNGENESIA. LIN. SYST.

50. *Cotula multifida. D. C.* Herbaceous, ascending, smooth, branchy. *Leaves* semi-amplexicaul at base, pinnatifid ; lobes trifid, acute. *Flower-heads* discoid, terminal, yellow Scales of the *involucre* blunt, with a membranaceous margin.

This plant grows in the district of Uitenhage, and is used by the Hottentots (who call it *t'Kamso*) in rheumatism, scalds, and in cutaneous affections.

ARTEMISIA. Lin.
(*Compositæ*.)
XIX.—SYNGENESIA. LIN. SYST.

51. *Artemisia afra. Jacq.* Suffrutescent. *Stem* erect, branchy. *Branches* angular, furrowed, her-

baceous, leafy. *Leaves* interruptedly bipinnatifid, stalked, smooth above and tomentose beneath; lobes linear-lanceolate, falcate. *Petioles* bearing stipules at base. *Flower-heads* peduncled, racemoso-paniculate, one-sided, hemisphærical, drooping. Scales of the *involucre* ovate, lanceolate, scarious. *Recepticle* naked.

The whole of the *Wormwood* (Alsem.) has a strong, balmy smell, and a bitter, aromatic, but nauseous taste, owing to a green essential oil which it contains. The herb is tonic, antispasmodic, and anthelmintic, and very useful in debility of the stomach, visceral obstructions, jaundice, hypochondriasis, or similar evils, while its efficacy as a vermifuge is generally admitted. The best forms for using it are the infusion, the decoction, and tincture, the latter being preferred by the colonists. A strong infusion is used externally as a collyrium in weakness of the eyes, and the pounded leaves and stalks are employed as a discutient in œdema and sugillations.

TANACETUM. Lin.
(*Compositæ.*)
XIX.—SYNGENESIA. LIN. SYST.

52. *Tanacetum multiflorum.* *Thbg.* *Root* woody. *Stem* herbaceous, angular, erect. *Branches* fastigiate, pubescent. *Leaves* alternate, rough, pinnatifid ; pinnæ linear, inciso-dentate. *Capitula* terminal, corymbose, many-flowered, small, yellow.

This species, like all other plants of the same genus, contains a great deal of resin, and a specific, ethereal oil, of a very strong and peculiar odour. It has a bitter, aromatic, acrid taste, and is used as a tonic, antispasmodic, and anthelmintic, in flatulency, gout, amenorrhœa, and dropsy ; but particularly for expelling lumbrici and other intestinal worms. It is administered in the form of powder or infusion, which latter promotes perspiration and acts as a mild diuretic. Applied as a fomentation, it is resolvent and anodyne, and is used also for making injections. This plant, called *Worm-kruid*, grows very abundantly in sandy soil, close to the sea-shore.

ERIOCEPHALUS. Lin.
(*Compositæ.*)
XIX.—SYNGENESIA. LIN. SYST.

53. *Eriocephalus umbellulatus.* *D. C.* Shrubby.

Branches erect, one-sided, divaricating, smooth. *Leaves* fasciculate, linear, axillary, entire, silky. *Flower-heads* subterminal, stalked, corymbose. *Pedicels* somewhat longer than the capitula. *Ray-flowers* white.

This shrub (*Wild Rosemary*) inhabits the mountainous parts of the colony, and has received its colonial name on account of its smell, which somewhat resembles that of the Rosemary. According to Thunberg, it is diuretic, and used by the farmers and Hottentots in various forms of dropsy.

HELICHRYSUM. D. C.

(*Compositæ.*)

XIX.—SYNGENESIA. LIN. SYST.

54. *Helichrysum nudifolium. Less. Root* perannual, fibrous. *Stem* single, tomentose. *Radical leaves* stalked, amplexicaul, unequal at base, ovato-lanceolate, reticulated, 5-nerved, smooth, but scabrous at the margin and on the upper surface. *Cauline* leaves narrow, lanceolate, sharp-pointed. *Capitula* terminal, corymbose, yellow. Scales of the *involucre* blunt.

A plant pretty common in the colony, and to be met with even in the vicinity of Cape Town, on Devil's Mountain. The whole of this plant, here called *Caffer-tea*, is demulcent, and, in the form of infusion, recommended in catarrh, phthisis, and other pulmonary affections.

55. *Helichrysum serpyllifolium. Less. Stem* suffrutescent. *Branches* filiform, spreading, tomentose. *Leaves* alternate, sessile, obovate, entire, blunt, somewhat curled, glabrous above and tomentose beneath. *Capitula* corymbose, conglomerated, many-flowered, white.

This species also appears to possess demulcent and emollient properties, and to be of service in the various diseases of the chest. It goes by the name of *Hottentot's tea*, and grows near the watercourses on the Cape mountains, has a pleasant smell, and is much liked by the coloured people, who infuse it as tea. Sometimes the *Helichrysum auriculatum. Less.*, is used for the same purpose, and under similar circumstances.

56. *Helichrysum imbricatum. Less. Root* fibrous. *Stem* suffrutescent, erect. *Leaves* semi-amplexical,

ovato-oblong, apiculate and clothed, as well as the spreading branches, with white short down. *Capitula* terminal, corymbose, many-flowered, stalked ; scales of the *involucre* membranaceous, imbricated, obtuse ; the outer ones of a brownish hue, the inner ones snow-white at top.

Like the two former species, this likewise is recommended as a demulcent in coughs and other pulmonary affections. It is used in the form of tea, and called *Duinen-thee* (tea from the Downs). Common in the Cape Downs.

LEONTONYX. Cass.

(*Compositæ.*)

XIX.—SYNGENESIA. LIN. SYST.

57. *Leontonyx augustifolius. D. C.* Covered all over with a snow-white woolly down. *Stems* suffruticose at base, branching, leafy, erect. *Leaves* sessile, linear-oblong, blunt. *Capitula* solitary. Scales of the *involucre* purple, linear, straight, pointed. D. C.

The whole of this little plant, called *Beetbosjes* by the Boers, has an aromatic smell, and when pounded and mixed with lard or fat, is applied to ulcers. Frequent in sandy soil, chiefly near St. Helena Bay and vicinity.

ELYTROPAPPUS. Cass.

(*Compositæ.*)

XIX.—SYNGENESIA. LIN. SYST.

58. *Elytropappus Rhinocerotis. Less.* Shrubby. *Stem* erect, tomentose. *Branches* many, drooping. *Leaves* very small, imbricated, appressed, erect, sessile, filiform, smooth. *Capitula* racemose, 3-flowered.

A bush, called *Rhinosterboschjes*, which covers immense tracts of waste land in the Western districts. The whole of this shrub is bitter and resinous The tops of the branches, when infused in wine or brandy, furnish a superior kind of stomachic bitters, which have a green colour, and are frequently used as a tonic in dyspepsia and other complaints, arising from impaired digestion. The tops are also given in powder to children affected with diarrhœa.

59. *Elytropappus glandulosus. Less. Stem* shrubby, downy, erect, branched. *Branches* aggregate, patent, very leafy. *Leaves* linear, acuminate, spirally twisted, bearing stalked glands on the lower surface. *Capitula* terminal, clustered, 2–4 flowered.

This small shrub is the *Slangenbosch* (Snake-shrub) spoken of by Thunberg (Trav. I., p. 268) as a good remedy for the expulsion of intestinal worms, when used in the shape of decoction.

LEYSSERA. Lin.

(*Compositæ.*)

XIX.—SYNGENESIA. LIN. SYST.

60. *Leyssera gnaphaloides. Lin. Root* fibrous. *Stem* suffruticose, downy. *Branches* silky, nearly umbellate. *Leaves* aggregate, imbricato-erect, sessile, linear-subulate, furrowed, more or less tomentose, glandularly scabrous. *Capitula* solitary, terminal, peduncled. *Involucre* turbinate ; its scales scarious, blunt, shining. *Rays* yellow.

Very few of our indigenous plants are so much in domestic use as this one, known as *Geele-bloemetjes-thee.* When pounded, or rubbed between the fingers, it gives an agreeable scent, and the infusion has a pleasant, sweetish taste. It is emollient, and for that reason is highly recommended in catarrh, cough, and even consumption. Some of our apothecaries have added this plant to the *species pectorales.*

OSMITOPSIS. Cass.

(*Compositæ.*)

XIX.—SYNGENESIA. LIN. SYST.

61. *Osmitopsis asteriscoides. Cass. Stem* fruticose, erect, tomentose, little branched. *Branches* leafy to the apex. *Leaves* crowded, sessile, imbricated, lanceolate, pointed, entire, dotted, shaggy. *Capitula* on short pedicels, solitary, terminal, aggregate. *Involucre* unequal ; scales ovate. *Rays* white, *disk* yellow.

A native of Table Mountain, where it grows abundantly. The whole plant, called *Bellis,* is impregnated with a great deal of an aromatic volatile oil, which, from its odour and taste, seems to contain camphor.* Hence its virtues as an antispasmodic, tonic, and resolvent. In the form of infusion, it is frequently and advantageously employed in cough, hoarseness, and in diseases of the chest generally, and is said to be also very serviceable in flatulent colic. Infused in spirit, it acts as a powerful external remedy, and Thunberg relates, that he has successfully cured paralysis with embrocations of the *Spiritus Bellidis*. It would be worth while to distil the essential oil, with which this plant abounds, and which, from its peculiarity, shows an affinity to cajeput-oil.

The *Osmites hirsuta. Less.*, a plant common on the mountains of Fransche Hoek and Drakenstein, having a similar smell, is known in the colony as *Van der Merwe's Kruiden*.

EURYOPS. Cass.

(*Compositæ*.)

XIX.—SYNGENESIA. LIN. SYST.

62. *Euryops multifidus. D. C.* Shrubby. *Stem* smooth, very branchy. *Branches* alternate, divaricating. *Leaves* glabrous, linear, entire at base, bifid or multifid above. *Peduncles* alternate, axillary, much longer than the leaves, one-headed. *Ligulæ* oblong, yellow. *Achænia* villose.

From the stem and branches of this little shrub, which grows plentifully near the Olifant's River, in the district of Clanwilliam, exudes a yellowish, semi-transparent, resinous substance, which in every respect resembles the *mastic* of the Pharmacopœia, and seems to possess almost the same properties.

The existence of this gummiferous shrub has been known for many years, and was noticed by Mr. Burchell, who in his Travels, I., p. 259, mentions it in these words :—

" The inhabitants of the Roggeveld, when in want of resin, use as a substitute a gum, which exudes from different shrubs, which they call *Harpuis-bosch* (Resin-bush) Of this gum a considerable quantity may be collected."

---

* A chemical analysis of this oil has since been made.[1] It is liquid, of a yellowish-green tint, and easily soluble in ether and alcohol. In its qualities, it resembles cajeput-oil and Borneo camphor.[2]

[1] Ueber das ætherische Oel von *Osmitopsis asteriscoides* von E. v. Gorup Bezanez. (Annals of Chemistry and Pharmacy, vol. 89, p. 211—218.)

[2] Prepared from a Malayan tree (Dryobalanops Camphora. Colcb)

STOBÆA. Thunb.

(Compositæ.)

XIX.—SYNGENESIA. LIN. SYST.

63. *Stobæa rubricaulis. D.C. Root* woody. *Stem* erect, purple. *Leaves* amplexicaul, eared, rigid, smooth above, tomentose beneath, pinnatifid ; lobes lanceolate, acuminate, spiny, with prickly fringes on their margin. *Pedicels* short, bracteate, subracemose. Scales of the *involucre* spreading, ovato-lanceolate, having two spines at base, which outreach the *disk.* *Achænia* downy.

The colonial name of *Graveel-wortel,* given to this plant, fully implies the nature of its effects. It is a native of the district of Swellendam, where it grows on hills and uncultivated fields. A tincture prepared from the bruised roots is diuretic, and of great service in gravel.

LOBELLA. Lin.

(Campanulaceæ.)

V.—1. PENTANDRIA MONOGYNIA. LIN. SYST.

64. *Lobelia pinifolia. Lin. Stem* frutescent, erect, smooth. *Leaves* crowded, alternate, sessile, linear-lanceolate, acute, entire, keeled. *Peduncles* with short bracts, silky, few-flowered. Tube of the *calyx* half-round. *Flowers* blue, subterminal, hairy outside.

The resinous root of this little shrub is stimulant and diaphoretic. A decoction of it is sometimes used as a domestic remedy in cutaneous affections, chronic rheumatism, and gout. This plant is common in the mountainous parts of the Western division of the colony, where it flowers during the greater part of the year.

WAHLENBERGIA. Schrad.

(Campanulaceæ.)

V.—1. PENTANDRIA MONOGYNIA. LIN. SYST.

65. *Wahlenbergia procumbens. D. C. fil.* Herbaceous ; procumbent, diffused, entirely smooth. *Leaves* opposite, ovate, subsessile, blunt, entire or obsoletely crenate. *Pedicels* axillary, longer than the leaves.

Tube of the *calyx* egg-shaped, its lobes acute. *Flowers* erect, solitary, white.

Common about watercourses, ditches, &c., in the summer. It is an emollient, and used accordingly as an ingredient in poultices. Its smell, when dried, resembles that of *Trigonella foenum graecum.*

STAPELIA. Lin.

(*Asclepiadeæ.*)

V.—2. PENTANDRIA DIGYNIA. LIN. SYST.

66. *Stapelia pilifera. Lin. Root* fibrous. *Stem* simple or branchy, leafless, succulent, round, furrowed, tubercled ; *tubercules* hair-pointed. *Flowers* stalked, solitary. *Calyx* 5 cleft ; *corolla* 5 fid, its segments ovate, acuminate, patent.

The stem of this plant, which grows in the dreary wastes of the Karroo, is fleshy and of the size and form of a cucumber. It has an insipid, yet cool and watery taste, and is eaten by the natives, who call it *Guaap,* for the purpose of quenching their thirst. Infused with brandy, this plant is said to be a useful remedy for *piles.*

GOMPHOCARPUS. R. Br.

(*Asclepiadeæ.*)

V.—2. PENTANDRIA DYGYNIA. LIN. SYST.

67. *Gomphocarpus crispus. R. Br. Stem* erect, hispid. *Branches* alternate. *Leaves* on short petioles, subsessile, opposite, linear-lanceolate, round or subcordate at base, crisp and wavy at the margin, rigid, acuminate. *Flowers* stalked, axillary, or terminal, umbellate. *Pedicels* bracteolate, hairy. *Corolla* reflexed; *leaves* of the *corona* pointed upwards, oblong, toothed at base. *Follicles* compressed, beaked, downy. *Ribs* naked.

This plant, the *Bitter-wortel* of the farmers, is found among hilly places in the western part of the colony. The root, formerly known to the Dutch apothecaries as the *Radix Asclepiadis crispæ,* is extremely bitter and acrid, and on account of its diuretic virtues, a decoction or infusion of it has been recommended in various kinds of dropsy, and a tincture prepared of it, is said to be a valuable remedy in colic.

DATURA. Lin

(*Solanaceæ.*)

v.—1. PENTANDRIA MONOGYNIA. LIN. SYST.

68. *Datura Stramonium. Lin.* Herbaceous. *Stem* round, branchy. *Leaves* ovate, unequally sinuato-dentate, smooth. *Flowers* large, white, funnel-shaped, plaited, axillary, solitary ; *peduncles* short. *Calyx* tubular, 5-toothed, deciduous. *Stamens* 5 ; *style* fili-form. *Capsule* fleshy, ovate, erect, prickly, 4-celled at base, 2-celled at the apex. *Seeds* numerous, kidney-shaped.

This common weed, originally a native of America, but now naturalized in most parts of the civilized world, is well known to Englishmen as the *Thorn-apple*, so named on account of its spiny fruit. Having a foetid, nauseous smell, it is called *Stinkblaren* by the Cape colonists. Every part of this plant is highly narcotic, and pharma-ceutical preparations made from it require, in their adminis-tration, the greatest care and circumspection. In South Africa, the fresh warmed leaves of the plant, or the vapour of an infusion, are successfully used as a sedative in violent pains, caused by rheumatism (zinkens) or rheumatic gout. In the shape of poultices also they are applied to carcino-matous ulcers, and it is said that the smoking of the dried leaves affords great relief in spasmodic athma.

SOLANUM. Lin.

(*Solanaceæ.*)

v.—1. PENTANDRIA MONOGYNIA. LIN. SYST.

69. *Solanum niveum. Thbg. Root* perannual. *Stem* fruticose, 6 feet high, erect, snow-white, tomentose, thorny. *Branches* prickly. *Leaves* alternate, stalked, ovate, attenuate at both ends, entire, nerved. *Flowers* blue, in a lateral, decompound, panicle. *Pedicels* dichotomous, drooping. *Fruit* a red glabrous berry.

The leaves of this Solanum are smooth on the upper, and woolly on the lower surface. The application of the latter to foul ulcers cleanses them, and a cure is afterwards effected by applying the upper surface. Hence their Dutch name of *Geenesbláren*. The fresh juice of the berries and leaves, when formed into an ointment with lard or fat, are also in use amongst the farmers for the same purpose.

70. *Solanum nigrum. Lin. Stem* and *branches* herbaceous, erect, angular. *Leaves* ovate, bluntly-toothed and waved, attenuate at base. *Flowers* umbellate, lateral, drooping, white. *Berries* globose, black.

The common *Nightshade* (Nacht-schaduwen) grows wild in almost all parts of the globe. It has a nauseous smell, and is slightly narcotic. In South Africa the expressed juice of the herb, and its decoction, made with fat and wax into an ointment, are often successfully employed in cleaning and healing foul ulcers.—Frequent amongst garden weeds, under walls, on dunghills, etc.

LYPERIA. Benth.

(*Scrophulariaceæ.*)

XIV.—2. DIDYNAMIA ANGIOSPERMIA. LIN. SYST.

71. *Lyperia crocea. Eckl.* A little branchy shrub. *Leaves* very small, wedge-shaped, fasciculate, obtuse, entire, smooth. *Peduncles* elongated, axillary. *Flowers* sub-racemose, yellow. Tube of the *corolla* much longer than the calyx.

This bush deserves notice as a drug, and in all probability will, ere long, become an article of colonial export. It grows abundantly in some parts of the Eastern districts, whence it has found its way into the dispensary. The flowers, which are called *Geele bloemetjes*, closely resemble *Saffron* in smell and taste ; they possess similar medical properties, and as an antispasmodic, anodyne, and stimulant, ought to rank with the *Crocus sativus.* Here, they have as yet been only used with success in the convulsions of children, but they deserve a more general trial. On account of the fine orange colour which they impart, they are in daily request among the Mohamedans, who use them for the purpose of dying their handkerchiefs. This drug has been observed to be sometimes adulterated by the admixture of other plants of the same genus, which are less efficacious.

MENTHA. Lin.

(*Labiatæ.*)

XIV.—1. DIDYNAMIA GYMNOSPERMIA. LIN. SYST.

72. *Mentha capensis. Thbg. Stem* erect, 4-edged, covered all over with a white shag. *Branches* alternate, divaricating. *Leaves* opposite, sessile, subcordate

at base, linear-lanceolate, pointed, entire or often unequally toothed, hoary beneath, penninerved. *Floral
leaves* awl-shaped. *Flowers* whorled, spiked. *Spikes*
cylindrical, subsolitary. *Calyx* tomentose. *Corolla*
white. *Stamens* longer than the corolla.

Like other *Mints*, this one contains an ethereal oil, which
is sharp and bitter to the taste. It grows plentifully in
moist mountainous regions, and is valued as a most excellent antispasmodic and carminative. It is used in the form
of infusion in flatulent colic, meteorism, cardialgia, hysteria,
and amenorrhœa, and externally to sugillations, glandular
swellings, indurations, or similar complaints.

SALVIA. Lin.

(*Labiatæ.*)

II.—1. DIANDRIA MONOGYNIA. LIN. SYST.

73. *Salvia africana. Lin. Stem* shrubby, erect,
2 feet high, scabrid, very branchy. *Branches* divaricating, four-edged, shaggy. *Leaves* decussate, stalked,
opposite, obovate, mucronate, serrate, wrinkled with
veins, truncate at base, green above, whitish beneath.
Leaf-stalks short, amplexicaul. *Flowers* in whorls,
terminal, bracteate, peduncled. *Peduncles* opposite,
short, hairy. *Bracts* 3-leaved, unequal. *Whorls* 4-6
flowered. *Calyx* campanulate villose. *Corolla* blue,
hairy, double as long as the calyx. Upper lip 3-lobed,
nearly entire, round ; lower 2-lobed ; lobes ovate,
acute.

Like those of the common Sage, the leaves of this
species (known as the *Wild Sage*) are fragrant, astringent,
and bitter. They possess nearly the same medical properties as the *Salvia officinalis*, and are used in the same
way, and under similar circumstances.

BALLOTA. Lin.

(*Labiatæ.*)

XIV.—1. DIDYNAMIA GYMNOSPERMIA. LIN. SYST.

74. *Ballota africana. Benth.* **Shaggy.** *Stem*
erect, one to a foot and a half high. *Leaves* stalked,
orbicular, cordate, irregularly notched. *Flowers* small,

crowded in distant axillary whorls. *Corolla* almost smooth ; *bracts* awl-shaped. *Calyx* ribbed, with 10 setaceous, pointed teeth.

This plant, the whole of which is covered with soft hairs, bears an affinity to, and possesses the medical properties of the European Horehound (Marrubium vulgare. Lin.). It has an aromatic, bitter taste, and as a tonic, discutient, and expectorant, decoctions and infusions of its leaves are often successfully employed in chronic pulmonary diseases, obstinate coughs, and particularly in asthmatic affections. The colonists know this plant as *Katte-kruiden*** (Cat-herbs).

LEONOTIS. R. Br.

(*Labiatæ.*)

XIV.—1. DIDYNAMIA GYMNOSPERMIA. LIN. SYST.

75. *Leonotis Leonurus. R. Br. Stem* shrubby, 5 feet high. *Branches* tomentose. *Leaves* oblongo-lanceolate, whorled, obtuse, serrate from the middle to the apex, narrowed at base, slightly shaggy beneath. *Flowers* in crowded axillary whorls. *Calyx* dentate, pubescent. *Bracts* linear-lanceolate, acute, shorter than the calyx. *Corolla* tube-shaped, curved, densely hairy, bright orange, or rarely buff.

This plant, the *Wild Dagga*, is, on account of its beautiful flowers, a fine garden ornament. It grows wild in the sandy Cape Flats, and often at the roadside. It has a peculiar scent and a nauseous taste, and seems to produce narcotic effects if incautiously used. It is employed in the form of decoction in chronic cutaneous eruptions, and may be tried even in cases of leprosy. The usual dose is a wineglass-full three or four times a-day. The Hottentots are particularly fond of this plant, and smoke it instead of tobacco, and take a decoction of its leaves as a strong purgative ; they likewise give it as an emmenagogue in amenorrhœa. In the Eastern districts, the *Leonotis ovata* is used for the same purpose.

---

* In the famous trial of C. A. van der Merwe for the murder of his wife (1838), this herb has been represented (but erroneously) by a medical witness as narcotic.

CHENOPODIUM. Lin.

(*Salsolaceæ.*)

V.—2. PENTANDRIA DIGYNIA. LIN. SYST.

76. *Chenopodium ambrosioides. Lin.* Herbaceous. *Stem* erect, rough, branchy. *Leaves* stalked, oblong, narrowed at both ends, unequally sinuato-dentate, glandular beneath, upper ones linear-lanceolate, entire. *Racemes* leafy, glomerate, subspicate, terminal and axillary.

The whole of this plant has a strong aromatic smell, caused by an ethereal oil which it contains, and a pungent, bitter taste. Its properties are antispasmodic, diaphoretic, and anthelmintic, and the best form for its administration is that of tea or infusion.—Grows chiefly on waste ground, under walls, by way-sides, or upon rubbish near towns and villages.

CASSYTA. Lin.

(*Laurineæ.*)

IX.—1. ENNEANDRIA MONOGYNIA. LIN. SYST.

77. *Cassyta filiformis. Lin.* Parasitical. *Branches* filiform, leafless, twining, having papillæ instead of roots. Perianth 6-cleft. *Flowers* bisexual, clustered, greenish. *Fruit* a red berry.

A small, twining leafless parasite, known as *Vrouwenhaar,* and common all over the colony. It is employed, but not often, as a wash in scald head, and for the destruction of vermin. Some people pretend, that it makes the hair grow.

PROTEA. Lin.

(*Proteaceæ.*)

IV.—1. TETRANDRIA MONOGYNIA. LIN. SYST.

78. *Protea mellifera. Lin.* A shrub 7—8 feet high, perfectly smooth. *Stem* bushy, erect. *Branches* purplish. *Leaves* lanceolate, attenuate at base, blunt, quite entire, glossy. *Involucre* in the axils of the branches, obovate, oblong, pink or white, scaly, imbricated. Inferior scales small, ovate, appressed ; upper ones lanceolate, erect, concave, bituminous.

During the time of the inflorescence of this common, but beautiful shrub (*Suikerbosch*), the involucra or its showy flowers are filled with a sweet, watery liquor, which is an allurement to the laborious bee, and to a host of various insects. This liquid contains a great deal of honey. It is therefore collected by many farmers, who prepare from it by inspissation, a delicious syrup, which is known as the *Syrupus Proteæ* (*Boschjes-stroop*), and which is of great use in cough and pulmonary affections. The *Protea Lepidocarpon, R. Br.* and some other Proteæ also supply the same savoury juice.

RICINUS. LIN.

(*Euphorbiaceæ.*)

XXI.—10. MONOECIA MONADELPHIA. LIN. SYST.

79. *Ricinus lividus. Jacq. Stem* arborescent, branchy *Leaves* peltate, palmated, coloured; their lobes oblong, serrato-dentate.

It is scarcely necessary to say much of a remedy so universally known as the one derived from this plant. As a mild purgative, the *Castor-oil* excels all other preparations, and is daily prescribed in all parts of the globe. It is desirable, however, that instead of importing this medicine, the colonists should prepare it themselves for exportation to those countries, where this useful plant does not grow spontaneously.

HYÆNANCHE. LAMB.

(*Euphorbiaceæ.*)

XXI.—9. MONOECIA POLYANDRIA. LIN. SYST.

80. *Hyænanche globosa. Lamb.* An arborescent shrub 8—10 feet high. *Branches* wrinkled, rifted, knotty. *Leaves* standing by fours on short stalks, whorled, oblong, reticulated, obtuse, leathery, quite entire, glabrous. *Peduncles* corymbose, axillary. *Flowers* monoecious.

Though the fruit of this shrub (*Wolveboon*) has not been introduced into the Materia medica of the Cape, yet it deserves particular attention. It is highly poisonous, and its four-celled nuts, when pounded, are used to destroy hyænas, or other beasts of prey, and seem to contain *Strychnium*. This fatal bush is an inhabitant of the Maskamma mountain, in the neighbourhood of the Olifants River.

GUNNERA. Lin.
(*Urticaceæ.*)
II.—2. DIANDRIA DIGYNIA. LIN. SYST.

81. *Gunnera perpensa.* **Lin.** Herbaceous. *Radical leaves* large, stalked, kidney-shaped, unequal, veined, obsoletely lobed, cordate at base, serro-dentate. *Petioles* elongated, compressed, streaked, hairy, as the leaves are. *Scape* tall, bearing a compound panicle of very small crowded flowers. *Fruit* a glabrous juicy berry.

This plant (*Wilde Ramanas*) grows in moist and watery parts of the colony. A decoction of the root is used by the farmers in the interior as a tonic in dyspepsia, and a tincture from it as an efficient remedy in gravel. The leaves infused as tea are said to act as a demulcent in pulmonary affections, and to cure ulcerations and wounds when applied fresh.

PIPER. Lin.
(*Piperaceæ.*)
II.—1. DIANDRIA MONOGYNIA. LIN. SYST.

82. *Piper capense.* **Lin.** Herbaceous, smooth. *Stem* erect, articulated, branchy, climbing. *Branches* geniculate, forked, one-sided, spreading. *Leaves* alternate, stalked, cordate, acute, entire, 3-nerved above, 7-nerved beneath, netted. *Nerves* downy. *Flowers* in spikes, opposed. *Spikes* peduncled, cylindrical. *Fruit* a berry.

The dense forests of Swellendam and George produce a kind of pepper (*Boschpeper*), which partakes of the properties peculiar to the genus. The berries have a hot pungent taste, and an aromatic smell, and, infused in spirits, yield a tincture which is prescribed as a stomachic, stimulant, and carminative in indigestion, flatulency and colic. In appearance and taste they greatly resemble the *Cubebs*, and very likely possess similar virtues.

WIDDRINGTONIA. Endl.
(*Coniferæ.*)
XXI.—10. MONOECIA MONADELPHIA. LIN. SYST.

83. *Widdringtonia juniperoides.* **Endl.** *Branches* purplish, squarrose, twiggy. *Leaves* opposite, minute,

decussate, densely imbricate, appressed, ovate, connate, bluntly pointed, glabrous, glanduliferous. *Flowers*
dioecious. *Male catkins* terminal, solitary ; female
ones, lateral. *Cones* globose, 4-valved ; *calves* woody,
erect, mucronate.

From the branches and cones of this fine tree, *Ceder-
boom* (Cedar-tree), which grows plentifully in the mountainous regions of Clanwilliam, exudes a gum, which soon
hardens in the air, becomes solid, yellowish, and transparent, and scarcely differs from the *Gummi Olibanum*,
an article well known in commerce. This gum is successfully used in the form of fumigations, in gout, rheumatism, or œdematous swellings, and is also employed for
the purpose of compounding plasters or preparing varnish.
—*Widdringtonia cupressoides. Endl.* (Thuia cupressoides
Thbg.), a shrub pretty common in the neighbourhood of
Cape Town, exudes the same substance.

HOMERIA. Vent.

(*Irideœ.*)

XVI.—1. MONADELPHIA TRIANDRIA. LIN. SYST.

84. *Homeria collina. Sweet. Root a corm* or tuberous bulb, covered with a fibrous, reticulated, hardened
coat. *Shaft* erect, smooth, paniculately branched.
Branches 2–3 flowered. *Spathe* 2-valved, awned.
Radical-leaf, strap-shaped, narrow, caudate, concave,
abruptly-pointed, outreaching the shaft. *Cauline
leaves* 2-3 much smaller. *Corolla* ephemerous, of a
yellow or vermilion colour.

I introduce this plant, the *Moraea collina. Thbg.,* (which
is known to almost every child in the colony as the *Cape
Tulip,*) not for its therapeutical use, but for its obnoxious-
ness. The poisonous qualities of its bulbs appear to have
been known to some extent years ago, but judging from
the rapidity with which death ensued in a recent case,
when they had been eaten by mistake, it must be of a
very poisonous kind. To Dr. Laing, Police Surgeon
of Cape Town, I am indebted for the particulars of a
most melancholy case of poisoning caused by this bulb.

A malay woman, somewhat advanced in years, with her
three grand-children, respectively of the ages of 12, 8, and
6, partook, on the 18th September last (1850), of a supper,
consisting of coffee, fish, and rice, and ate along with this,

a small basinful of the bulbs of the Homeria collina. The exact quantity which each ate, is not well known. They appear to have supped between 7 and 8, and retired to bed at 9 o'clock, apparently in good health.

About one in the morning the old woman awoke with severe nausea, followed by vomiting, and found the children similarly affected. She endeavoured to call for assistance, but found herself too weak to leave her bed, and when, at 5 o'clock, assistance arrived, the eldest girl was found *moribund*, and expired almost immediately. The little boy of 8 years died an hour afterwards, and the youngest child was found in a state of collapse, almost insensible, with cold extremities, pulse scarcely 50 and irregular, pupils much dilated. The symptoms of the grandmother were nearly similar, but in a lesser degree, accompanied by constant efforts at vomiting. By using diffusible stimulants, she and this child eventually recovered.

The body of the eldest child was examined twelve hours after death. Marks of intense gastritis were found, particularly about the cardiac and pyloric orifices. The inflammation extended throughout the whole course of the small intestines, and there was great venous congestion of the brain.*

---

* About a year after the publication of the first edition of this little work, the author received the following communication from the late RICHARD FRYER, Esq., then Justice of the Peace for Clanwilliam :—

Clanwilliam, 9th February, 1852.

Dear Sir,—On perusing your "Flora Capensis Medica" the other day, the circumstance stated at page 26, of the poisonous effects of the bulb of the "Cape Tulip," brought to my recollection a dreadful accident which occurred in Hantam, in this district, many years ago, and, as I was called upon at the time, in a judicial way, to examine some of the bodies and take evidence upon the causes of death, I can vouch for the accuracy of what I shall here relate. It appears that one of the shepherds of a farmer residing there, brought home in the evening, a bundle of bulbs, which the Dutch call "Uyntjes;" that towards dusk these were put under the ashes to roast, and when the other servants assembled in the kitchen, they were taken out and eaten amongst them,—the party consisting of three Hottentots, two women, and one male slave. About half an hour after they had partaken of them, they were all seized with dreadful nausea, followed shortly afterwards by severe vomiting, and a speedy prostration of strength. The farmer being called, ascertained immediately from some of the bulbs still unconsumed, that they had been eating of the "Homeria collina," of the yellow sort. Wilde Dagga, sweet oil, milk, and everything thought good, were immediately administered, but before midnight, the three Hottentots and one woman had died, in excruciating agonies. The male slave was got through, although, for a year afterwards, he looked like a skeleton, and the surviving woman ascribed her safety to only having ate one bulb.—&c.,

R. F.

It is remarkable that in cases of poisoning from *Fungi*, violent diarrhœa is present along with vomiting, whereas in the present case obstinate constipation prevailed.

Most probably, all plants belonging to this genus partake of this poisonous property, which, in the case mentioned above, was not dissipated by boiling.

HÆMANTHUS. Lin.

(*Amaryllideæ.*)

VI.—1. HEXANDRIA MONOGYNIA. LIN. SYST.

85. *Hæmanthus coccineus. Lin. Root* a large tunicated bulb. *Radical leaves* 2, lying flat on the ground, broad, thick, coriaceous, tongue-shaped or ovate, entire, smooth. *Scape* flat, erect, coloured, bearing a densely-flowered *umbel. Involucre* 4-leaved, blood-red ; its segments ovate. *Fruit* a red berry.

The bulb of this beautiful plant is used on account of its diuretic effects. It is cut into slices, digested in vinegar, and with the addition of honey, boiled down to the consistence of an oxymel, which is given as an expectorant and as a diuretic in asthma and dropsy. The fresh leaves are used externally as an antiseptic in foul flabby ulcers and in anthrax, and are known by the name of *Veldschoenblâren.*

GETHYLLIS. Lin.

(*Amaryllideæ.*)

VI.—1. HEXANDRIA MONOGYNIA. LIN. SYST.

86. *Gethyllis spiralis. Lin. Bulb* ovate, scaly, *Leaves* fascicled, upright, linear, channelled, glabrous, spirally twisted, appearing after the flower has decayed. *Flower* solitary, salver-shaped, white, spotted beneath with confluent purple dots ; its *tube* very long, stalk-like, partly under ground. *Fruit* cylindrical, scented.

The elongated, club-shaped, orange-coloured fruit of this plant has a peculiar fragrance, and still preserves its old Hottentot name of *Kukumakranka.* Infused in spirits, the liquor partakes of its pleasing scent, and is employed in colic and flatulency.

ASPARAGUS. Lin.

(*Asparagineæ*.)

VI.—1. HEXANDRIA MONOGYNIA. LIN. SYST.

87. *Asparagus laricinus. Burch.* Perannual. *Stem* twining, waving, smooth. *Branches* alternate, bent backward, armed at base and in the axils of the leaves with solitary, short, reflexed prickles. *Leaves* sub-verticillate, clustered, awl-shaped, sharp-pointed, stipulate, longer than the *internodes. Peduncles* 2, very slender, one-flowered, pendulous, nodulose above base. *Flowers* bell-shaped, patent, white, small.

The young succulent shoots of this kind of *Asparagus* furnish a most excellent dish. Its roots are *diuretic*, impart a peculiar smell to the urine, and are of service in dropsy, and in all cases where the secretion of the kidneys is scanty or anomalous

SANSEVIERA. Thbg.

(*Asparagineæ.*

VI.—1. HEXANDRIA MONOGYNIA. LIN. SYST.

88. *Sanseviera thyrsiflora. Thbg.** *Root* horizontally creeping, jointed. *Leaves* radical, broad, ensiform, smooth, coriaceous, marginate with a callous point at the apex. *Scape* 2 feet high, sheated at intervals by membranaceous bracts of an ovate-lanceolate form. *Flowers* racemoso-spicate, stalked, white, standing in pairs ; *anthers* yellow ; *style* lengthened, capitate.

Not uncommon in forests and on Karroo-like hills between the Zwartkops and Bosjesman Rivers (Uitenhage) Fl. Dec. Jan. In the Eastern districts, the fleshy root of this plant, when boiled, is made use of internally in piles, and is called *t'Kay* by the natives.

ALOE. Lin.

(*Asphodeleæ.*)

VI.—1. HEXANDRIA MONOGYNIA. LIN. SYST.

89. *Aloe ferox. Lam.* Stem very lofty. *Leaves* perfoliate, thick, juicy, sword-shaped, deflexed, glau-

---

* This species has been referred by most authors to *Sanseviera guineensis. Willd.* as a mere variety. Whether this be truly correct I cannot decide, not having had an opportunity of examining both in a fresh state.

cous, prickly throughout, but bearing larger and sharper spines along the margins. *Flowers* racemose, crowded. *Stamens* double as long as the corolla.

The Cape Aloes are procured from several species of this extensive genus, so peculiar to South Africa. The *Aloe ferox. Lam.*, a native of Swellendam, is generally acknowledged to yield the best extract. That obtained from the *Aloe africana. Mill.* is almost equally good, but not so bitter, nor so powerful as a drastic. It is the produce of the eastern districts, whence large quantities are annually exported. The Aloe commonly used by the Colonists, is prepared from the *Aloe plicatilis. Mill.*, whose extract is a much milder purgative, and much resembles the Barbadoes Aloes. It inhabits the mountainous range near the Paarl, Drakenstein, and Fransche Hoek. It is much to be regretted, that the farmers do not take more trouble in purifying this valuable drug.

ORNITHOGALUM. Lin.

(*Asphodeleæ.*)

VI.—I. HEXANDRIA MONOGYNIA. LIN. SYST.

90. *Ornithogalum altissimum. Lin.* *Bulb* very large, round, tunicated. *Leaves* (appearing after the scape has withered) strap-shaped and lanceolate, convolutely-mucronate. *Scape* solitary, glaucous, racemose, elongated. *Raceme* cylindrical, lengthened, crowded with white scentless flowers.

The fleshy bulb of this plant often grows as large as a child's head. It is diuretic, and a kind of oxymel, like that obtained from the *Hæmanthus coccineus*, is prepared from it, and employed as a demulcent in catarrh, asthma, consumption, and hydrothorax. It resembles the *Scilla maritima* in its effects, is common in Zwartland, where it is called *Mayerman*, and may be prescribed as a substitute for Scilla.

TULBAGHIA. Thbg.

(*Asphodeleæ.*)

VI.—I. HEXANDRIA MONOGYNIA. LIN. SYST.

91. *Tulbaghia alliacea. Thbg.* *Root* fasciculated, imperfectly bulbous, fibrous. *Leaves* sheating at base, two-rowed, strap-shaped, linear, obtuse, streaked, smooth. *Scape* simple, longer than the leaves, ending

in a loose, few-flowered umbel, surrounded by a dry 2-valved involucre. *Flowers* 6-7, on long peduncles, drooping, dark purplish. *Perianth* double, outer-one funnel-shaped, limb 6 partite, interior 3-leaved, fleshy.

This bulbous plant has a very pungent, offensive odour, very like that of garlic, and a somewhat acrimonious taste, and has received the name of *wilde Knoflook* (wild garlic). Its bulbs, boiled in milk, are recommended in phthisis, and for expelling intestinal worms. In the eastern districts, *Tulbaghia cepacea* and *T. violacea* serve the same purpose.

IDOTHEA. KUNTH.

(*Asphodeleæ.*)

VI.—1. HEXANDRIA MONOGYNIA. LIN. SYST.

92. *Idothea ciliaris. Kth. Root* a scaly bulb. *Radical leaves* (appearing after the flowers have faded) strap-shaped, pointed, and fringed with short marginal hairs. *Scape* straight, spotted, smooth, much longer than the leaves. *Flowers* racemose, greenish-white; *flower-stalks* spreading.

The bulb of this plant greatly resembles that of the *Scilla maritima;* it is of a dingy, purplish colour, and its juice is so very acrid as to cause inflammation and even blisters, when applied to the skin. It is called *Jeukbol* (itching bulb) by the Colonists, and used by them when dried, like the common Squill is in Europe, as an emetic, expectorant, and diuretic.

Found in the district of Swellendam, where it flowers in the month of September.

Idothea elata, Kth., closely allied to this species, has the same properties, and was already known to *Breynius*[*] as the "Bulbus liliaceus vomitorius Capitis bonæ Spei."

ERIOSPERMUM. JACQ.

(*Asphodeleæ.*)

VI.—1. HEXANDRIA MONOGYNIA. LIN. SYST.

93. *Eriospermum latifolium. Jacq. Root* tuberous, roundish, knobbed, blood-red inside. *Radical-leaf*

---

[*] *J. Breynius* Exoticarum, aliarumque minus cognitarum plantarum Centuria. Gedani 1678. Fol. (Tab. 40.)

broad, ovate, pointed, entire, coriaceous, nervy, transversely veined, smooth, involute at base, dotted beneath, stalked. *Scape* simple, erect. streaked, racemose, many-flowered. *Flowers* pedicellate, bracteate, white.

The scarlet coloured tuber of this species, which grows on the sides of the Lion's Rump, near Cape Town and elsewhere, is very muculent, and used externally, in abrasions of the skin and in superficial ulcers. It is also employed by the Mohamedans, in the form of decoction, in amenorrhœa. Its Cape name is *Baviaans-oren.*

RICHARDIA. Ктн.

(*Aroideæ.*)

XXI.—1. MONOECIA ANDROGYNIA. LIN. SYST.

94. *Richardia africana. Kth. Root* thick, fleshy. *Leaves* radical, glossy, arrow-shaped, cordate at base, stalked ; *leaf-stalks* sheating, clasping the scape ; *scape* nearly three-cornered, erect; *spathe* petal-like, hooded, covering the flower-bearing *spadix. Fruit* a berry.

More than a century ago, this hardy plant, the *Ethiopian Calla,* has, on account of its large, ornamental, white, caplike spathe, been cultivated in all the gardens of Europe. In this Colony, where it is indigenous, the fresh leaves, when applied warm to parts affected with gout or rheumatism, allay the pain by producing local perspiration. The roots afford good nourishment for the porcupine (Hystrix cristata) *Yster-vark,* and therefore probably, this conspicuous plant has received the Cape vernacular, but ugly name of *Varkens-blaren* (pig's-leaves.)

MOHRIA. Sw.

Filices.

XXIV.—CRYPTOGAMIA. LIN. SYST.

95. *Mohria thurifraga. Sw. Caudex* creeping, fibrous. *Stipe* filiform, hispid, erect. *Fronds* bipinnate, covered beneath with chaffy scales. *Pinnæ* alternate, stalked ; *pinnules* ovate, the upper fruit-bearing-ones, crenate ; the barren-ones deeply incised.

This fern grows abundantly on the Cape Mountains. The plant, when bruised, is fragrant and smells of *Oli-*

banum. In some parts of the Colony, the dry leaves are pulverised, and with fat made into an ointment, which is cooling, and very serviceable in burns and scalds. The vernacular name of this plant is *Brand-boschjes.*

LASTREA. Presl.

(*Filices.*)

XXIV.—CRYPTOGAMIA. LIN. SYST.

96. *Lastrea athamantica. Moore. Stipe* erect, flexuose, covered at base with long linear deciduous scales. *Fronds* leathery, smooth, lanceolate, three-pinnate. *Pinnæ* stalked, oblong, acuminate. *Primary pinnules* sessile, ovato-oblong, wedge-shaped at base, decurrent ; *secondary,* sickle-shaped, oblong, blunt, veiny. *Sori* round, solitary *Involucre* kidney-shaped.

A fern, growing on grassy hills and in moist places, near Port Natal. The Zoolu Kafirs, who know it by the name of *Uncomocomo,* use it as a vermifuge, and its *caudex,* given in the form of powder, infusion, or electuary, has been proved to be excellent in helminthiasis, and especially in the cure of the tape-worm.

ADIANTHUM. Lin.

(*Filices.*)

XXIV.—CRYPTOGAMIA. LIN. SYST.

97. *Adianthum æthiopicum. Lin. Caudex* fibrous. *Stipe* compressed, waving, purplish. *Fronds* very delicate, transparent, decompound, smooth. *Pinnæ* alternate on capillary stalks. *Pinnules* rhomboidal, crenate at apex, traversed by forked nerves.

An infusion of this herb is sometimes used as an emollient in coughs, and in diseases of the chest. A syrup is also prepared from it, and it forms part of the *species pectorales* of the pharmacopœia. The Basuto Kafirs, who call this fern *Ma-o-ru-metsoo,* employ its caudex in the shape of decoction for promoting parturition.

FUCOIDEÆ.

XXIV.—CRYPTOGAMIA (ALGÆ). LIN. SYST.

98. The peculiar substance called *Iodine,* and now so universally appreciated as a powerful remedy, is

derived from the ashes or kelp of the *Fucoideæ.* With these our shores are well strewed; and amongst them are found *Algæ,* distinguished both for extraordinary frequency and gigantic size. It is certain that the *Ecklonia buccinalis. Hornm.* (Zee-bambocs), *our Sargassa, Laminariæ,* and *Iridaeæ,* the *Macrocystis planicaulis. Ag.,* the *Desmarestia herbacea. Lamour,* and many more of our large marine plants, would easily yield a vast quantity of *Iodine,* if the experiment of preparing it, were thought worth a due trial.

SUHRIA. J. Ag.

(*Florideæ.*)

XXIV.—CRYPTOGAMIA (ALGÆ). LIN. SYST.

99. *Suhria vittata. I. Ag.* Base callous, fixed parasitically on the stems of larger *Algæ. Frond* leaf-like, linear-lanceolate, branchy, mid-ribbed at base, prolificating. *Prolifications* issuing chiefly from the margin of the frond as fringes, or in the form of small obovate leaves, which contain the fructification. *Substance* cartilaginous; colour deep purple.

Like the Carrageen, or Irish moss, the whole of this handsome sea-weed is soluble in boiling water, and transformed into a gelatinous mass. In the shape of *jelly* or *blanc mange,* it is advantageously employed in pulmonary complaints, scrofula, rickets, irritation of the bladder, &c., as a demulcent and nutritive.

Common in Table Bay, particularly on the gigantic stems of the Sea-trumpet (Ecklonia buccinalis. Horn.)

PODAXON. Desv.

(*Fungi.*)

XXIV.—CRYPTOGAMIA. LIN. SYST.

100. *Podaxon carcinomatis. Fr.* Club-shaped; *peridium* dehiscent at base. *Stipe* erect, cylindrical, white. *Cap* ovate, tapering upwards, nearly as long as the stipe.

A mushroom of an oblong club-shaped form, which grows gregariously on ant-hills. It contains a blackish powder (seeds), which is used occasionally for curing carcinomatous ulcers.

APPENDIX.

I subjoin to the above enumeration of medical plants, a remedy derived from the *animal Kingdom,* one, which, if tried properly, will in all probability become an article of commerce. I allude to the

HYRACEUM,[*]

much valued by many farmers, and well known amongst them, by the rather harsh name of *Dasjespis.* Thunberg, and other travellers, mistook it for a kind of bitumen ; but it is in fact the secretion of a quadruped, which is common throughout the Colony, and that lives gregariously on the rocky summits of mountains, viz., the *Klipdas* or *Hyrax capensis.* It is worthy of note that this production has baffled the researches of eminent Zoologists, who have failed from even minute dissection, in discovering any specific secretory organ, from which this matter could be derived. It may be asserted, however, that the *Hyraceum* is produced by the uropoetical system of the animal just named, and in order to explain this seeming anomaly, it must be observed that the Hyrax drinks very seldom, if ever. Its urine, like that of the *Hare,* is not thin and limpid, as in other quadrupeds, but thick and of a glutinous nature. From a peculiar instinct, these animals are in the habit of secreting the urine always at *one* spot, where its watery parts evaporate in the sun, while its more tenacious portions stick to the rock, and harden in the air. The fresh urine of the Hyrax is of a reddish tint, and this has given rise to the opinion of those, who took this production for a kind of menstrual secretion.

This substance is common on our mountains, and

---

* Cf. *Dr L. Fikentscher,* Das Hyraceum in historischer, chemischer, pharmaceutischer, and therapeutischer Beziehung. Erlangen, 1851. Octvo.

is to be found, mixed with earth and dirt, near the caves or crevices, where these animals have their haunts.

In smell, and in its therapeutical effects, the *Hyraceum* resembles most the *Castoreum*, a remedy which is decreasing in quantity every year, and may therefore be replaced by the former. A new article of export would thus be gained. Amongst the farmers, a solution of this substance is highly spoken of as an antispasmodic in hysterics, epilepsy, convulsions of children, St. Vitus's dance ; in short, in spasmodic affections of every kind.

Dr. A. Brown, who has employed the *Hyraceum* in a great number of cases, has communicated to me the following remarks of its effects, as the result of his experience :—

Hyraceum is a mild stimulant and antispasmodic. The tincture, when well and properly prepared, appears to be a remedy of considerable power. It is regarded as an emmenagogue among the country people. In hysterical, nervous, and spasmodic affections, *Hyraceum*, in the form of tincture, is a very valuable remedy, and one highly deserving of trial. It is daily prescribed by myself. It is advantageously combined with the Tr. Valerianæ. I can speak highly of its efficacy in this class of cases. My common formula for its use is

Tinct. Hyracei.
　　,,　　　,,　Valerianæ.
Spir. æther sulph., two drams of each.
Aq cinnamon, two ounces.

M. D. S.—A tea-spoonful thrice a-day, or 30 drops every two or three hours.

In Epilepsy, I have also tried, and can recommend it. In spasmodic asthma, I have often derived decided advantage from a combination of equal parts of Tinctura Hyracei and Tinct. Lobeliæ inflatæ.

In a long-standing case of Hypochondria, accompanied by strong hysterical symptoms, and which had baffled myself and several other practitioners, a teaspoonful of the tincture produced a rapid and decided cure. As an emmenagogue in amenorrhœa and chlorosis, its effects have been beyond all conception. In one case of chlorosis, where the catamenia had been absent eleven months, in another of amenorrhœa of eighteen months, and where the patient had been confined to bed for months, expectorating pus and blood, had hectic fever, cold clammy perspiration at night, complete loss of appetite, and was given up as altogether hopeless, Hyraceum effected a complete cure, for she has now for years continued fat and plump, and menstruates regularly.

In all cases where Castoreum is recommended, I have found Hyraceum far preferable as an antispasmodic ; in hysteria itself, it is invaluable.

A. B.

Abortive and *abortion*, terms used where the symmetry of the flower is not complete, or imperfectly developed.

Achænium, the fruit of the family of the *Compositæ*, which is one-seeded, and does not open, but the *pericarp* of which is separable.

Acuminate, tapering at top ; sharp-pointed.

Acute, pointed, not tapering.

Alternate, placed one above another.

Amplexicaul, embracing the stem.

Angular, having angles on the margin.

Anther, a membranaceous body, borne by the filament, containing a dust-like powder.

Apiculate, having a soft terminal point.

Articulated, jointed.

Attenuate, gradually diminishing in breadth.

Axillary, growing in the axil.

Baccate, berried, covered with a soft flesh.

Bipinnate, if a compound leaf is divided twice in a pinnate manner.

Bract, a floral leaf ; a leaf from which flowers proceed.

Bractlet, a small bract at the base of a separate flower.

Callous, hardened, indurated.

Calyx, flower-cup, the exterior covering of a flower.

Campanulate, bell-shaped.

Cap, the uppermost part of a fungus.

Capitate, formed into a head.

Capitulum, a head of flowers in *Compositæ*.

Capsule, a membranaceous seed-vessel opening by valves.

Cartilaginous, hard and tough.

Catkin, a deciduous unisexual spike, whose flowers are destitute of calyx and corolla, but supplied with bracts.

Caudate, having a tail or appendage.

Caudex, the stem of ferns.

Channelled, concave, so as to resemble a gutter.

Ciliated, fringed with short, stiff, marginal hairs.

Compound, composed of several parts.

Compressed, flattened.

Cone, a dry fruit formed by scales, covering naked seeds.

Connate, united at base.

Cordate, heart-shaped.

Coriaceous, leathery.

Corolla, the inner envelope of the flower, constituting what is commonly called *the flower*.

Corona, scaly or petal-like bodies, intervening between the petals and the stamens.

Corymb, a raceme, in which the lower stalks are longest, and the upper ones so shortened, that the flowers are placed in one horizontal plane.

Crenate, having rounded marginal teeth.

Crested, having an elevated appendage, a crest.

Cylindrical, having a cylindrical shape.

Deciduous, falling off after having performed its functions.

Decompound, having compound branchings.

G

Decussate, crossing at right angles.

Dehiscent, opening, bursting.

Dentate, toothed.

Dichotomous, divided by twos, forked.

Dioecious, a plant is so called when male and female organs appear separate upon different individuals.

Discoid, having the form of a flattened sphere.

Divaricating, straggling, spreading.

Drupe, a fleshy fruit, enclosing a nut.

Elliptical, pointed at both ends.

Emarginate, having a notch at the point.

Ensiform, sword-shaped.

Entire, without marginal teeth or incisions.

Ephemerous, short-lived.

Falcate, bent like a sickle.

Farinaceous, mealy.

Fascicled, standing in bundles.

Fastigiate, having a pyramidal shape, from *the branches* being parallel and erect.

Filiform, thread-like, slender.

Flexuous, waving, bent in a zig-zag manner.

Follicle, a fruit, formed by a single carpel, and opening by one suture.

Frond, the leaflike development of ferns bearing the fructification.

Geniculate, bent like a knee; knee-jointed.

Glabrous, smooth, bald.

Glandulous, bearing glands at the tip.

Glaucous, covered with a pale-green bloom.

Globose, round, spherical.

Hispid, covered with long rigid hairs.

Imbricated, sessile parts covering or overlapping each other like tiles.

Impari-pinnate, unequally yoked; pinnate-leaves ending in an odd leaflet.

Incised, deeply cut down.

Internode, the portion of a stem between two nodes or leaf-buds.

Involucre, bracts, surrounding a head of flowers in a whorl.

Leaflet, the division in a compound leaf.

Legume, a seed-pod with two valves, the seeds of which are fixed on one and the same suture, but alternately upon the two valves.

Ligula, the ray-flowers of a capitulum in *compositæ*.

Linear, very narrow; when the length much exceeds the breadth.

Limb, the broad part of a petal, or a leaflet, forming part of the calyx.

Lobed, divided into segments.

Membranaceous, having the appearance and structure of a membrane.

Monoecious, when male and female flowers are separated from each other, but grow upon the same individual plant.

Mucronate, abruptly terminating in a hard sharp point.

Nodulose, with a thickened knot.

Oblong (oval), elliptical, obtuse at each end.

Obovate, reversely ovate.

Obtuse, blunt, not pointed.

Opposite, placed on opposite sides.

Orbicular, rounded, with the stalk attached to the centre.

Ovate, egg-shaped, broadest at base, narrowed upwards.

Palmated, 5-lobed, resembling a hand.

Perfoliate, surrounding the stem at base.

Panicle, an inflorescence, where subordinate stalks are again divided.

Patent, spreading horizontally.

Peltate, shield-like, flattened and expanded at top.

Pedicel, the stalk supporting a single flower.

Peduncle, the general flower-stalk.

Pendulous, hanging down.

Penni-nerved (leaf), whose ribs are disposed like the parts of a feather.

Perianth, a term used where the calyx and corolla are combined, partaking of the nature of both.

Pericarp, the covering of the fruit.

Peridium, the cover of the fructification in *fungi*.

Petals, flower-leaves; leaves forming the corrolline whorl.

Petiole, the leaf-stalk.

Pinna, a leaflet.

Pinnate (leaf), a compound leaf, having leaflets arranged on each side of the central rib.

Pinnatifid (leaf), a simple leaf, cut into lateral segments to about the midrib.

Pinnulæ, the small pinnæ of a bipinnate or tripinnate leaf.

Polygamous (plants), bearing hermaphroditical, as well as distinct male and female flowers.

Procumbent, lying on the ground.

Pubescent, covered with short and soft hair.

Quadrangular, four-sided, four-angled.

Raceme, a cluster of flowers, where from one common stalk undivided flower-stalks arise.

Receptacle, the expanded part of the fruit-stalks, which bears the parts of fructification.

Reflexed, bent backwards.

Reniform, kidney-shaped.

Repand, slightly waved at margin.

Reticulated, netted.

Rigid, stiff, inflexible, not easily bent.

Rugose, wrinkled.

Rhomboid, oval, somewhat angular in the middle.

Scabrid, rough, covered with short stiff hairs.

Scape, a leafless flower-stalk.

Scarious, dry, shrivelled.

Serrate, toothed, like the indentations of a saw.

Sessile, stalkless.

Setaceous, bristle-like.

Simple, not divided.

Sinuated, the margin having obtuse or blunt indentations.

Sorus, a cluster of sporangia, organs of propagation in *ferns*.

Spadix, a fleshy spike, bearing male and female flowers.

Spathe, a membranaceous bract, surrounding the flowers.

Spatulate, shaped like a spattle.

Spike, an inflorescence, where stalkless flowers are arranged on a common axis.

Stamen, the male organ of a flower, formed by the *filament*, or stalk, and the *anther*.

Stellate, arranged like a star.

Stipe, the stalk of cryptogamic plants.

Stipule, a leaf-like appendage, situated at the base of real leaves, or of leaf-stalks.

Striated, marked by streaks.

Stoloniferous, having creeping runners, which root at the joints.

Style, the columnar or filiform elongation of the pistil, which supports the stigma, and proceeds upwards from the ovary.

Subulate, awl-shaped.

Succulent, fleshy.

Suffruticose, having the character of an undershrub.

Ternate, composed of three leaflets.

Terminal, on the summit.

Tomentose, covered with dense, entangled, rigid, short hairs.

Trifid, divided into three segments.

Trifoliate, consisting of three leaflets.

Truncate, lopped off; terminating abruptly.

Tubular, cylindrical, fistular.

Tunicated, covered by thin scales.

Turbinate, formed like a top.

Umbel, an inflorescence in which numerous stalked flowers arise from one point.

Valves, the portions which separate self-opening capsules.

Verticillate, ranged in whorls.

Villose, shaggy, covered with long, weak hairs,

Viscid, clammy.

Whorl, a kind of inflorescence, in which the flowers are placed around the stem or branch on a common axis.

INDEX.

SYNOPSIS

FILICUM AFRICÆ AUSTRALIS:

OR,

AN ENUMERATION OF THE SOUTH AFRICAN FERNS HITHERTO KNOWN.

BY

L. PAPPE, M.D.,

AND

THE HON. RAWSON W. RAWSON, ESQ.

CAPE TOWN:

W. BRITTAIN, 44, ST. GEORGE'S-STREET.

1858.

CAPE TOWN:
SAUL SOLOMON AND CO., STEAM PRINTING OFFICE.
LONGMARKET-STREET.

INTRODUCTION.

§ 1. THE natural family of Ferns comprises cryptogamic, mostly perennial, plants, the leaves or fronds of which are, in the early stage of their growth, coiled up in a particular way, so as to represent a scroll. Their fronds show a great variety of form and texture, and generally bear on the veins of the under surface, or along their edges, the organs of the fructification.

§ 2. These consist of *capsules* or spore-cases *(sporidia)*, which burst in various ways, and are either continuous, spread about irregularly, grouped together in heaps *(sori)*, or more rarely collected into spikes or racemes, formed by the contraction of part of the frond.

§ 3. These capsules are one-celled, stalked or sessile, generally surrounded by an articulated elastic ring, and discharge, when mature, the *spores*, or minute seeds, which they contain. The *sori* or clusters of sporidia are, in a great many genera, protected by a peculiar membrane, or scale, called the *indusium* or involucre, which is deciduous or persistent, derives its origin from the epidermis of the frond, and covers the sori entirely or in part; while in other cases, the borders of the frond, being dilated and reflexed, perform the function of that membrane.

§ 4. The Ferns arise from a subterraneous root-stock *(rhizome)*, which for the most part is creeping and of a woody nature. Their stem, or that portion of the rhizome which rises above ground *(caudex)*, is almost ever upright and simple, and but rarely climbing *(Stenochlæna Meyeriana)*, or branched *(Gleicheniaceæ)*. It is very short, and nearly wanting

B

in some species, yet becomes arborescent in others, and often attains a considerable height (*Cyathea*, *Alsophila*). This caudex, which is hollow within, and not possessed of a fibrous inner bark (*liber*), is generally hard from without, and of a glossy appearance. Both the root-stocks and the stems of some of these plants contain peculiar resinous substances which have anthelmintic properties, and serve as vermifuges, (*Lastrea athamantica*, etc.,)—a fact, already known to the ancients.—Theophr. Hist. Plantar, 18, 8.

§ 5. In the formation of the leaves, nature has displayed her wondrous charms. These leaves are called *fronds* by botanists, and are either stalked, or more rarely sessile, or sometimes jointed to the caudex, or root-stock, by articulations. They are persistent and evergreen within the tropics and temperate zones, but deciduous in cold climates, in which case the frond is yearly renewed. Their texture is herbaceous, membranaceous, or leathery ; their upper surface, generally dark, smooth, glazed or shining ; the under side, on the contrary, paler, very veiny, often clothed with short hair, and furnished with minute breathing pores (*stomata*). In a few genera, only, both surfaces are nearly alike (*Vittaria*, *Hymenophylleæ*). The fronds are rarely simple and entire, much oftener lobed, digitate, or pinnatifid, but mostly pinnate or further divided. Their *pinnæ* and *pinnules*, again, are entire, notched, sawed, toothed, incised, or pinnatifid, and frequently unequally shaped at their bases.

§ 6. The *stipes*, which in this family represents the leaf-stalks of phanerogamous plants, is connected with the stem or the rhizome by articulation. It is of different size : almost wanting in some species, or of considerable length in others ; mostly herbaceous, but sometimes woody, and covered by an epidermis, which in the course of growth becomes brittle, glossy, and of a dark-brown or blackish hue. The continuation of the stipes through simple fronds goes by the name of rib, or *costa*, while its further ramifications in pinnated fronds are called *rachises*.

§ 7. The root-stocks, stems, stalks, and rachises of Ferns are often clothed, especially in their youth, with a peculiar kind of deciduous, membranaceous, chaffy scales, which are decidedly hygroscopical (absorbing water), scarious, dispersed, or imbricated, erect, twisted, filiform, lanceolate, oval, etc., and of a brown, black, or yellow colour. They are called *Paleæ*, differ in size, and their edges are either entire, sawed, fringed, or irregularly torn.

§ 8. The process of fecundation in this family of plants has been the speculative task of many naturalists. Some skilful hypotheses have been advanced on the subject by eminent authors, in order to establish sexuality amongst them ; but as nature has mysteries of her own to hide from mortal view, so these theories, however intelligent, are only to be looked upon as ingenious suppositions. That young Ferns may be reared from spores, or seeds, is sufficiently known, as well as that some of them are propagated by leaf buds. (*Asplenium gemmiferum.*)

§ 10. For the purpose of systematic classification, the filical tribe has been divided into *sub-orders*, the chief characters of which are to be found in the construction, shape, dehiscence, or position of the *sporidia ;* the presence or absence of an *involucre*, the form of the *spores*, the vernation, etc. In *Hymenophylleæ* (small Ferns with very delicate, almost transparent, fronds, *without stomata*), the marginal spore-cases are placed upon the top of an extended vein, and covered with a cuplike involucre, formed by the lobes of the frond ; while the capsules in *Ophioglosseæ* are spiked on the margin of a contracted leaf, possess no ring at all, and have a straight vernation.

§ 11. If the graceful Fern trees of tropical or sub-tropical climes approach *Cycadeæ*, and remind us of the majestic growth of *Palms*, then the small order of *Lycopodiaceæ* or club-mosses show, in the structure and shape of their leaves, an affinity to the muscal alliance. These plants form indeed a family of their own, but are commonly classed with Ferns as an intermediate group. They have creeping or erect stems; their leaves are small, sessile, whorled, or imbricated, and their fructification, which is spiked or axillary, consists of bivalved cases, containing minute powdery spores. Of this order, but few representatives are known to inhabit South Africa.

§ 12. In most true Ferns, but especially in the dorsiferous ones, the peculiar course, position, distribution, and ramification of the nerves and veins, placed at the back of their fronds, are highly important for the supply of superior *generic characters*, being, as they are, closely connected with the insertion of the organs of fructification. They, therefore, are very valuable also in the arrangement of fossil Ferns, which, as we learn from geology, abounded in great number and variety during the carboniferous epoch of the earth, and of which some hundred species, belonging to different genera, have been described.

§ 13. Although Ferns exist in nearly all parts of the globe, yet countries situated within or somewhat beyond the tropics, seem to be most genial to their growth and development. They generally delight in warm, moist, shady localities, and thrive best in woody, mountainous regions. In the western districts of the colony of the Cape of Good Hope they are proportionally rare for that reason, but increase in species towards the east, and become frequent and distinct in the dense woods, mountain ravines, and near the cascades of Natal. The aboriginal forests of British Kaffraria, as yet unexplored, undoubtedly conceal strange forms, quite new to the scientific world.

§ 14. If we estimate (by moderate calculation) the entire number of South African plants at about 12,000 species, out of which one thousand, at least, are cryptogamic or cellular, it then becomes apparent, that the Ferns are but poorly represented in this great and imposing assemblage, forming hardly one-sixtieth part of the whole Flora, and scarcely one-fifth part of the plants of the lower classes, known to exist in so wide and rich a tract of territory.

§ 15. It is rather remarkable that, up to this date, not one single genus of Ferns has been discovered which could be said to be exclusively peculiar to this country, while even eighty-eight of the species described in this treatise, or about the half of them only, could claim that privilege. The rest of them are widely diffused, for we find thirty-one out of the number inhabiting the Mascarenhas (Mauritius and Reunion). Fifteen are found in Europe; fifteen grow in the West Indies, eleven in New Holland, ten in North America, nine in South America, eight in the Brazils, seven in the East Indies, six in the barren island of Tristan d'Acunha, six in the Canaries and Azores, five at Java, five in Central America, five in the north of Asia, six in the Sandwich Islands, three in North Africa, two in New Zealand and Tasmania, two at Luzon, one in Amboyna, Singapore, Fernando Po, China, and Japan. The rare *Cyrtomium falcatum*, a native of the lastnamed country, has but recently been found by Capt. Espinasse in the forests of British Kaffraria.

§ 16. Collectors of Ferns should not be satisfied with gathering fertile specimens alone, but secure, in like manner, sterile fronds and young shoots, which often greatly differ from perfect plants in their general aspect. The root-stocks and caudices also are of importance, and ought to be preserved.

§ 17. To persons who take an interest in the natural history of South African Ferns, a short review of the principal works treating on that topic may be acceptable. Thunberg,* whose writings on the Flora of this country are invaluable, described only thirteen genera and twenty-nine species of Ferns as indigenous. At a later period, Professor de Schlechtendal, encouraged by the examination of the valuable collections brought home by several zealous botanical travellers, and deposited in the Royal Herbarium of Berlin, issued a work on South African Ferns.†

* Prodromus Plantarum Capensium, 2d volume. Upsalæ, 1800, 8vo., and Flora Capensis, ed. Schultes, Stuttg. 1823, 8vo.

† Adumbratio Filicum in Promontorio Bonæ Spei provenientium. Part 1-5. Berl. 1825–26, 4to., with 24 engraved plates.

Here the author not only gives his own elaborate descriptions of many new, rare, or little known species, but also inserts Dr. Schrader's remarks on Cape Ferns, hitherto concealed in a learned periodical,* little accessible to botanical students. This important publication, which unhappily has been left unfinished, contains the descriptions of twenty-three genera and sixty-nine species. The latest monograph on the subject we owe to the pen of one of the ablest Pteridologists of our time. The rich collections made in this country by Ecklon and Zeyher, Drege, Gueinzius, and others, supplied the late and much lamented Professor Kunze (of Leipzic) with ample materials for his treatise on South African Ferns. This appeared under the title of " Acotyledonearum Africæ Australioris recensio nova. I. Filices, in the Linnæa † for 1836 and 1844, and contains thirty-three genera and one hundred and eleven species, many of which were perfectly new. Some of them are also figured in Kunze's continuation of Schkuhr.‡ Since then, the number of South African Ferns has been on the increase, a fact borne out by the contents of the following pages.

* Gœttinger gelehrte Anzeigen, 1818.

† Linnæa. Ein Journal für die Botanik in ihrem ganzen Umfange.

‡ G. Kunze, Die Farrnkraeuter in colorirten Abbildungen. Leipz. 1840 sq. 4to.

AN ENUMERATION

SOUTH AFRICAN FERNS.

SYNOPSIS OF SOUTH AFRICAN GENERA OF FERNS.

The classification adopted in the following description is mainly that established by Professor Presl, in his admirable "Tentamen Pteridographiæ," published in 1836, and followed by Sir Wm. Hooker, in his exquisitely illustrated "Genera Filicum," published in 1842.

The latter author, in his subsequent, more detailed, work, commenced in 1846, under the title of "Species Filicum," has somewhat modified Presl's arrangement, and other later authors have introduced more extensive changes; but as none of these have been generally accepted, and as Sir Wm. Hooker's work on the species of Ferns is still incomplete, it has been deemed preferable to adhere generally to the classification of Presl.

This author excludes from the order of Ferns (Filices) the group Hymenophylleæ of Endlicher, containing the two genera of Hymenophyllum and Trichomanes, which Sir William Hooker has restored, placing them between the tribes Dicksoniaceæ Pr., and Davalliaceæ Pr. He also excludes the order of Lycopodiaceæ, and others akin to, but not comprised in, the order of "Filices." The same arrangement will be adopted in the following synopsis.

Presl admitted two sub-orders, established by Bernhardi, dependent upon the character of the elastic ring surrounding the capsules (sporangia), viz., Helicogyratæ, having an eccentric ring, and Cathetogyratæ, having a marginal ring seldom complete. The former embraces only the first two tribes of the order. The distinction cannot easily be detected without a magnifying glass, and need not be attended to in a study of the Ferns of South Africa.

ORDER FILICES.

SUB-ORDER, HELICOGYRATÆ.

TRIBE 1.

Gleicheniaceæ. Kunze. *Fronds* creeping, spreading, gene rally dichotomous, pinnate, coriaceous, with gemmæ in axils. *Pinnules* small, linear. *Involucre* none. *Sori* globose, solitary or few.

Gen. 1.—*Gleichenia.* Swartz. *Sori* immersed.

Gen. 2.—*Mertensia.* Willd. *Sori* superficial, on a raised dotlike receptacle.

To this tribe belong the genera Platyzoma, Brown, and Calymella, Presl, which are not, as far as is known, represented in South Africa.

TRIBE 2.

Cyatheaceæ. Endlicher. *Plant* arborescent. *Stem* erect. *Involucre* cup-shaped, inferior, or wanting.

Gen. 1.—*Cyathea.* Smith. *Sori* on fork of veins, with an involucre.

Gen. 2.—*Alsophila.* Br. (Hemitelia, Presl). *Sori* at base of veins, with spurious involucre.

Schizocæna, I. Smith., Cnemidaria, Pr., Trichopteris, Pr., Metaxya, Pr., and Gymnosphæra, Blume., are not represented in South Africa.

SUB-ORDER CATHETOGYRATÆ.

GROUP 1, having an involucre (true or spurious.)

TRIBE 1.

Peranemaceæ. Pr. *Sori* globose, pedunculate, or on middle of superior veinlet. *Involucre* inferior, covering the *sori.*

This tribe, containing Peranema, Don., Diacalpe Blume, Woodsia, Br., and Hypoderris, Br., is not represented in South Africa.

TRIBE 2.

Aspidiaceæ. Pr. *Sori* globose, on middle, seldom on apex, of veins. *Involucre* superior, free, except at point of insertion; deciduous. *Rhizome* creeping, or sub-globose.

SECT. 1.—*Nephrodiariæ.* Pr. *Involucre* kidney-shaped.

Gen. 1.—*Lastrea.* Pr. *Veins* simple or forked.

Gen. 2.—*Oleandra*. Cavanilles. *Veins* numerous, close, parallel; root creeping.

Gen. 3.—*Nephrodium*. Schott. *Lower veins* arching.

Nephrolepis, Schott is not represented in South Africa.

SECT. 2.—*Aspidiariæ*. Pr. *Involucre* round or elliptic; entire.

Gen. 1.—*Polystichum*. Schott. *Sori* round; *veins* simple or forked; *fronds* coriaceous.

Gen. 2.—*Cyrtomium*. Pr. *Sori* round; *veins* irregularly reticulate.

Gen. 3.—*Didymochlæna*. Desvaux. *Sori* elliptic; sub-immersed.

Phanerophlebia., Pr., Cyclodium, Pr., Sagenia., Pr., Fadyenia., Hooker., Mesochlæna., Br., Aspidium., Schott, Pleocnemia., Pr., and Matonia., Br., are not represented in South Africa.

TRIBE 3.

Aspleniaceæ. Pr. *Sori* globose, oblong, or linear, on back of veins. *Involucre* suborbiculate, or linear, lateral, persistent, skinny; free at margin opposite point of insertion. *Rhizome* globose, seldom creeping.

SECT. 1. *Cystopterideæ*. Pr. *Sori* globose. *Involucre* suborbiculate, becoming reflex and wrinkled.

Gen. 1.—*Cystopteris*. Bernh. *Sori* on middle of veinlets.

Acrophorus, Pr., Leucostegia, Pr., and Onoclea., Linn., are not represented in South Africa.

SECT. 2. *Blechnaceæ*. Pr. *Sori* oblong, short, or linear long. *Involucre* corresponding, flat.

Gen. 1.—*Athyrium*. Roth. *Sori* oblong, short, curved, on middle of veins.

Gen. 2.—*Blechnum*. L. *Sori* linear, contiguous or confluent, on transverse veinlets uniting veins, parallel to rachis.

Woodwardia, Sw., Doodia, Br., and Salpichlæna, I. Sm., are not represented in South Africa.

SECT. 3. *Aspleniariæ*. Pr. *Sori* linear, long, in some species (Cænopteris, Bernh., or Darea, Auct), marginal or sunk in margin. *Involucre* corresponding, flat.

Gen. 1.—*Asplenium*. L. *Sori* linear, long. *Involucre* lateral on vein.

c

Gen. 2.—*Cetcrach.* Willd. The same, with underside of *frond* densely covered with scales.

Plenasium, Pr., Allantodia, Br., Neottopteris, I. Sm., and Hemidictyum, Pr., are not represented in South Africa.

Sect. 4. *Diplazieæ.* Pr. *Sori* linear, long, the lowest upper, and sometimes all, bilateral or double.

This tribe, containing Diplazium, Sw., Anisogonium, Pr., Digrammaria, Pr., and Oxygonium, Pr., is not represented in S. Africa.

Sect. 5. *Scolopendrieæ.* Pr. *Sori* linear, long, opposite, on adjoining opposite veins. *Involucre* corresponding, flat, open sides facing one another.

Gen. 1.—*Scolopendrium.* Sm. *Veins* close and parallel.

Antigramma, Pr., and Camptosorus, Link., are not represented in South Africa.

TRIBE 4.

Davalliaceæ. Gaudichaud. *Sori* infra-marginal, globose or linear, on ends of veins or veinlets. *Receptacle* dot-shaped, club-shaped, or linear. *Involucre* lateral, semi-orbiculate, oblong, or linear, persistent, skinny, free at upper margin. *Rhizome* sub-globose, or creeping.

Sect. 1. *Davalliæ.* Pr. *Sori* globose or longitudinally linear. *Involucre* semi-orbiculate or longitudinally linear.

Gen. 1.—*Microlepia.* Pr. *Sori* removed from margin. *Involucre* truncated, covering half the sorus.

Gen. 2.—*Davallia.* Sm. *Sori* infra-marginal, on back of teeth or sinus.

Saccoloma, Kaulf., Humata, Cav., and Loxsoma., A. Cunningham, are not represented in South Africa.

Sect. 2. *Lindsæaceæ.* Pr. *Sori* transversely linear, submarginal, generally continuous. *Involucre* lateral, linear, thin, membranaceous, free towards margin.

Gen. 1.—*Lindsæa.* Dryander. *Sori* and *involucre* continuous, parallel to margin. *Veins* much forked.

Isoloma, I. Sm., Schizoloma, Gaudich., Synaphlebium, I. Sm., and Dictyoxyphium, Hook., are not represented in South Africa.

TRIBE 5.

Dicksoniaceæ. Pr. *Sori* globose, sub-marginal on end of veins or veinlets. *Receptacle* globose. *Involucre* lateral, persistent, bivalve; the true one being the lower valve, affixed laterally by semi-circular line, the accessory one being like a cap, formed of teeth of frond, and covering the sori.

This tribe, containing Balantium, Kaulf, Cystodium, I. Sm., Culcita, Pr., Leptopleuria, Pr., Dicksonia, Pr., Patania, Pr., Cibotium, Kaulf., Thyrsopteris, Kze., and Deparia, Hooker, is not represented in South Africa.

TRIBE 6.

Adiantaceæ. Pr. *Sori* linear, or oblong, or globose; marginal, seldom sub-marginal; fixed on underside of involucre, springing from end of veins or veinlets. *Receptacle* linear or dot-shaped. *Involucre* formed of reflexed margin, bearing the capsules, linear, oblong, semi-orbiculate, or semi-lunate.

SECT. 1. *Adiantariæ*. Pr. *Sori* separate, but soon confluent, covering the margin of the whole pinnæ, on edge of teeth or segments.

Gen. 1.—*Pteris*. L. *Sori* linear, marginal, continuous. *Veins* simple or forked. *Involucre* broad.

Gen. 2.—*Lomaria*. Willd. *Fertile frond* contracted; *veins* ditto; *sori* sub-marginal.

Gen. 3.—*Campteria*. Pr. Like *Pteris*, but lower veins anastomosing and arching at sinus.

Gen. 4.—*Allosorus*. Bernh. *Sori* roundish, separate, then confluent and linear, hid by folded margin and involucre.

Gen. 5.—*Cryptogramma*. Br. *Sori* linear, on oblique veins, hid by folded margin; no involucre.

Gen. 6.—*Adiantum*. L. *Sori* marginal, globose, kidney-shaped, oblong or linear; distinct, or confluent, or continuous. *Involucre* corresponding to sori, formed of reflexed margin of underside of frond, and bearing the capsules beneath.

Gen. 7.—*Cheilanthes*. Sw. *Sori* marginal, globose, generally upon a lobe or tooth of the margin of frond, which becomes reflexed, solitary, contiguous or confluent. *Involucre* kidney-shaped or oblong.

Haplopteris, Pr., Litobrochia, Pr., Amphiblestra, Pr., Ceratodactylis, I. Sm., Onychium, Kaulf., Jamesonia, Hook. *et* Greville, Hewardia, I. Sm., and Ochropteris, I. Sm., are not represented in South Africa. Platyloma, I. Sm., is included in Allosorus, Bernh., and Cassebeera, Kaulf., in Cheilanthes, Sw.

SECT. 2. *Lonchitideæ.* Pr. *Sori* globose or linear, occupying sinus of teeth and segments. *Involucre* semi-lunate or linear, marginal.

Gen. 1.—*Hypolepis.* Bernh. *Sori* punctiform, sub-globose. *Veins* simple or forked.

Gen. 2.—*Lonchitis.* L. *Sori* linear, semi-lunate. *Veins* anastomosing.

GROUP 2, having no involucre. *Sori* naked.

TRIBE 7.

Vittariaceæ. Pr. *Sori* sunk in margin, linear, or globose. *Rhizome* creeping.

Gen. 1.—*Vittaria.* Sm. *Sori* linear. *Frond* simple, linear.

Prosaptia, Pr., (a doubtful genus) is not represented in South Africa.

TRIBE 8.

Polypodiaceæ. Pr. *Sori* globose on apex or back of veins in disc of frond; seldom confluent. *Receptacle* dot-shaped. *Rhizome* creeping, seldom sub-globose.

SECT. 1. *Struthiopterideæ.* Pr. *Fertile fronds* contracted.

This tribe, containing only one genus, Struthiopteris, Willd., is not represented in South Africa.

SECT. 2. *Polypodieæ.* Pr. Margin of frond uniform with disc, flat. *Fronds* often simple or digitate.

Gen. 1.—*Polypodium.* Lin. *Sori* at end of simple or forked veins, or on mid-veins or veinlets.

Gen. 2.—*Goniopteris.* Pr. *Sori* on mid-veins; first four opposite veins anastomosing in acute angled arch.

Gen. 3.—*Marginaria.* Bory. *Sori* 1-3 serial, at end of primary, or secondary, veinlets, in hexagonal maculæ.

Gen. 4.—*Pleopeltis.* Humboldt and Boupland. *Sori* large, serial, veinlets anastomosing, the middle maculæ containing two or three secondary veinlets, making an oblong macula, bearing sorus at the end. Pedicellated scales in sorus.

Gen. 5.—*Phymatodes.* Pr. *Veins* anastomosing, secondary veinlets clubbed. *Sori* at end of veinlets.

Gen. 6.—*Niphobolus.* Kaulf. *Sori* multi-serial, contiguous, covering upper part of frond.

Stenosemia, Pr., Goniophlebium, Pr., Campyloneurum, Pr., Dictyopteris, Br., Phlebodium, Br., Aglaomorpha, Schott., and Dryostachyum, I. Sm., are not represented in South Africa.

SECT. 3.—*Lecanopterideœ.* Pr. *Sori* sub-globose, sub-marginal in the teeth of the frond, extended into broad cartilaginous lobes, bearing the sori.

This tribe, containing only one genus, Lecanopteris, Bl., is not represented in South Africa.

TRIBE 9.

Grammitaceœ. Pr. *Sori* linear long, seldom linear oblong, short, on back of veins or veinlets. *Receptacle* linear. *Rhizome* creeping or sub-globose.

SECT. 1.—*Grammitideœ.* Pr. *Sori* on back of simple veins, or of upper veinlet, or of one secondary veinlet.

Gen. 1.—*Grammitis.* Sw. *Sori* small on mid-veins, or upper veinlets.

Synammia, Pr., Monogramme, Schkuhr., Stegnogramme, Bl., Meniscium, Schreber., Microgramma, Pr., Loxogramme, Pr., Polytænium, Desv., Antrophyum, Kaulf., Diblemma, I. Sm., and Selliguea, Bory., are not represented in South Africa.

SECT. 2.—*Hemionitideœ.* Pr. *Sori* confluent on all the veinlets of branching veins, long, linear, narrow.

Gen. 1.—*Gymnogramma.* Desv. *Sori* small and covering frond.

Hemionitis, L., is not represented in South Africa.

TRIBE 10.

Tœnitideœ. Pr. *Sori* linear, generally continuous, on veins, veinlets, or parenchyma, or extending to the rib on each side laterally, or on the mid disc of each side, or on margin of frond. *Rhizome* sub-globose, or creeping. *Frond* often simple.

Gen. 1.—*Notholœna.* Br. *Sori* linear, marginal, continuous; sometimes with a narrow revolute margin.

Gen. 2.—*Pteropsis.* Desv. *Sori* linear, sub-marginal. *Receptacle* elevated.

Pleurogramme, Pr., Jenkinsia, Hook., Tæniopteris, Hook , Tænitis, Sw., Lomagramma, I. Sm., and Drymoglossum, Pr., are not represented in South Africa.

TRIBE 11.

Acrostichaceæ. Pr. *Sori* superficial, covering the whole of the underside of frond. *Fertile frond* generally contracted. *Rhizome* creeping or sub-globose.

Gen. 1.—*Stenochlæna.* I. Sm. *Fertile frond* contracted, with revolute margins.

Gen. 2.—*Olfersia.* Raddi. *Fertile frond* contracted, with flat margin. *Veins* of sterile frond parallel, close.

Gen. 3.—*Acrostichum.* L. *Fertile frond* not contracted. *Veins* anastomosing regularly in long hexagons.

Polybotrya, Humb. and Bonp., Elaphoglossum, Schott., Aconiopteris, Pr , Campium, Pr., Platycerium, Desv., Pæcilopteris, Pr., Gymnopteris, Bernh., and Photinopteris, I. Sm., are not represented in South Africa.

TRIBE 12.

Hymenophylleæ. Endlicher. *Sori* marginal, lateral or terminal, at end of vein. *Involucres* monophyllous. *Receptacle* elongated, columnar, or filiform. *Capsules* sessile, covering more or less the receptacle. *Caudex* creeping, filiform, slender.

This tribe, " chiefly founded upon the complete transverse ring of the capsules, the very much elongated, columnar or filiform receptacle, and the delicate texture of the frond," is placed by Sir W. Hooker next to the genus Loxsoma, in his tribe Dicksoniaceæ.

Gen. 1.—*Hymenophyllum.* Sm. *Receptacle* generally · included. *Involucre* bivalved, cup-shaped, or orbicular.

Gen. 2.—*Trichomanes.* Linn. *Receptacle* generally exserted. *Involucre* tubular, sub-cylindrical, generally entire.

ORDER PARKERIACEÆ. Hook. *Aquatic Ferns,* with spore cases very thin, surrounded by a broad, imperfect, or obsolete ring.

This order, containing Ceratopteris, Brongniart , and Parkeria, Hook., is not represented in South Africa.

ORDER SCHIZÆACEÆ. Mart. *Spore cases* dorsal, with a complete terminal contracted ring. *Spores* pyramidal or conical.

Gen. 1.—*Schizæa.* Sm. *Spore cases* oval, sessile, vascular, reticulate, placed on linear or pinnated appendages.

Involucre formed of reflexed margin. *Fronds* cæspitose, linear, simple or dichotomous.

Gen. 2.—*Anemia.* Sw. *Spore cases* the same, placed on one-sided spikes, densely panicled, biserial. No *involucre.* Fertile portion of *frond* dissimilar.

Gen. 3.—*Mohria.* Sw. *Spore cases* sub-globose, sessile, reticulate, placed near concave margins of under side of frond. *Fertile frond* partially contracted.

Actinostachys, Wallich., Lygodictyon, I. Sm., Lygodium, Sw., Anemidictyon, I. Sm., and Trochopteris, Gardner., are not represented in South Africa.

ORDER OSMUNDACEÆ. Mart. *Spore cases,* dorsal or panicled, stalked, with a broad dorsal incomplete ring.

Gen. 1.—*Osmunda.* Linn. *Spore cases,* heaped on lateral or terminal pinnæ, contracted.

Gen. 2.—*Todea.* Willd. *Spore cases,* heaped on veins, upon under side of frond, thickly or thinly spread.

ORDER MARATTIACEÆ. Kaulf. *Spore cases,* without a ring, dorsal, combined in masses, and splitting by a central cleft.

Gen. 1.—*Marattia.* Sw. *Sori* oblong, sessile on forked veinlet, in single series, near the margin. *Involucre* coriaceous.

Eupodium, I. Sm., Angiopteris, Hoffmann., Danæa, Sm., and Kaulfussia, Bl., are not represented in South Africa.

ORDER OPHIOGLOSSEÆ. Br. *Spore cases,* ringless, distinct, bivalved, formed on margin of a contracted leaf.

Gen. 1.—*Ophioglossum.* Linn. Spike undivided in two rows.

Botrychium, Sw., and Helminthostachys Kaulf. are not represented in South Africa.

ORDER LYCOPODIACEÆ. Sw. *Spore cases* axillary, one to three-celled.

Gen. 1.—*Lycopodium.* Linn. *Spore cases,* 1 to 4-lobed, sessile ; often in spikes.

Gen. 2.—*Psilotum.* Sw. *Spore cases,* 3-lobed, globose, sessile, solitary, at base of minute leaves.

Tmesipteris, Bernh., is not represented in South Africa.

SYNOPSIS OF SOUTH AFRICAN SPECIES OF FERNS.

I. GLEICHENIACEÆ. Kze.

I. GLEICHENIA. Sw. (2 Species.)

1. *Gleichenia polypodioides.* Sw. *Frond* dichotomous, much branched, proliferous; *branches* pinnate, spreading; *pinnae* pinnatifid; *segments* ovate, more or less glaucous beneath, smooth; *capsules* 3-4, immersed on the underside of the frond, forming flat-topped *sori.* *Stipes* and *rachises* rather smooth. *Caudex* creeping.—Hook. Spec. Filic. vol. 1, p. 3, Schkuhr. Filic. t. 149.

Var. *glauca.* *Pinnae* somewhat longer and closer; fronds more glaucous beneath.

Common on Table Mountain, and in many parts of the Colony, and Natal.—*v. v. & s.**

2. *Gleichenia argentea.* Kaulf. *Fronds* dichotomous, branching; *branches* pinnate, spread; *pinnæ* pinnatifid; *segments* wedge-shaped, very blunt, rounded at the apex, silvery beneath; *rachises* clothed in a thick woolly ferruginous shag. *Capsules* about 4. *Caudex* creeping, surrounded with stellate bristly scales.—Kaulf, Enum. Filic., p. 36.

In moist shady places, amongst rocks on Table Mountain (Chamisso.), at Genadendal (Rev. C. R. Kölbing), near the Van Staden's River, Uitenhage (Ecklon and Zeyher), *v. s.*

II. MERTENSIA. Willd. (1 Species.)

3. *Mertensia umbraculifera.* Kze. *Fronds* repeatedly dichotomous, much branched, pinnatifid; segments linear, comb-shaped, blunt or slightly pointed, glabrous above, and glaucous beneath; *ribs* and *rachises* clad with ferruginous woolly shag. *Stipes* long erect, channelled naked; *rhizome* horizontal, paleaceous.—Kze Linnæa., vol. 18, p. 116.

In British Kaffraria, and on the grassy banks of the Omnaroti River, Natal.—(Gueinzius.) *v. s.*

* V. V. and S.—Vidi vivam et siccam.

II. CYATHEACEÆ. Endl.

III. CYATHEA. SMITH. *(Arborescent.)* (2 Species.)

4. *Cyathea Dregei.* Kze. Unarmed, *fronds* 2 pinnate, coriaceous ; *pinnules* lanceolate, pointed, deeply pinnatifid, smooth above, paler below, and rufo-tomentose on and near the *rachis* beneath; *segments* oblong-ovate, subfalcate, obtuse, entire or serrated ; *sori* on the lower half of the segments immersed in rufous wool ; *involucre* hemispherical, breaking irregularly; *Stipes* short, rough, scaly.—Hook. Spec. Filic., vol. 1, p. 23., Tab. 10, fig. B., and Tab. 17, fig. A. Kunze Linnæa, vol. 10, p. 551.

In forests near Bethel (Kaffraria), and the Magalisberg (Zeyher), in a rocky valley at the great cataract between Omzam-woobo and Omzamcaba (Drege), near the Moore River. (Natal. Plant.) *v. s.*

5. *Cyathea Burkei.* Hook. *Fronds* 2-pinnatifid, membranaceous ; *pinnules* lanceolate, bluntly acuminate, 2-pinnatifid ; *rachis* partially woolly, smooth above ; *segments* oblong-ovate, obtuse, entire, the *costa* hairy at the base. *Sori* few, often solitary ; *involucre* globose, with an irregular opening at the top. *Stipes* tubercled with small prickles, and at its base, and that of the main rachis, clothed with glossy brown, chaffy scales.—Hooker Spec. Filic., vol. 1, p. 23, Tab. 17, B.

In forests at Magalisberg. (Zeyher.) *v. s.*

IV. ALSOPHILA. R. BR. *(Arborescent.)* (1 Species).

6. *Alsophila Capensis.* J. Smth.* Unarmed ; *fronds* 3-pinnate ; *pinnæ* lanceolate-acuminate, membranaceous, deeply pinnatifid ; *segments* narrow-oblong, acute falcate serrated (rachis and costa, with small deciduous scales), veins simple, or rarely forked. *Sori* cylindrical, generally solitary at the bases of the lowest veins, on the upper half of the segment.—

---

* Very curious leaflike appendages issue luxuriantly from the base of the stipes in this species. They are flaccid 3-pinnate *abortive fronds* six or eight inches in length. Their pellucid membranaceous *pinnæ* are dichotomously branched, and their narrow, linear acute lobes, forked, or irregularly split. Their appearance is that of a parasitical *Trichomanes* in its barren state; and they were described erroneously as Trichomanes incisum, by Thunberg and as T. cormophilum, by Kaulfuss.

D

Hook. Spec. Filic., vol. 1, p. 36. *Hemitelia Capensis.* R. Br. *Amphocosmia riparia.* Gardner. *London Journal of Botany,* vol. 1, p. 441, Tab. 12.

Common in the woody ravines and forests of South Africa.— *v. v.* and *s.*

III. ASPIDIACEÆ. PRESL.

V. LASTREA. PRSL. (7 Species.)

7. *Lastrea Thelypteris.* Prsl. *Fronds* pinnate ; *pinnæ* pinnatifid, linear-lanceolate smooth ; *segments* ovate, acute, nearly entire, the fertile-ones revolute. *Sori* marginal, contiguous, at length confluent. *Stipes,* with or without scales, downy at the apex. *Caudex* creeping. *Aspidium Thelypteris.* Sw. Schlecht. Adumbr. Filic. Capens, p. 23, Tab. 11.

In moist localities, near rivulets, in the Cape flats, on Devil's Mountain, near the Paarl, Swellendam, Tulbagh, Uitenhage, &c., also at Natal.—(*v. v.* and *s.*)

8. *Lastrea patens.* Presl. *Fronds* pinnate; *pinnæ* pinnatifid ; *segments* subfalcate-lanceolate, acute, the lower ones of the inferior pinnæ pinnatifido-incised. *Sori* small, round, in a double line ; upper portion of the *stipes,* costa, and rachises downy.—*Aspidium patens.* Sw. Schlecht, l. c., p. 22. Hook. Genera Filic., t. 45 a.

In shady localities, at the foot of Table Mountain (Kirstenbosch), and in the forests of Stellenbosch, George, Uitenhage, British Kaffraria, and Natal.—*v. s.*

* 9. *Lastrea Catoptera.* Nob. *Fronds* 2-pinnatifid ; *pinnæ* stalked, distant, erect, oblong-lanceolate sharp-pointed ; *pinnules* oblong, the lower ones blunt, deeply pinnatifid ; *segments* ovato-oblong, subfalcate, obtuse sinuato-subdentate, downy on both sides ; the basal-one triangular, wedge-shaped, decurrent. *Sori* sub-marginal ; *rachis* and *stipes* downy. *Aspidium catopteron.* Kze. Linnæa., vol. 10, p. 550.

In the forests between Omzamcaba and Omzamwoobo, also at Koratra, Natal. (Drege. Gueinzius.) *v. s.*

10. *Lastrea inæqualis.* Presl. *Fronds* 2-pinnate, smooth ; *pinnæ* confluent and pinnatifid at the apex, bipinnatifid at the base ; *pinnules* oval, obtuse, obliquely cuneate, inciso-dentate

and pinnatifid. *Sori* solitary, distant. *Stipes* and *rachis* somewhat scaly; *rhizome* thick, creeping. *Aspidium inæquale.* Schlecht. 1. c., p. 23, Tab. 12.

Moist and shady spots on Devil's Mount; at Hottentot's Holland, Swellendam (Voormansbosch), British Kaffraria, Natal, &c.— *v. v.* and *s.*

11. *Lastrea spinulosa.* Presl. *Fronds* 2-pinnate, erect, oblong-lanceolate; *pinnæ* elongated, oblique, opposite; *pinnules* oblong, acute, decurrent, inciso-serrate or pinnatifid, with sharp-toothed lobes. *Sori* round in a double row. *Stipes* slightly scaly.—*Aspidium spinulosum.* Sw. Schkuhr. Filic. T. 48.

In shady rocky localities in the Du Toit's Kloof, Swellendam (Drege.)

12. *Lastrea pentagona.* Moore. *Fronds* 2-pinnate coriaceous, smooth, ovato-pentagonal; *pinnæ* acuminate, the lower pairs triangular, unequal-sided; the *inferior pinnules* of the lowest pinnæ longest, pinnate with distant oblong-obtuse, duplicato-serrate decurrent secondary pinnules, with mucronate teeth; the *superior pinnules* and those of the upper part of the frond pinnatifid, with oblong mucronato-serrate lobes. *Sori* distinct, forming two lines near the mid-vein on the pinnules; *stipes* and *rachises* scaly.—Moore, p. 227. in Hook. Journ. of Botan., and K. G. Miscellany, vol. 5., p. 227.

In ravines and moist places near the Umvoti, Natal (Plant.)

* 13. *Lastrea athamantica.* Nob. *Fronds* 3-pinnate coriaceous, lanceolate, smooth, *pinnæ* ¿stalked, oblong, acuminate. *Primary pinnules* sessile, ovato-oblong cuneate, at base decurrent; *secondary* falcate, blunt, veiny. *Sori* round, solitary. *Stipes* short, erect, flexuose, covered at base with long linear deciduous scales. *Aspidium athamanticum.* Kze. Linnæa, vol. 18, p. 123. *Lastrea Plantii* Moore in Hook. Journ. of Botan., etc., vol. 5, p. 226.

On grassy hills and in boggy localities at Natal (Gueinzius), and in deserted holes of the jackal near Moore River, Natal (Gueinzius, Plant.) *v. s.*

The natives, who call this fern *Umkomo-Komo* use its rootstock as a vermifuge, especially for the cure of the tape-worm.

VI. OLEANDRA. CAV. (1 Species.)

14. *Oleandra articulata.* Presl. *Fronds* simple, entire, lanceolate, acuminate, membranaceous; *Sori* round, scattered.

Stipes short, nodose, articulated ; *rhizome* horizontally creeping, climbing, clothed with numerous awl-shaped imbricated scales, which have a black spot at their bases. *Aspidium articulatum.* Sw. Kunze Linnæa, vol. 18, p. 123.

Climbing rocks in woody ravines in the Magalisberg (Zeyher), and in similar localities at Natal. (Gueinzius) *v. s.*

VII. NEPHRODIUM. SCHOTT. (2 Species.)

* 15. *Nephrodium Ecklonianum.* Nob. *Frond* pinnate, lanceolate, coriaceous; the *lower pinnæ* distant, almost opposite, the *upper ones* alternate, approximate; all shortly stalked, lanceolate, sharp-pointed, inciso-pinnatifid, bearing small scattered resinous dots on the under surface ; *segments* ovate, subfalcate, rounded ; *costæ* slightly scaly beneath, channelled above, and as well as the angular *rachis* downy. *Sori* nearly marginal, continuous; *involucre* smooth. *Stipes* long, smooth ; *root-stock* covered with brown scales. *Aspidium Ecklonii.* Kze. Linnæa, vol. 10, p. 546.

Around the hot springs at Brandvalley (Worcester), at the Zwartkops River (Uitenhage), Van Staden's River, the Knysna, &c., also at Natal. (Plant) *v. s.*

* 16. *Nephrodium Plantianum.* Nob. (New Species.) *Frond* pinnate, oblong-lanceolate, coriaceous; *pinnæ* shortly stalked, alternate, approximate, erect patent, lance-shaped, pinnatifid, smooth ; *segments* ovate, obtuse, notched; *stipes* and *rachis* angular, naked.

In the dense forests of Natal. (Plant No. 341) *v. s.*

VIII. POLYSTICHUM. SCHOTT. (4 Species.)

17. *Polystichum pungens.* Presl. *Frond* 2-pinnate ; *pinnules* oblong-ovate, obliquely cuneate, auricled, subfalcate, acute, doubly inciso-dentate, teeth mucronate. *Sori* irregularly scattered. *Stipes* and *rachises* scaly. *Aspidium pungens.* Kaulf. Schlecht, l. c., p. 21, Tab. 10.

Common in shady moist places throughout the Colony. *v. v.* and *s.*

* 18. *Polystichum luctuosum.* Nob. *Frond* 2-pinnate. lance-shaped, coriaceous, smooth ; *pinnæ* alternate, stalked, patent, erect, lanceolate acute, pinnate, pinnatifid at the apex ; *pinnules* ovate-trapeziform subfalcate, aristato-serrate, mucronate, eared at base. *Sori* small ; *stipes* and *rachises* clothed with blackish scales. *Aspidium luctuosum.* Kze., vol. 10, p. 548.

In a mountain kloof at Bedford (Dr. Atherstone) on the wood-clad mountains near Philipstown, Kat River (Bartels, Ecklon, and Zeyher), in the forests of British Kaffraria. (Captain Espinasse) *v. s.*

19. *Polystichum angulare.* Presl. *Frond* 2-3-pinnate, rigid, coriaceous, acuminate, glossy above, paler beneath; *pinnæ* alternate, distant, stalked, spreading, linear-lanceolate, acute, pinnate, pinnatifid at the apex, perfectly smooth; *pinnules* alternate oblong-lanceolate deeply incised, sharp-pointed, cuneate at the base, the lowermost lobe or segment 3-4 toothed, largest, eared. *Sori* small, solitary in the axils of the indentations. *Rachises* and the angular-furrowed *stipes* fringed sparingly with short scales. *Aspidium angulare.* Kitaibl.

In swamps near the Natal coast. (Gueinzius. Plant.) *v. s.*

20. *Polystichum coriaceum.* Schott. *Fronds* 3-pinnate, coriaceous; *pinnules* ovate, wedge-shaped at the base, bluntly serrate, smooth; lower-ones pinnatifid, upper ones confluent. *Sori* solitary, placed near the bases of the serratures. *Stipes* and margined *rachises* glabrous; *rhizome* thick, horizontally creeping, clothed with broad ferruginous scales. *Aspidium coriaceum.* Sw. Schkuhr, Filic., Tab. 50.

Common in moist woody localities all over the Colony, as well as in the forests of Kaffraria and Natal.—*v. v.* and *s.*

IX. CYRTOMIUM. PRESL. (1 Species.)

21. *Cyrtomium falcatum.* Presl. *Fronds* pinnate, smooth coriaceous; *pinnæ* shortly stalked, alternate, broad ovate, rounded at the base, falcate, acuminate, distant, blunt, repando-crenate or serrate, the terminal one tri-lobed. *Sori* globose, copious, scattered. *Stipes* scaly. *Aspidium falcatum.* Sw.

In the aboriginal forests of British Kaffraria. (Captain Espinasse, 1856.) *v. s.*

X. DIDYMOCHLÆNA. DESV. (1 Species.)

22. *Didymochlæna dimidiata.* Kze. *Frond* 2-pinnate, coriaceous; *pinnæ* approximate stalked, oblong-lanceolate, patent, erect; *pinnules* dimidiate obliquely ovate; the superior margin sinuato-crenate, revolute, soriferous; the inferior one entire, here and there bristly along the costa. *Stipes* and

rachises, fringed with ferruginous scales.—Linnæa, vol. 18, p. 122, Kunze Supplem. to Schkuhr's, Filic., T.84.

In moist shady ravines near the great cataract between the Omfondi and Togela Rivers, Natal. (Gueinzius.) *v. s.*

IV. ASPLENIACEÆ. PRESL.

XI. CYSTOPTERIS. BERNH. (1 Species.)

23. *Cystopteris fragilis.* Bernh. *Fronds* lanceolate 2-pinnate, slender, smooth. *Pinnæ* ovate or lanceolate, toothed, lobed or pinnatifid. *Segments* more or less acute, entire or much dentate. *Sori* scattered, often crowded and almost confluent. *Rachis* winged. *Stipes* glabrous, scaly at base. Hook. Spec. Filic., vol. 1, p. 197. *Aspidium fragile.* Sw. Schkuhr. Icon. Filic. tables 54, 56.

In a mountain kloof near Bedford (Dr. Atherstone) and in shady places on the Kat River mountains. (Ecklon.) *v. s.*

XII. ATHYRIUM. ROTH. (1 Species.)

*24. *Athyrium laxum.* Nob. (N. sp.) *Fronds* 2-pinnate, flaccid, membranaceous. *Pinnæ* alternate remote, ovate-lanceolate acuminate, smooth. *Pinnules* ovate-oblong, pinnatifid; their *segments* incised, serrate, acute. *Sori* round. *Rachises* flexuose, somewhat margined. *Stipes* long, chaffy only at the base.

In woods and shady places at Natal. (Gueinzius.) *v. s.*

XIII. BLECHNUM. LIN. (2 Species.)

25. *Blechnum radiatum.* Presl. *Fronds* much divided, radiating, stiff. *Segments* linear, erect, dichotomous, toothed at the apex, perfectly smooth. *Stipites* clustered, much longer than the fronds. *Rhizome* short, scaly at the base, *roots* fibrous. *Adiantum radiatum.* Kœnig. *Acropteris radiata.* Link.

On rocks at the Magalisberg (Zeyher), and in Griqualand. (Mr. Robt. Moffatt.) *v. s.*

*26. *Blechnum Atherstoni.* Nob. (N. sp.) *Frond* pinnate, coriaceous. *Pinnæ* alternate, rigid, sessile, sub-auriculate cordate, linear-lanceolate, acute, slightly waved at the margins.

Lower pinnæ remote. *Stipes* and glabrous *rachis* destitute of scales.

This species much resembles and stands close to Blechnum cartilagineum. Sw.

On the southwest of Graham's Town, near the blockhouse. (Dr. Atherstone, 1856.) *v. s.*

XIV. ASPLENIUM. LIN. (29 Species.)

27. *Asplenium gemmiferum.* Schrad. *Fronds* pinnate, smooth, membranaceous, often gemmiferous towards the apex. *Pinnæ* alternate stalked, lanceolate ovate, elongated, acute, crenate or sub-serrate, obliquely cuneate and decurrent at base. *Sori* oblong distant. *Stipes* channelled above and scaly below. *Caudex* paleaceous. *Roots* densely clothed with ferruginous shag. *Asplenium lucidum.* Schlecht. (not Forster), Adumbr., p. 25, table 14, f. 1.

In the dense forests of the Knysna, Tsitzikamma, and near the great cataract of the Omzamcaba River (Natal) *v. s.*

28. *Asplenium Prionites.* Kze. *Fronds* pinnate, ovate, oblong, coriaceous. *Pinnæ* alternate, stalked, patent, lanceolate, acuminate, cuneate at the base, sharply and unequally toothed, glabrous; the lowermost shorter, smaller, almost auricled. *Sori* oblong, cushioned, often irregular. *Stipes* angular, *rachis* winged at the apex, and both of them scaly. *Rhizome* creeping. Linnæa, vol. 10, p. 511.

In Blockhouse-kloof, near Graham's Town (Dr. Atherstone), and in the forests of Natal. (Drege, Gueinzius.) *v. s.*

* 29. *Asplenium discolor.* Nob. (N. sp.) *Fronds* pinnate lanceolate, elongated, acuminate, membranaceous smooth, sometimes gemmiferous. *Pinnæ* alternate, remote, stalked, patent, spreading, oblong-lanceolate, acute, sub-pinnatifid, dark green above, paler beneath, cuneate at base. *Segments* confluent at the apex, wedge-shaped, obtuse, 2-crenate recurved, the lowermost remote, decurrent, almost auricled. *Sori* linear-oblong. The channelled *stipes* and flexuose marginate *rachises* sparingly scaly. *Asplenium lucidum.* Schlecht., var. b. Adumbr., table 14, f. b.

In the forests of the Knysna (Miss Dalgairns), Albany (Dr. Atherstone), and in the mountain-woods near Philipstown, Kat River. (Ecklon and Zeyher.) *v. s.*

30. *Asplenium anisophyllum.* Kze. *Fronds* pinnate, linear-lanceolate, membranaceous. *Pinnæ* nearly opposite, smaller at both ends, ovate-lanceolate, acuminate, bluntly serrate and incised, upwardly truncate with an unequal base, wedge-shaped below, decurrent. *Sori* elliptical, scattered. *Stipes* and winged *rachis* scaly. Linnæa., vol. 10, p. 511.

In shady mountains near the fountains of the Kat River (Ecklon and Zeyher), in British Kaffraria (Capt. Espinasse), and near the great cataract between the Omzamwoobo and Omzamcaba Rivers, Natal. (Drege.) *v. s.*

31. *Asplenium brachyotus.* Kze. *Fronds* pinnate, lanceolate, acuminate, membranaceous. *Pinnæ* stalked lanceolate, more or less falcate, blunt, irregularly and obtusely 2-serrate, sub-auricled and truncate at the base. *Sori* oblong. The slender *stipes*, as well as the *rachises*, downy. *Rhizome* naked. Linnæa., vol. 10, p. 512.

Found in the same localities with the former. (Drege. Gueinzius.) *v. s.*

32. *Asplenium protensum.* Schrad. *Fronds* pinnate, erect, coriaceous. *Pinnæ* alternate, distant, patent, linear-lanceolate, acuminate, pinnatifid, unequally cuneate at base. *Segments* remote, oblong, obtuse, 2-3-toothed; the lowermost broadest, incised, nearly auricled. *Sori* numerous, oblong, at length confluent. *Stipes* and the under side of the *fronds* downy. Schlecht., Adumb., p. 20, tab. 16.

Near rivulets in the forests of the Knysna and the Dœkamma; near Graham's Town (Dr. Atherstone); also at Natal. *v. s.*

33. *Asplenium erectum.* Bory. *Fronds* pinnate, membranaceous. *Pinnæ* shortly stalked, lanceolate, sub-falcate, acuminate, bluntly serrate. *Upper pinnæ* cuneate with an unequal base, and auricled on the upper edge; lowermost remote, eared at both ends. *Sori* solitary, placed close to the costa *Stipes* margined, glossy, smooth. Schlecht., Adumbr., p. 28, tab. 15.

Common in moist, shady, rocky localities throughout the whole colony. *v. v.* and *s.*

* 34 *Asplenium Zeyheri.* Nob. (N. sp.) *Fronds* pinnate, membranaceous smooth. *Pinnæ* shortly petioled, alternate, sub-falcate, oblong-ovate, bluntly incised, cuneate at the base. *Segments* obtusely crenate; the lowermost remote, erect, ob-ovate, cuneate, rounded, notched, auricled. *Sori* elliptical, irregular, distant. *Rachis* and channelled *stipes* not margined,

glabrous. *Asplenium polymorphum*. Eckl. and Zeyh. Herb. (Asplenii erecti var. Kze, Linnæa, vol. 10, p. 513, in note.)

Amongst rocks, and in shady ravines, Uitenhage (Dr. Rubidge), near Philipstown, Kat River. (Eckl. and Zeyh.) *v. s.*

35. *Asplenium lunulatum*. Sw. *Fronds* pinnate, slender, curved. *Pinnæ* alternate, sub-sessile, patent, oblong-ovate, more or less falcate, blunt, notched, confluent at the apex, truncate and auricled at the base. *Sori* oblong, numerous. *Stipes* and *rachises* margined. Kze. Linnæa, vol. 10, p. 514.

In the woods near Uitenhage (Eckl. and Zeyh.); also at Kat River and Natal. (Drege.) *v. s.*

36. *Asplenium monanthemum*. Smth. *Fronds* pinnate, linear lanceolate, erect, smooth. *Pinnæ* oblong-trapeziform, sessile, blunt, truncate at the lower base; apex and upper margin crenate-serrate. *Sori* generally solitary, linear, sub-marginal. *Stipes* almost quadrangular, and, as well as the *rachis* black, polished. *Rhizome* tufted. J. E. Smith, Plant. Icon. inedit., tab. 73.

Common in shady places in many parts of the colony. *v. v.* and *s.*

37. *Asplenium ebeneum*. Ait. *Fronds* pinnate, smooth, linear lanceolate. *Pinnæ* sessile, oblong, obtuse; upper ones auricled, bluntly crenate at the margin; *lower pinnæ* cordate, hastate. *Sori* oblong, approximate. *Stipes* and *rachis* smooth, ebenous, glossy. *Rhizome* creeping. *Roots* fibrous.

In the forests of the Krakakamma, Uitenhage. (Eckl. and Zeyh.) *v. s.*

38. *Asplenium Trichomanes*. Lin. *Fronds* pinnate, slender, smooth. *Pinnæ* irregularly oblong-ovate, crenate, truncate and cuneate at the base, and obtuse at the apex. *Sori* linear, at length confluent, and placed in a single row on each side of the costa. *Stipes* and *rachis* purplish-black, glossy. Schkuhr., Filic., t. 74.

In rocky, shady places in the Du Toit's Kloof, Swellendam (Drege); near Bedford (Dr. Atherstone); in the Winterberg, Kaffraria. (Eckl. and Zeyher.) *v. s.*

39. *Asplenium dentatum*. Lin. *Fronds* pinnate, glabrous; *pinnæ* obovate-oblong, blunt, unequally cuneate and attenuate at base; irregularly and obsoletely toothed on the margins. Willd. Spec. Plant. vol. 5, p. 324.

Among rocks on the mountains of the Bosjesmansrand, Natal. (Dr. F. Krauss.)

E

40. *Asplenium præmorsum.* Sw. *Fronds* 2-pinnate, sub-coriaceous ; *pinnæ* pinnate, stalked, patent ; *pinnules* alternate, oblong-cuneate, truncate, the extreme-one elongated, trifid, the lowermost erect, lobed, auricled, all of them inciso-serrate, striated. *Sori* linear ; *rachises* flexuose, not margined ; *stipes* channelled purple, fringed here and there with short downy scales. *Caudex* creeping, paleaceous; *roots* fibrous. Schkuhr. Filic., t. 29, fig. 1.

In the forests of the Tzitsikamma, Uitenhage. (Dr. Krauss) at Natal. (Gueinzius) *v. s.*

41. *Asplenium ruta muraria.* Lin. *Frond* 2-pinnate at the lower, singly pinnate at the upper portion ; *pinnæ* stalked, opposite or alternate, remote ; *pinnules* rhomboid-oblong, cuneate at base, blunt, striated ; crenate and inciso-lobate. *Sori* confluent. *Stipites* aggregate, flaccid, flexuose, perfectly smooth. *Roots* filiform, clothed with ferruginous shag. Willd. Enum. Plant, vol. 5, p. 341. Schkuhr's Filic. tab. 80. b.

On the top of Muizenberg mountain, in crevices of rocks (Hon'ble R. W. Rawson, March, 1857.) *v. v.* and *s.*

42. *Asplenium furcatum.* Thbg. *Fronds* 2-pinnate; *pinnæ* lanceolate attenuated at the apex; *pinnules* distant, cuneate-lanceolate 3-fid and pinnatifid; *segments* inciso-serrate. *Sori* linear, confluent. *Stipes* and *rachis* clothed below with scaly down. *Caudex* thickly paleaceous; *rhizome* creeping.

Very variable in its forms, some of which have been described as distinct species.

In woods and shady localities ; very common within the Colony and Natal. *v. v.* and *s.*

43. *Asplenium fimbriatum.* Kze. *Fronds* sub-2-pinnate, membranaceous, oblong, smooth ; *pinnæ* distant, stalked, ovate-rhomboidal ; *pinnules* obovate-cuneate, with a cartila-ginous edge, and elevated veins on the upper surface, incised and lobed at the apex; *segments* curved, apiculate ; *involucres* membranaceous ; *sori* confluent ; *rachises* and short *stipes* purplish ; *rhizome* tufted, paleaceous. Kunze. Linnæa., vol. 18, p. 117.

On rocks in the woods between the Omfondi and Togela Rivers, Natal. (Gueinzius.) *v. s.*

44. *Asplenium cuneatum.* Lam. *Fronds* 2-pinnate, mem-branaceous, smooth ; *pinnæ* stalked, pinnate, alternate ; *pin-*

nules obovate-cuneate, blunt, unequally inciso-serrate, striate, auricled at base; *rachis* margined at its upper extremity. *Sori* linear, often confluent. Willd. Spec. Plant., vol. 5, p. 344.

In Blockhouse Kloof, near Graham's Town (Dr. Atherstone, also Ecklon and Zeyher). In the forests of Natal (Plant.); Kaffraria (Capt. Espinasse.) *v s.*

45. *Asplenium solidum.* Kze. *Fronds* sub-2-pinnatifid, lanceolate coriaceous, smooth, glossy; *pinnæ* lanceolate-ovate, attenuated; *pinnules* and *segments* wedge-shaped, incised, armed with pungent teeth. *Sori* convex scattered. The margined *rachis* and furrowed *stipes* glabrous. *Caudex* creeping, scaly. Kze. Linnæa, vol. 10, p. 520.

In the vicinity of Algoa Bay (Forbes), on mountains near Ruig-tevalley, amongst shrubs (Drege); near Alice, (Mr. Stewart) *v. s.*

46. *Asplenium splendens.* Kze. *Fronds* 2-pinnate, ovate, acuminated; *pinnæ* lanceolate, sharp-pointed, alternate remote, stalked; lower *pinnules* ovate-rhomboidal, cuneate at base, crenato dentate, more or less lobed and rounded at the apex; *terminal-one* elongated incised; all of them veiny, smooth and glossy above, clothed here and there with blackish scales at the underside. *Sori* irregular, linear; base of the *stipes,* and the *rachis* paleaceous. *Caudex* creeping. Linnæa, vol. 10, p. 516.

In the woods of the Krakakamma and Kat River. (Ecklon and Zeyher) at Natal. (Plant.) *v. s.*

47. *Asplenium Adiantum nigrum.* Lin. *Fronds* 2-3-pinnate coriaceous, glossy; upper *pinnæ* pinnatifid, uppermost confluent, lower ones 2-pinnatifid; *segments* obliquely cuneate, acutely toothed. *Sori* linear elongate, at length confluent. *Stipes* purple, ebenous. *Caudex* thick, tufted. Schlecht. Adumb. p. 31, Tab. 17. A. *argutum* Bory.

On walls, amongst rocks, &c., in many parts of the Colony.— *v. v.* and *s.*

48. *Asplenium aspidioides.* Schlecht. *Fronds* 2-3-pinnate smooth; *pinnæ* stalked, patent, lanceolate; *pinnules* ovate lanceolate, pointed, wedge-shaped and pinnatifid at the base; *segments* more or less 2-dentate. *Sori* solitary, oblong;

rachises and the angular, striped *stipes* scaly. Schlecht. Adumbr., p. 24, t. 13.

Within the Colony, at places unknown. (Bergius. Mundt.) and in a swampy forest near Port Natal. (Gueinzius.)

* 49. *Asplenium lobatum.* Nob., n. sp. *Fronds* 2-pinnate, membranaceous ; *pinnæ* alternate, shortly stalked, ovate-oblong, obtuse ; *pinnules* obovate-cuneate, inciso-crenate, the basal-one broader, remote, 3-lobed. *Sori* oblong-ovate, confluent; *partial rachises* margined, smooth ; *stipes* slightly scaly.

In woods of British Kaffraria (Captain Espinasse), Albany (Mr. Hutton and Dr. Atherstone), in the Tzitsikamma (Dr. Rubidge.) *v. s.*

* 50. *Asplenium gracile.* Nob. n. sp. *Fronds* 2-pinnate, membranaceous, smooth ; *pinnæ* alternate, stalked, patent, ovate-oblong, rounded at the apex; *pinnules* obovate-cuneate decurrent, bluntly incised, *upper-ones* confluent, *lowermost* broader, auricled, stalked. *Sori* solitary, remote, irregular, elliptical. The channelled *stipes* and flexuose winged *rachises* perfectly naked

In the primæval forests of Natal. (Gueinzius.) *v. s.*

51. *Asplenium Dregeanum.* Kze. *Fronds* pinnate linear-lanceolate, acute, membranaceous, smooth ; *pinnæ* alternate short-stalked, obliquely sub-ovate blunt, those of the *apex* smaller, cuneate-obovate ; all of them truncate and more or less auricled at the upper, quite entire at the lower base; inciso-pinnatifid at top and the upper margin ; *segments* oblong, rounded, incised, the lowermost wedge-shaped, 2-3-fid. *Sori* solitary ; *stipes* short ; *rachis* partly flexuose, sub-margined, scaly. *Caudex* creeping. Kze. Linnæa, vol. 10, p. 517. Suppl. to Schkuhr, Tab. 27.

In a shady valley on a cataract near the Omzamcaba River, Natal. (Drege) *v. s.*

52. *Asplenium Thunbergii.* Kze. *Fronds* pinnate, linear lanceolate acuminated, membranaceous; *pinnæ* alternate, ovate-oblong, deeply pinnatifid, erect, somewhat curved, blunt; *segments* oblong-cuneate, entire; lower ones 2-fid; lowermost broad lobed. *Sori* solitary, linear-oblong, sub-marginal; *stipes* short, channelled; *rachis* margined. Kze. Linnæa, vol. 10, p. 517. *Cænopteris auriculata* Thbg. *Darea auriculata* Willd.

In forests at Natal. (Gueinzius.) *v. s.*

53. *Asplenium Odontites.* R. Br. *Frond* pinnate ; *pinnæ* alternate, lanceolate, acuminated, pinnatifid ; *segments* remote, linear lanceolate, acute ; the inferior ones 2-fid. *Sori* sub-marginal. R. Brown. Prodrom. Flor. Nov. Holland, p. 151. *Cænopteris Odontites.* Thbg. Schkuhr. Filic., tab. 82.

Found by Thunberg ; locality not recorded.

54. *Asplenium stans.* Kze. *Frond* 2-pinnate, glabrous ; *pinnæ* deeply pinnatifid, almost opposite ; *segments* spathulate-linear, obtuse, lower ones 2-partite. *Sori* sub-marginal ; *rachis* winged. *Stipes* compressed, nearly 4-angular, smooth. *Caudex* sub-globose, clothed with stiff, acute, imbricated, blackish-brown scales. Kunze. Linnæa., vol. 10, p. 521. *Cænopteris furcata.* Berg. *Darea stans.* Bory.

In the forests of Swellendam, George, Uitenhage, and Kaffraria. *v. s.*

55. *Asplenium rutæfolium.* Kze. *Fronds* 2-pinnate, smooth; *pinnæ* and *pinnules* alternate, remote ; the inferior *pinnules* deeply pinnatifid ; the middle ones 2-3-partite ; terminal ones simple ; *segments* linear, obtuse. *Sori* sub-marginal ; *rachis* not winged. *Stipes* compressed, glabrous. *Caudex* paleaceous. Kze. Linnæa., vol. 10, p. 521. *Cænopteris rutæfolia.* Berg. *Darea rutæfolia.* Willd.

In the forests of Swellendam, George, Uitenhage, and Natal. *v. s.*

XV. CETERACH. WILLD. (3 Species.)

56. *Ceterach officinarum.* Willd. *Fronds* pinnatifid ; the *segments* oblong, obtuse, thickly covered at the underside with entire, rufous scales. Willd. Spec. Plant., vol. 5, p. 136. Schkuhr. Filic. tab. 7, f. b.

In crevices of rocks near the Baviaan's River. (Krebs.)

57. *Ceterach capensis.* Kze. *Fronds* pinnate or pinnatifid, oblong, obtuse ; the *pinnæ* and *segments* decurrent, ovate oblong, blunt, crenate, incised, sub-cordate at the auricled base, and clothed beneath (as well as the flexuose *rachis* and the *stipes*) with rufous scales. Kze. Linnæa, vol. 10, p. 496. *Gymnogramme cordata.* Hook. & Grev. Icon. Filic., tab. 156.

On rocks and walls near Cape Town ; also at the entrance of the forests near Olifant's Hoek and Bushman's River (Uitenhage) ; at the stems of old trees in Albany ; at the Kat River, etc. *v. v.* and *s.*

58. *Ceterach cordata.* Kze. *Fronds* pinnate; *pinnæ* sessile, cordate, oblong, crenate or lobed, paleaceous beneath; the *inferior pinnæ* small, more remote; *lobes* rounded, crenate-dentate. Kze. Linnæa., vol. 10, p. 497. *Gymnogramme cordata.* Schlecht. Adumbr. p. 16.

Amongst rocks in almost all parts of South Africa. *v. v* and *s.*

XVI. SCOLOPENDRIUM. SM. (1 species).

59. *Scolopendrium Krebsii.* Kze. *Fronds* coriaceous, lanceolate, acuminate pinnate. *Pinnæ* sessile, cordate, and auricled at base, lanceolate, acute, falcate, margined, and reflexed at the margin; *lower pinnæ* smaller, ovate; *terminal-ones* confluent. *Involucres* and *sori* oblique, placed near the mid-rib. *Stipes* short, angular, scaly at its base. *Rhizome* horizontally creeping, paleaceous. Kunze Linnæa, vol. 18, p. 119. Suppl. to Schkuhr, Filic., tab. 74.

In moist, shady places, and between rocks, near Graham's Town (Krebs. & Dr. Atherstone); in the forests of Natal (Gueinzius) *v. s.*

V. DAVALLIACEÆ. GAUDICH.

XVII. MICROLEPIA. PRESL. (1 species.)

60. *Microlepia polypodioides.* Presl. *Fronds* ovate or deltoid, acuminate, 3-pinnate, flaccid, more or less hairy or downy, especially on the veins and costæ beneath. Primary *pinnæ* and lower secondary ones acuminate, distant. *Pinnules* oblong or rhomboid-lanceolate, blunt, deeply pinnatifid. *Lobes* ovate or ob-ovate, entire or irregularly inciso-lobate, or again pinnatifid, sub-oblique, very obtuse. *Sori* large usually solitary on the entire lobes, several, on the pinnatifid-ones, and in the sinuses within the margin. *Involucres* small, half cup-shaped, smooth. *Rachis* downy on the underside. Hook. Spec. Filic., vol. 1, p. 181. *Davallia polypodioides.* Don.

In the forests of the Magalisberg. (Zeyher.) *v. s.*

XVIII. DAVALLIA. SM. (2 Species.)

61. *Davallia nitidula.* Kze. *Fronds* triangular sub-coriaceous, nearly glabrous, paler beneath, sub-3-partite, 3-pinnate; *pinnæ* alternate, stalked, patent, ovate, pointed, slightly curved; *lowermost* remote, nearly opposite; *secondary pinnules* from a cuneate base unequally ovate, obtuse, pinnatifid or incised; *segments* cuneate-oblong, retuse or sub-

marginate, and sub-incised at the apex, bearing *sori; involucres* obovate, truncate; *rachis* and *stipes* flexuose, glabrous; *caudex* creeping, chaffy. Kunze. Linnæa., vol. 10, p. 545. Suppl. to Schkhr. Filic., tab. 75, f, 2. Hook. Spec. Filic., vol. 1, p. 165, tab. 44, f. A.

In shady and rocky localities at Natal. (Drege, Gueinzius.) *v. s.*

62. *Davallia concinna.* Schrad. *Fronds* lanceolate-oblong, obtuse, curved, coriaceous, glabrous above, clothed beneath with scattered brown scales, more or less deeply pinnate-pinnatifid; *pinnæ* alternate, patent, ovate-cuneate at base; *segments* linear-spathulate, curved, margined; *margin* thickened, reflexed, retuse, 2 or 3 fid; *sori* and *involucres* semi-orbicular; *rachis* flattened, costate, margined; *stipes* short, ascending; *caudex* creeping, densely covered with brown, rigid scales. Hook. Spec. Fil., p. 193 *D. campyloptera.* Kunze. Linnæa., vol. 10, p. 544. Suppl. to Schkuhr. Filic., tab. 75, f. 1.

On the trunks of old trees in Plettenberg's Bay, George (Drege.) and in Blockhouse Kloof, Albany (Dr. Atherstone.) *v. s.*

XIX. LINDSÆA. DRYAND. (1 species.)

63. *Lindsæa ensifolia.* Sw. Firm and rigid. *Caudex* very short, creeping. *Stipes* (as well as the *rachis*) glabrous, as long as, or longer than the *pinnatid frond. Pinnæ* 5-13 linear-ensiform or lanceolate, patent, erect, sub-membranaceous; *sterile ones* sub-serrate; *veins* reticulated. *Sorus* continuous round the margin. Hook. Spec. Filic., vol. 1, p. 220. *Lindsæa membranacea.* Kze. Linnæa, vol. 18, p. 121. *Schizoloma ensifolium.* J. Smith.

At the base of high trees in the forests of Natal. (Gueinzius.) *v.s.*

VI. ADIANTACEÆ. PRESL.

XX. PTERIS. LIN. (5 Species.)

64. *Pteris pedata.* Willd. *Fronds* deeply lobed, pedate, coriaceous, smooth, dark green above. *Lobes* pinnatifid, acute; lateral ones parted in two, the lowermost reflexed. *Stipes* round, slightly pubescent at base, and, as well as the *rachises,* ebenous, glossy. *Rhizome* descendent. *Roots* fibrous. Willd. Sp. Plantar., vol. 5, p. 358.

Near Tamacha-post (Kaffraria), and along the sources of the Kat River (Eckl. & Zeyher); also at Natal. (Gueinzius.) *v. s.* Presl refers this to *Litobrachia;* but none of the South African specimens we have seen, show the venation of that genus.

65. *Pteris cretica.* Lin. *Fronds* either ternate or pinnate, glabrous. *Pinnæ* opposite acuminate; the lower ones more or less stalked, often 2-fid; middle ones confluent, sub-decurrent; *terminal pinna* lanceolate 3-fid; *sterile pinnæ* lanceolate, serrate at the sub-cartilaginous edge; *fertile ones* linear, entire. *Caudex* destitute of scales. Schlecht. Adumb., p. 40. Schkuhr. Filic., tab. 90. *Pteris Serraria.* Sw.

On the wood-clad mountains of Swellendam, George, and Uitenhage, at the Kat River, in the Winterberg, and at Natal. *v s.*

66. *Pteris arguta.* Sw. *Fronds* 2-pinnatifid, glabrous; *pinnæ* pinnatifid, lanceolate-ovate, falcate, acuminate, patent; *upper ones* sessile, somewhat decurrent; *lower ones* stalked; *segments* lanceolate-oblong, sub-falcate, acutely serrate at the apex; *basal ones* irregularly 3-4-lobed. *Sori* placed at the inferior half of the *segments* below the serratures; *margin* of *involucre* entire; *rachises* and *stipes* naked, very smooth. Schlecht. Adumb. p. 43. *Pteris flabellulata.* Thbg. (?)

In shady mountain localities; common in all parts of the colony, as well as at Natal. *v. v.* and *s.*

67. *Pteris catoptera.* Kze. *Fronds* pinnate, membrana-ceous, smooth, somewhat pale on the under surface; *pinnæ* sub-sessile; *segments* confluent (bearing short, stipule-like spines on the mid-rib of the upper side), oblong-linear, blunt, entire; *rachises*, *ribs*, and *stipes* glabrous, straw-coloured. Kze. Linnæa., vol. 18, p. 119. *Pteris biaurita.* Kze. Lin-næa., vol. 10, p. 436.

In the forests of Natal (Drege, Gueinzius); at the Magalisberg. (Zeyher.) *v. s.*

68. *Pteris incisa.* Thbg. *Fronds* 2-pinnate, membrana-ceous, glabrous; *pinnæ* opposite, sessile, many-yoked; *pin-nules* lanceolate, pale underneath; *lower ones* opposite, pinnatifid; *terminal ones* confluent; *segments* lanceolate-ovate, sinuate or entire; *stipes* round, stramineous. Schlecht. Adumb., p. 44. Thunb. Flora Capens., p. 733.

On the Devil's Mountain near the waterfall; in shady ravines at Hottentots' Holland; in the Du Toit's Kloof, etc. *v. v.* and *s.*

This Fern has not the venation of *Litobrachia*, to which genus it is referred by Presl.

21. LOMARIA. WILLD. (11 Species.)

69. *Lomaria capensis.* Willd. *Fronds* pinnate, membranaceous; *sterile pinnæ* approximate, sessile, obliquely cordate, lanceolate, notched, acuminate, not decurrent, smooth; *fertile ones*
linear, crenate, mucronate; *ribs* and *stipes* furrowed, paleaceous.
Caudex covered with large, broad, lanceolate, acute, ferruginous scales. *Blechnum capense.* Schlecht. Adumb., p. 34
tab. 18.

Common in moist, shady places and near rivulets; on the Table
and Devil's Mountains, and in many parts of the colony. *c. c.*
and *s.*

70. *Lomaria Boryana.* Willd. *Fronds* pinnate, coriaceous; *sterile pinnæ* alternate, remote, narrow, linear-lanceo-
olate, entire, attenuated; *lower ones* stalked; *upper ones*
adnate, cuneate at base, decurrent; all of them smooth and
opaque on the upper surface, pale, and clothed with ferruginous scaly wool beneath; *fertile pinnæ* stalked, linear, erect,
involute; *rachis* furrowed, very wooly in the upper half;
involucres continuous, rent and articulated at length. *Stipes*
long, surrounded at its base by awl-shaped, comose, twisted,
ferruginous scales. *Blechnum Boryanum.* Schlecht. Adumb.,
p. 35, tab. 19. *Lomaria coriacea.* Schrad. (not Kze).
Lomaria cinnamomea. Kaulf. Enum. Filic., p. 153.

In the forests of the Krakakamma, Uitenhage, and near the
Kat River (Eckl. and Zeyher); in the DuToit's Kloof. (Drege) *v s*

* 71. *Lomaria Dalgairnsiæ.* Nob. (N. sp.) *Fronds*
pinnate, membranaceous; *sterile pinnæ* alternate, remote,
sessile, lanceolate-oblong, narrowed at both ends, pale beneath,
glabrous; *terminal ones* confluent at their bases; *fertile pinnæ*
linear, straight, erect, sharp-pointed; *involucres* involvent,
lacerato-ciliate. *Stipes* and *rachises* clothed with wooly, ferruginous scales.

In the dense forests of the Knysna. (Miss Dalgairns, 1856.) *c. s*
This appears to be the Fern collected by Drege in the Du Toit's
Kloof, and noticed by Kunze (Linnæa, vol. 10, p. 506) as a
variety of *L. Boryana.* It does not, however, answer satisfactorily
to the short diagnosis, and seems to be distinct.

72. *Lomaria heterophylla.* Desv. *Fronds* pinnate, coriaceous, smooth; *sterile pinnæ* rigid, alternate, broad at base,
adnate, linear-lanceolate, acuminate, sub-falcate, entire, patent,

glaucous; margin dotted, revolute; *lowermost* small, remote, oblong, cuneate, rounded; *terminal one* often pinnatifid; *fertile pinnæ* narrow, linear, sharp-pointed; *involucres* more or less gnawed. *Stipes* and the *creeping caudex* paleaceous. *Blechnum heterophyllum.* Schlecht. Adumb. p. 37, tab. 20 and 22, fig. 1. *Lomaria gigantea* and *L. hamata.* Kaulf., l. c., p. 150.

In the bushes at the foot of Table Mountain, Kirstenbosch (Bergius); in forests of George (Drege.); Albany (Dr. Atherstone); and Natal (Gueinzius.) *v. s.*

* 73 *Lomaria cycadoides.* Nob. (N. sp.) *Fronds* pinnate, coriaceous; *pinnæ* alternate, remote, erect, sessile, glabrous, auricled at base; *sterile ones* lanceolate, oblong, blunt, very veiny, revolute, glossy, entire, dotted at the margin; *fertile pinnæ* linear-lanceolate, recurved at the apex; *rachises* and angular *stipes* smooth; *caudex* scaly, comose.

In the woods of Natal. (Plant No. 335.) *v. s.*
A sterile specimen of the same Fern, from Madagascar, is preserved in Dr. Pappe's collection.

74. *Lomaria attenuata.* Willd. *Sterile fronds* pinnatifid; *segments* lanceolate-oblong, attenuate, acuminate, entire, the *uppermost* elongated; *fertile pinnæ* pinnate; *pinnæ* linear; *involucres* torn, denticulated; *caudex* oblique, clothed with long, ferruginous scales. Willd. Spec. Plantar., vol. 5, p. 290. Kze. Linnæa., vol. 18, p. 116.

In shady places at Natal. (Gueinzius.)

75. *Lomaria inflexa.* Kze. *Fronds* pinnate, lanceolate, coriaceous, smooth; *sterile pinnæ* adnate, alternate, approximate, patent, somewhat auricled, oblong, falcate, blunt, pale at the underside; *fertile pinnæ* stalked, erect, linear-oblong, obtuse, mucronate, curvato-inflexed; *rachis* purple, paleacous. *Stipes* short, dark-purple, ebenous, surrounded at base by large subulate, lanceolate, brown scales. Kunze. Linnæa., vol. 18, p. 117. Suppl. to Schkuhr's Filic., tab. 65.

In moist places at Natal. (Gueinzius.) *v. s.*

76. *Lomaria punctulata.* Kze. *Fronds* pinnate, glabrous; *sterile pinnæ* alternate, sessile, sub-imbricated, linear-lanceolate, auriculato-cordate, acuminate, sub-falcate, entire, reflexed and dotted at the margins; *lowermost pinnæ* smaller, oblong, obtuse; *fertile pinnæ* patent, remote, linear, mucronate.

Stipes short, scaly at its base. *Blechnum punctulatum.*
Schlecht. Adumbr., p. 37, tab. 21 and 22, fig. 2. *Lomaria
densa.* Kaulf., l. c., p. 151.

Common in moist, shady places throughout the colony and
Natal *v. v.* and *s.*

77. *Lomaria pumila.* Kaulf. *Fronds* pinnate, smooth;
sterile pinnæ alternate, sessile, oblong, obtuse, submucronate,
auriculato-cordate, scabrous at the margins; *fertile ones*
linear-lanceolate, falcate, mucronate. *Stipes* short, and at its
base, as well as the creeping *caudex* paleaceous. Kaulf.
Enum. Filic., p. 151. *Blechnum australe.* Schlecht., p 38.
Schkuhr., Filic., tab. 110, b.

Common between rocks and moist mountainous spots in almost
all parts of the colony; also at Natal. *v. v.* and *s.*

78. *Lomaria Spicant.* Desv. *Fronds* pinnate, destitute of
scales; *sterile pinnæ* lanceolate, pectinato-pinnatifid; *segments*
alternate, linear-lanceolate, rather blunt, entire, somewhat
falcated, the *lowermost* rounded, short, remote, *uppermost*
confluent; *fertile pinnæ* pinnate; *pinnæ* linear, narrow, acuminate; *involucres* curled. *Stipes* scaly at base. *Blechnum
boreale.* Lin. Schlecht. Adumb., p. 38. Schkuhr. Filic.,
tab. 110.

Found somewhere in the colony. (Mr. Riche.)

* 79. Lomaria decipiens. Nob. N. sp. (?) *Sterile fronds*
deeply pinnatifid, smooth; *segments* alternate, oblong, obtuse,
quite entire; *lower ones* short, rounded; *terminal one* elongated,
lanceolate, acuminate; all of them dotted at the margin.
Fertile fronds unknown.

A puzzling species, and perhaps the juvenile plant of *Lomaria
heterophylla*, Desv., but very close also to *L. Spicant.*
Near Graham's Town, parasitical on the caudex of *Alsophila
capensis* (Dr. Atherstone), and between crevices of rocks near the
mouth of the Klein River, Caledon. (Zeyher.) *v. s.*

XXII. CAMPTERIA. PRESL. (1 Species.)

80. *Campteria biaurita.* Hook. *Fronds* pinnate, membranaceous, smooth; *pinnæ*, sub-opposite, sessile, pinnatifid,
lanceolate oblong, acute (bearing short stipule-like spines on
the midrib of the upperside), *lowermost* 2-partite; *segments*
confluent, oblong, blunt and rounded at the apex, all of them

quite entire. *Stipes* glossy, stramineous. *Campteria Rottleriana.* (Presl.?) *Pteris nemoralis.* Willd. (?)

In shady localities and clifts. Magalisberg. (Zeyher.); in the forests of Natal. (Plant.) *v. s.*

Very like *Pteris Catoptera.* Kze., but sufficiently different by the venation.

XXIII. ALLOSORUS. BERNH. (8 Species.)

81. *Allosorus hastatus.* Presl. *Fronds* 2 or sometimes 3-pinnate at the lower extremity; *pinnæ* and *pinnules* stalked, alternate, ovate-lanceolate, blunt, eared, or 3-lobed at base, notched, smooth or downy at the *ribs*, crenate and revolute at the margin. *Stipes* half round, channelled on the upper side, glabrous, glossy or paleaceous, and covered at its base with large linear-acute black-purplish scales. *Pteris auriculata.* Thbg. *Pteris hastata.* Schlecht. Adumb., page 42. *Cheilanthes hastata.* Kze. Linnæa, vol. 10, p. 532.

In the forests of Swellendam, George, Uitenhage, Albany, &c. *v. s.*
Of this very variable Fern, the following two are the most striking forms.

1st var. *macrophylla.* Kze. *Fronds* pinnate, or sometimes 2-pinnate at base; *pinnæ* and *pinnules* ovate, cordate, or sub-hastate, somewhat falcate, auricled, very smooth, often $3\frac{1}{2}$ inches long and $2\frac{1}{2}$ inches broad. Linnæa, vol. 10, p. 532.

In the aboriginal forests of the Krakakamma. (Ecki. & Zeyher), and at Natal (Gueinzius. Plant.) *v. s.*

2nd var. *stenophylla.* Kze. *Fronds* 2-pinnate; *pinnæ* and *pinnules* linear-lanceolate, acuminate, narrow, hastate, middle lobe elongated, nearly two inches long; *petioles* short, and as well as the *rachises,* downy. Kze. Linnæa, l. c. p. 533. *Pteris hastæfolia.* Schrad.

Near Philipstown, Kat River. (Eckl. & Zeyh.) *v. s.*

82. *Allosorus Calomelanos.* Presl. *Fronds* 2-pinnate, or 3-pinnate in the lower half; *pinnæ* and *pinnules* stalked, alternate, 3-angular-cordate, obtuse; terminal ones cordate, often 5-angular, all of them coriaceous, smooth. *Stipes* flexuose, slightly paleaceous at base, and like the *rachises* brittle, polished and ebenous. *Caudex* tufted, sub-globose, and thickly clothed with narrow ferruginous scales; *roots* fibrous,

shaggy. *Pteris hastata.* Thbg. *Pteris Calomelanos.* Sw. Kunze & Schlecht. Adumb., p. 43, tab. 30.

Between fissures of rocks; very common all over South Africa. *v. v.* and *s.*

83. *Allosorus auriculatus.* Presl. *Fronds* pinnate smooth; *pinnæ* either alternate or opposite, sub-sessile, ovate, or ovate lanceolate, auricled or sub-pinnatifid at base, entire or crenulated; *lower ones* rounded, *upper ones* oblong, all of them blunt; *margin* and *involucres* notched. *Stipes* smooth, or slightly paleaceous, purplish, glossy. *Caudex* clothed at base with pointed, linear ferruginous scales; *roots* fibrous, woolly. The whole fern little more than a span high. *Adiantum auriculatum.* Thbg. *Pteris auriculata.* Sw. Schlecht. Adumb. p. 41. tab. 23. *Cheilanthes auriculata.* Link. & Kze. Linnæa, vol. 10, p. 531.

Near water-courses, Rondebosch; in moist and shady places on Table and Devil's Mountains and elsewhere common. *v. v.* and *s.*

84. *Allosorus andromedæfolius.* Kaulf. *Fronds* 2-pinnate, 5-6 inches long; *pinnæ* remote, patent; *lower ones* 2-pinnate, *upper ones* pinnate; *inferior pinnules*, 3-foliate; *leaflets* stalked, oblong-ovate, blunt, revolute at the margin; *involucres* short. *Stipes* round, sparingly scaly. *Caudex* creeping, paleaceous; *roots* filiform, shaggy. Kaulf. Enum. Filic. p. 188.

In dry localities at Kendo. (Drege.)

*85. *Allosorus consobrinus.* Nob. *Fronds* 4-pinnate or 3-pinnate, pinnatifid, sub-triangular, straight, coriaceous, smooth; *pinnules* oblong-ovate, lower ones and those of the apex pinnatifid at base; terminal ones elongated, sterile ones, broad crenate, fertile ones narrow, quite entire. *Stipes* and *rachises* flexuose, furrowed, dark purple, glossy, the former covered at its base with comose paleaceous scales. *Pteris consobrina.* Kze. Linnæa, vol. 10, p. 526.

In the forests of the Knysna (Miss Dalgairns), Krakakamma, (Eckl. & Zeyher), near Fort England, Albany. (Dr. Atherstone), and in Kaffraria (Drege.) *v. s.*

*86. *Allosorus coriifolius.* Nob. *Fronds* 3-pinnate, coriaceous, glabrous, glossy above, pale below; middle and lower *primary pinnæ* and *pinnules* remote, terminal ones, short stalked, approximate, confluent at the apex, all of them patent, oblong, acuminate, flexuose or curved; *secondary pinnules* sessile, divergent, ovate oblong, blunt, sub-auriculate, slightly pinnatifid: *segments* ovate, rounded, rather notched. *Rachises* and the short *stipes* angular, flexuose, covered with rufous down. *Pteris coriifolia.* Kze. Linnæa, vol 18, p. 120.

In the dense woods of Natal (Gueinzius.)

87. *Allosorus capensis.* Presl. *Fronds* 2-3-pinnate, coriaceous, hairy on the under surface; *upper pinnules* entire or auricled at base, *lower* ones, divided down to the mid-rib; *segments* adnate, confluent at top; *margins of the pinnæ* and their *segments*, inflexed, crenulated; *involucres* fringed. The very robust *stipes* as well as the *rachises* muricated. *Caudex* descendant, woolly. *Pteris capensis.* Thbg. Schlecht. Adumb., p. 45.

Common in woody, rough, stony places, &c., in all parts of South Africa, *v. v.* and *s.*

88. *Allosorus aquilinus.* Presl. *Fronds* 3-partite coriaceous; branches 2-*pinnate; pinnules* sub-sessile, linear-lanceolate, the superior ones undivided, the inferior ones pinnatifid; *segments* remote, lanceolate-oblong, obtuse. *Stipes* smooth. *Pteris aquilina.* Lin. Schkuhr. Filic. Tab. 95.

In a forest on the sources of the Kat River near Philiptown. (Eckl. & Zeyher.)

XXIV. CRYPTOGRAMMA. R. BR. (1 Species.)

*89. *Cryptogramma robusta.* Nob. Fertile *frond* 3 inches high, 2-pinnate-pinnatifid, oblong, smooth; *pinnules* and *segments* oblong-ovate, blunt, wedge-shaped at base. *Rachises* and the short channelled *stipes* curved or flexuose, purple, glabrous. *Caudex* stout, creeping, paleaceous. *Allosorus robustus.* Kze. Linnæa, vol. 10, p. 502.

Between rocks near Goedemanskraal, Namaqualand. (Drege.) *v. s.*

XXV. ADIANTUM. LIN. (2 Species.)

90. *Adiantum Capillus Veneris.* Lin. *Frond* 3-4-pinnate ovate; *pinnules* delicately membranaceous, smooth, obliquely broad cuneate, tapering into a slender stalk; the superior edge deeply and irregularly inciso-lobate; *lobes* obtuse or truncate, soriferous. *Sori* as broad as the lobes, oblong or

sub-reniform. *Stipes* and *rachis* ebenous, glabrous, polished. Hook. Spec. Filic. vol. 2, p. 36., tab. 74, B.

Between rocks on Table Mountain, &c ; also in the woods near the Kat River, and at Natal. *v. v.* and *s.*

91. *Adiantum aethiopicum.* Lin. *Frond* 3-4-pinnate oblong-ovate, membranaceous, smooth : *pinnules* sub-orbicular, obliquely cuneate at base, stalked ; superior margin more or less lobed ; notches of the lobes soriferous ; *sori* large, *involucres* oblong-lunate. *Stipes* slender, compressed ; *rachis* ebenous, glabrous, glossy. *Caudex* fibrous. Hook., l. c., p. 37, tab. 77 A.

Common in moist, shady places in all parts of the colony. *v. v.* and *s.*

XXVI. CHEILANTHES. SW. (16 Species.)

92. *Cheilanthes pteroides.* Sw. *Fronds* 3-pinnate, coriaceous, smooth ; *pinnæ* and *pinnules* remote, the latter stalked, cordate, elliptical, obtuse, crenate, opaque : *involucres* contiguous, sub-round membranaceous, extending over the whole margin. *Stipes* and *rachises* woolly at their axils, stout, ebenous, glossy. *Caudex* creeping, scaly. Hook., Spec. Filic. vol. 2, p. 80, tab. 101, A. *Adiantum pteroides.* Lin.

In shady, damp places, and between rocks near Cape Town, the Paarl, Tulbagh, &c ; also at Natal. *v. v.* and *s.*

93. *Cheilanthes capensis.* Sw. *Fronds* 2-3-pinnate, deltoid, membranaceous, smooth ; *pinnules* adnate, decurrent, ovate, or oval-oblong, crenate-dentate, rarely pinnatifid ; *involucres* fringed at the margin ; *sori* numerous, approximate. *Stipes* ebenous, shining, scaly. *Caudex* creeping, paleaceous. *Adiantum capense.* Thbg. & Kze. *Hypolepis capensis.* Hook. Spec. Filic., vol. 2, p. 71, tab. 77, c.

In shady localities between rocks in many parts of the colony. *v. v* and *s.*

94. *Cheilanthes multifida.* Sw. *Frond* 3, below 4-pinnate, deltoid-ovate, acute, coriaceous, glabrous ; *primary pinnæ* rather opposite, broad-ovate, sub-deltoid, stalked : *pinnules* or segments oblong, pinnatifid, *lobes* sub-round, each bearing 2-4 involucres. *Stipes* and *rachises* brittle, deep ebony, black, glossy. *Caudex* clothed with black subulate scales. Hook. l. c., p. 90, tab. 100, b.

In rocky and stony places in most parts of South Africa. *v. v.* and *s.*

* 95. *Cheilanthes refracta.* Nob. (N. sp.) *Frond* 2-3-pinnate, deltoid, rigid, perfectly smooth; *pinnæ* alternate, remote, deltoid-ovate, patent, upper ones sub-sessile, middle and lower ones stalked; *petioles* more or less reflexed; *pinnules* lanceolate-oblong, sessile, confluent at the apex, and as well as the intermediate ones crenate; *lowermost* distant, pinnatifid. *Stipes* short, half round, channelled on the upper side, flexuose, and like the *rachises*, glossy.

In Griqualand (Mr. Robert Moffatt, 1857). *r. s.*

96. *Cheilanthes triangula.* Kze. *Frond* 3-pinnate, triangular, coriaceous, smooth; *pinnæ* and *pinnules* remote, patent, stalked; *secondary pinnules* or lobes oblong, obtuse, sinuate, lobate, margined; the *margin* inflexed, crenate; *involucres* marginal; *sori* contiguous. *Stipes* and *rachises* flexuose, stiff, purple, slightly hairy. *Caudex* short. Kze. Linnæa, vol. 10, p. 535. Hook. l. c., p. 91.

Rocky places in the Sneeuwbergen, Witbergen and Compasberg. (Drege) in similar localities at Natal. (Dr. F. Krauss.) *v. s.*

97. *Cheilanthes Bergiana.* Schlecht. *Fronds* 3-pinnate membranaceous, sparingly hairy on both sides; *primary pinnæ* ovate, sub-acuminate; *secondary ones* rather obtuse; *pinnules* and primary lobes subovate, almost oblique, entire, or pinnatifid; *involucres* small, situated at the inner margin of the lobe. *Stipes* and primary *rachises* deep purple, black, and as well as the secondary rachises and ribs clothed with rusty hairs. Schlecht. Adumbr., p. 51. *Hypolepis Bergiana.* Hook. l. c. p. 67.

In thickets and at the borders of the forests in the Swellendam, George, and Uitenhage districts; also at Kat River and Natal. *v. s.*

98. *Cheilanthes elata.* Kze. *Frond* 4-pinnate-pinnatifid, 3-angular, membranaceous; *pinnæ* and *primary pinnules* stalked, remote, erect, and as well as the *secondary ones* subsessile, ovate-lanceolate, acuminated; *tertiary ones* oblong, blunt, sinuate, or inciso-pinnatifid, slightly clothed with whitish hairs; *sori* and *involucres* semi-orbiculate. *Stipes* and *rachises* flexuose, rough, covered with reddish chaffy hairs. Kze. Linnæa, vol. 10, p. 542. *Hypolepis elata.* Hook, l. c., p. 67.

In woods at Koratra (Drege.)

99. *Cheilanthes hirta.* Sw. *Frond* 2-3-pinnate, lanceolate or oblong-lanceolate, sub-coriaceous, hairy on both sides;

primary pinnæ lanceolate, lower ones opposite, distant; *pinnules* oblong or pinnatifid-ovate or crenulate, the *lobes* with the margins recurved, soriferous; *sori* numerous, confluent. *Stipes* short, purplish-brown, glossy, very hairy, and more or less glandular, shaggy at the base with long subulate scales. *Caudex* almost creeping; *roots* tufted. Schlecht Adumbr. p. 50. Kze. Linnæa., vol. 10, p. 539. Hook, l. c., p. 92, tab 101, b.

Extremely changeable in form, according to the very different habitats of the species.

The following are the principal varieties enumerated by Kunze, l. c.

1st var. *contracta. Frond* 2-pinnate, rather rigid, often curved; *pinnules* approximate, oblong, erect; larger pinnules folded, and thickly clothed with rufous shag; *stipes* and *caudex* more or less smooth at base.

2nd var. *intermedia. Frond* 2-pinnate; *pinnæ* short, ovate, and as well as the minute and plane *pinnules* approximate; base of the *stipes* and *caudex* closely surrounded by long scales.

3rd var. *laxa. Frond* 2-3-pinnate; *pinnæ* and *pinnules* oblong-lanceolate, plane, remote, pinnatifid and incised; *stipes* and *rachises* fringed with rufous hairs. *Notholæna capensis.* A. Sprengel. Suppl. ad. Lin. Syst. Vegetab. p. 32.

4th var. *parviloba. Frond* 2-3-pinnate, calvescent, *pinnæ* lanceolate, elongated, distant; *pinnules* sub 3-lobed or auricled at base; *lobes* obtuse, convolute, middle one linear-oblong; *stipes* slightly paleaceous at base; *rachis* paleaceo-hirsute. *Cheilanthes parviloba.* Sw.

In rocky, shady, or open situations, and widely diffused over the whole of South Africa. *v. v.* and *s.*

* 100. *Cheilanthes glandulosa.* Nob. (N. sp.) *Frond* 2-3-pinnate, sub-coriaceous, linear-lanceolate; *primary pinnæ* remote, sub-opposite at base, alternate above, erect, pinnate, shortly stalked, oblong-ovate, obtuse, rough and opaque on the upper, paler and almost smooth on the under surface; *pinnules* subsessile, oblong, deeply lobed, blunt; *lobes* with the margins recurved, soriferous; *sori* copious, confluent. *Stipes* and *rachises* purple, fringed with delicate glandular shag.

G

Related to the preceding species, and very like *C. hirta* var. *laxa.* Kze. It seems however to be different.

In Griqualand (Mr. Robert Moffatt, 1857.) *v. s.*

101. *Cheilanthes induta.* Kze. *Frond* sub 4-pinnate, oblong, obtuse, coriaceous; *pinnæ* rather remote, stalked, ascending; *pinnules* shortly stalked, ovate, *secondary* oblong *tertiary*, and the *segments* roundish-ovate, all glabrous above, paleaceo-hirsute beneath; *involucres* marginal, crenulate, and as well as the *sori* continuous. *Stipes* flexuose, sparingly, and the *rachises* densely paleaceo-hirsute, purple. *Caudex* creeping. Kze. Linnæa, vol. 10, p. 538. Hook., l. c., p. 92, tab. 102, A.

In rocky, shady places in the Sneeuwbergen (Drege.)

102. *Cheilanthes deltoidea.* Kze. *Frond* 2-pinnate pinnatifid, 3-angular, sub-coriaceous, smooth; *pinnæ* obliquely ovate; *pinnules* and *segments* ovate, obtuse, with the cuneate base decurrent. *Stipes* smooth; *rachises* margined; *involucres* marginate, crenulated, continuous. *Sori* broad. Kze. Linnæa, vol. 10, p. 535. Hook, l. c., p. 106.

In the fissures of the rocks near Silverfontein, Little Namaqualand (Drege.) *v. s.*

103. *Cheilanthes profusa.* Kze. *Frond* pinnate, oblong-lanceolate, obtuse, sub-coriaceous; *pinnæ* often opposite, smooth, *uppermost* lanceolate, approximate, sub-connate, entire; *lower ones* ovate or deltoid, remote, acuminated, shortly stalked, deeply pinnatifid or sometimes pinnate at their bases; *pinnules* and *segments* lobed or pinnatifid; *costæ* hispid with narrow subulate scales; *involucres* continuous. *Stipes* and *rachises* hispid with paleaceous scales. *Roots* creeping, scaly. Kze. Linnæa, vol. 10, p. 535. Suppl. to Schkuhr's, Filic., tab. 17. Hook, l. c., p. 108.

Between rocks near Silverfontein (Drege) on Karroo-like hills at Buffeljagdsriver and Rietkuil. (Zeyher.) *v. s.*

104. *Cheilanthes cornuta.* Kze. *Frond* 2-pinnate, linear-lanceolate; *pinnæ* ovate approximate, the lowermost sub-opposite, stalked; *pinnules* sessile, sub-ternate, 2-3-fid, oblong, obtuse, coriaceous. *Sori* at length diffused. *Stipes* and *rachis* rigid, naked. Kze. Linnæa, vol. 10, p. 534. Hook, l. c., p. 109.

Near Hex River, Worcester (Eckl. & Zeyh.), and on dry stony hills near Enon, and the little Fish River (Drege.) *v. s.*

105. *Cheilanthes Atherstoni.* Hook. *Frond* 4-pinnate, deltoid, glabrous; *primary pinnæ* ovate-deltoid, and as well as the *secondary* and *tertiary pinnæ*, stalked; the lower ones distant, the upper ones more approximate; *pinnules* sessile, oblong, entire or pinnatifid in their lower half; *involucres* formed of the inflexed margins of the pinnules, pale and membranaceous at the edge, generally continuous; the edge more or less crenate or lobed. *Stipes* and principal *rachis* purple, ebenous, glossy. Hook, l. c., p. 107.

In the district of Somerset (Dr. Atherstone.)

106. *Cheilanthes firma.* T. Moore. *Frond* 3-4-pinnate, smooth, coriaceous, pentagonal acuminate, 1-1½ feet long; *inferior pinnules* of the lower pinnæ obliquely deltoid; *primary pinnæ* of lowest inferior pinnæ, pinnate, ovate-lanceolate, deeply pinnatifid, the *segments* oblong, bluntish, with notched margins; the lowest *secondary pinnules* stalked, the *intermediate ones* either stalked or sessile, lanceolate-oblong, scarcely pinnatifid; the uppermost ones connate, pointed. *Stipes* and *rachises* smooth, brown, shining, channelled. *Sori* continuous; *involucres* lobed, crenate. T. Moore, in Hook., Journ. of Botan. and K. G. Miscellany, vol. 5, p. 225.

According to Mr. Moore, nearly related to *C. Atherstoni.* Hook.

On the sides of mountain streams. Natal (Plant.)

107. *Cheilanthes linearis.* T. Moore. *Froud* 4-pinnate, deltoid, coriaceous smooth, 6 inches high; *ultimate pinnules* all distinct, small, linear, obtuse, the *terminal one* of the same form; *sori* numerous; *involucres* continuous, narrow, slightly waved. *Stipes* and *rachises* round behind, plane and margined in front, purple, glossy. T. Moore, l. c., p. 226.

In rocky places near Impafane, Natal (Plant.)

XXVII. HYPOLEPIS BERNH. (2 Species.)

108. *Hypolepis anthriscifolia.* Presl. *Fronds* 3-pinnate, hairy on the mid-rib and veins beneath, membranaceous; *primary pinnæ* oblong-ovate, acuminate; *secondary ones* broad, oblong; *pinnules* linear-oblong, sub-falcate, deeply pinnatifid; *segments* small, entire or toothed, bearing solitary *sori* in the inner margin; *involucres* squamiform. *Stipes* and *rachises* glabrous. *Cheilanthes sparsisora* Schr. *C. commutata.* Kze. Linnæa, vol. 10, p. 542. Hook. Spec. Filic., vol. 2, p. 66, tab. 95. A.

In the forests near Plettenberg's Bay, in the Zuurbergen (Albany), at Natal (Plant, No. 369), &c. *v. s.*

109. *Hypolepis aspera.* Prl. *Fronds* 3-pinnate, sub-coriaceous; *primary pinnæ* alternate, lanceolate, curved, erect, stalked; *pinnules* sub-sessile or shortly petioled, lance-shaped, pinnatifido incised; *segments* sub-dentate; *rachis* rough; *sori* solitary at the superior base of the segments; *involucres* sub-reniform. *Stipes* almost smooth, glossy. *Caudex* creeping, shaggy; *roots* filiform. *Cheilanthes aspera.* Kaulf. Linnæa, vol. 6, p. 186. Hook., l. c., p. 67.

In shady localities near the cataract on the Devil's Mountain, near Genadendal (Caledon), in the forests of George, Albany, &c. *v. v.* and *s.*

XXVIII. LONCHITIS. LIN.

110. *Lonchitis natalensis.* Hook. *Fronds* 2-pinnate, moderately hairy on both sides; *pinnæ* more or less stalked, the upper half, *pinnatifid*; *pinnules* sessile, broad lanceolate, acuminate, nearly entire or somewhat lobed in the lower half; *lobes* rounded, undivided, short, the sinuses and entire margins soriferous; *sori* small. *Stipes* and *rachis* downy. Hook. Spec. Filic., vol. 2, p. 57, tab. 89. B.

In the primæval forests of Natal. (Gueinzius.) *v. s.*

111. *Lonchitis glabra.* Bory. *Fronds* 2-pinnate membranaceous, with scattered fulvous hairs on the stipes, rachis, mid-rib, and veins on both sides; *pinnæ* sessile oblong-ovate, acuminate, pinnatifid at the apex; *pinnules* lanceolate, obtuse, lobed or pinnatifid, all of them decurrent, so as to constitute a broadly-winged rachis to the pinnæ; the *inferior pinnule* above (next to the main rachis), dwarfish; *lobes* round, entire; sinuses soriferous; *sori* small, lunate. *Stipes* paleaceous at the base. Schlecht. Adumbr. p. 47. Hook, l. c. p. 57. Kunze Suppl. to Schkuhr, tab. 66.

In the forests of the Tzitsikamma (Mundt, Dr. Alexander, Dr. Rubidge) at Natal. (Drege.) *v. s.*

VII. VITTARIACEÆ. PRESL.

XXIX. VITTARIA. SM. (1 Species.)

112. *Vittaria lineata.* Sw. *Fronds* linear, narrow, very long, membranaceous, pendulous. *Sori* solitary, intermarginal. *Caudex* bulbose, shaggy; *roots* fibrous. Schlecht. Adumbr., p. 33. Schkuhr. Filic., tab. 101 b.

In woods near Swellendam (Mundt), in the forests of George (Drege.), in Blockhouse Kloof, near Graham's Town (Dr. Atherstone), and at Natal (Gueinzius.) *v. s.*

VIII. POLYPODIACEÆ. PRESL.

XXX. POLYPODIUM. LIN. (3 Species.)

113. *Polypodium vulgare.* Lin. *Frond* deeply pinnatifid, its *segments* linear lanceolate, blunt, crenulate at the margins, approximate; upper ones gradually smaller. *Sori* circular, placed in a single line on each side of the midrib at the upper portion of the frond. *Rhizome* creeping, chaffy. Schkuhr's Filic., tab. 11.

In the fissures of rocks on Table Mountain; also at George, Albany, Kat River, and in Kafirland. *v. s.*

114. *Polypodium Ecklonis.* Kze. *Frond* lanceolate-ovate, deeply pinnatifid; *segments* broad at base, remote, alternate, patent, oblong, rather blunt, perfectly entire, glossy on the upper side, and covered below (as well as the *costa* and the *stipes*) with loose scales. *Sori* cushioned, submarginal. Kze. Linnæa, vol. 10, p. 498.

Parasitical on old trees in the forests of Uitenhage, Beaufort, and Kaffraria (Eckl. & Zeyh.); also at Natal (Drege.) *v. s.*

115. *Polypodium Bergianum.* Schlecht. *Fronds* hairy on both sides : *pinnæ* alternate or opposite, pinnatifid, acute ; *segments* alternate, oblong, obtuse, ciliated, slightly gnawed at the borders. *Stipes* and *rachises* clothed with shaggy down ; *sori* small in one row between the midrib and the margin. Schlecht. Adumb., p. 20, tab. 9.

In shady places at the foot of Table Mountain, Witteboom, and Kirstenbosch (Bergius, Mundt, Drege), near the cataract on the Devil's Peak (Ecklon), at Natal (Dr. Krauss.)

XXXI. GONIOPTERIS. PRESL. (1 Species.)

* 116. *Goniopteris silvatica.* Nob. *Frond* pinnate 3-4 feet high, smooth, dark green at the upper, pale at the underside, sub-coriaceous; *pinnæ* obliquely truncate at base, sessile, oblong-lanceolate, long and narrowly tapering towards the apex, acuminate, remote, inciso-pinnatifid ; *lower ones* nearly opposite, *upper ones* alternating ; *segments* oblong, falcate, obtuse ; *veins, rachises,* and the 3-cornered furrowed *stipes* slightly downy ; *sori* minute. *Gymnogramma unita.* Kze. Linnæa, vol. 18, p. 115.

In the primæval forests of Natal. (Gueinzius.) *v. s.*

XXXII. MARGINARIA. BORY. (1 Species.)

117. *Marginaria ensiformis.* Presl. *Frond* coriaceous,

smooth, ovate-oblong, wedge-shaped below, 3-fid, pinnatifid ; pinnate at base or sometimes simple ; *segments* of the *sterile frond* opposite, attenuated at top, rather acute ; those of the *fertile ones* linear ensiform, blunt, repando-crenate, decurrent ; *sori* circular in a single row. *Stipes* short ; *rhizome* creeping, paleaceous. *Polypodium ensiforme.* Thbg. Kze. Suppl. to Schkuhr's Filic., p. 117, tab. 54.

At the trunks of decayed trees in the forests of Swellendam and George ; also at Natal. *v. s.*

XXXIII. PLEOPELTIS. HUMB. & BONPL. (2 Species.)

118. *Pleopeltis lepidota.* Presl. *Frond* lanceolate, much narrowed towards the base, rather blunt at the apex, quite entire or sinuate, coriaceous, almost naked on the upper surface, and covered with minute scales below. *Sori* large, cushioned, solitary ; *rhizome* creeping, paleaceous. *Polypodium adspersum..* Schr. *P. lepidotum.* Schlecht. Adumb. p, 17, tab. 8.

In woods and shady spots near Cape Town, Kirstenbosch, Paradise, &c., and in the districts of Swellendam, George, Albany, &c.; also at Natal. *v. v.* and *s.*

119. *Pleopeltis lycopodioides.* Presl. *Frond* subsessile, lanceolate, or linear-lanceolate, narrowed at both ends, obtuse, glabrous. *Sori* large, placed in one row on each side of the midrib. *Caudex* creeping, scaly. *Polypodium lycopodioides.* Willd. Spec. Plant, vol. 5, p. 150. Schkuhr. Filic., tab. 8. c.

Creeping and climbing at the feet of old trees, in the forests of Natal (Gueinzius.) *v. s.*

XXXIV. PHYMATODES. PRESL. (3 Species.)

120. *Phymatodes vulgaris.* Presl. *Frond* simple, elongated 3-angular, coriaceous, smooth, deeply 3-lobed at the apex, decurrent at base ; *segments* lanceolate, patent, acuminate, quite entire ; *sori* almost circular, scattered, immersed. *Stipes* broadly winged in the upper portion of the frond. *Rhizome* creeping, scaly. *Polypodium phymatodes.* Lin. Willd. Spec. Plant, vol. 5, p. 167. Schkuhr. Filic., tab. 8. d.

On the trunks of old trees in the aboriginal forests of Natal· (Gueinzius Plant.) *v. s.*

121. *Phymatodes irioides.* Presl. *Frond* cartilaginous, simple, elongated, quite entire, oblong-lanceolate, sword-shaped, attenuated at the base, reticulated, perfectly smooth.

Sori minute, numerous, scattered. *Rhizome* creeping, scaly. ***Polypodium irioides.*** Poir. Spreng. Syst. Vegetab., vol. 4, p. 48.

In the forests of Natal (Gueinzius) *v. s.*

122. ***Phymatodes elongata.*** Presl. *Frond* linear-lanceolate, narrowed at both ends, entire, subcoriaceous, smooth. *Sori* impressed in one single row on each side of the costa. *Caudex* creeping. *Polypodium elongatum.* Schr. Schlecht. Adumb., p. 16, tab. 7.

On the stems of old trees in the forests of George (Mundt. Ecklon), near the bath of Olifant's River (Rev. Hesse.); in Blockhouse Kloof, Graham's Town (Dr. Atherstone); near Boontjes River, &c. (Drege.) *v. s.*

XXXV. NIPHOBOLUS. KAULF. (1 Species.)

123. ***Niphobolus africanus.*** Kze. *Frond* lanceolate, shortly stalked at base, costate, margined, stellate tomentose and hoary beneath, rather smooth above; top of the *sterile frond* shortened, blunt; *fertile one* narrowed into a long, obtuse, soriferous apex. *Sori* minute, confluent. *Caudex* creeping, densely scaly. Kze. Linnæa, vol. 10, p. 501. Suppl. to Schkuhr's Filic., tab. 33.

Between rocks and on the trunks of trees in the woods of Natal. (Drege.) *v. s.*

IX. GRAMMITACEÆ. PRESL.

XXXVI. GRAMMITIS. PRESL. (1 Species.)

124. ***Grammitis totta.*** Presl. *Fronds* pinnate, lanceolate, membranaceous (and as well as the *stipes* and *rachises*) hairy on both sides; *pinnæ* alternate, sessile, pinnatifid, lanceolate, acuminated; the upper ones adnate, confluent, the lower ones remote; *segments* opposite, ovate, blunt, gnawed, ciliated; *sori* linear, small. *Stipes* short; *rhizome* descending; *roots* filiform. *Gymnogramma totta.* Schlecht. Adumb., p. 15, tab. 6.

Near the cataract on the Devil's Mountain (Mundt. Pappe); in a wood near Koratra (Drege); in the forests of the Knysna (Dr. Krauss.)

XXXVII. GYMNOGRAMMA. DESV. (3 Species.)

125. ***Gymnogramma conspersa.*** Kze. *Frond* delicate, membranaceous, pale green on the upper surface, and covered beneath with a white mealy substance, ovate triangular,

acuminated, 3-partito 2-pinnatifid; *pinnæ* trapezoid, inciso-pinnatifid, wedge-shaped and decurrent at base; *segments* cuneate, 2-fid, blunt; *sori* few seeded. *Stipes* long; *rachises* and *ribs* purplish. *Caudex* tufted. Kunze. Linnæa., vol. 18, p. 116.

In the crevices of rocks near the cataract between Omfondi and Togela Rivers, Natal. (Gueinzius.) *v. s.*

* 126. *Gymnogramma namaquensis.* Nob. (N. sp.) Annual. *Frond* (about 4 inches long), membranaceous, smooth, pinnato-pinnatifid; *pinnæ* alternate, distant, lanceolate oblong, rough on the upper surface, glandular and scaly beneath; *segments* inciso-crenate. *Stipes* flexuose, erect, and as well as the *rachis* densely-paleaceous. *Caudex* short, cæspitose, obliquely descending.

Between rocks near Modderfontein, Namaqualand (Rev. H. Whitehead, 1856.) *v. s.*

127. *Gymnogramma leptophylla.* Desv. Annual. *Frond* slender, very delicate, 2-pinnate, smooth, 3 inches high; *pinnules* roundish-cuneate, sub-trilobed; *lobes* bluntly 2-dentate; *sori* confluent; *roots* filiform. *Grammitis leptophylla.* Sw. Willd. Spec. Plant., vol. 5, p. 143. Schkuhr. Filic., tab. 26.

In moist vegetable soil, near the cataract on the east side of the Devil's Mountain—rare. (Mundt, Dr. Alexander, 1848.) *v. s.*

X. TÆNITIDEÆ. PRESL.

XXXVIII. NOTHOLÆNA. R. BR. (3 Species.)

128. *Notholæna Eckloniana.* Kze. *Frond* 2-pinnato-pinnatifid, lanceolate, hoary above, clothed beneath with rufous shaggy scales; *pinnæ* opposite, 3-angular-ovate; *pinnules* oblong, the lowermost bent downwards, and as well as the middle ones deeply incised; *segments* ovate-oblong, blunt; the uppermost entire, confluent. *Caudex* short, ascending, paleaceous. Kze. Linnæa, vol. 10, p. 501.

In the mountains of Uitenhage, Beaufort, Kat River, Kaffraria and Natal. (Eckl. & Zeyher, Krebs, Drege, Dr Rubidge); and on hills along the Orange River, and Gamohana range, Griqualand. (Mr. Robt. Moffatt.) *v. s.*

* 129. *Notholæna Rawsoni.* Pappe. (N. sp.) *Frond* pinnate, linear oblong, stout, coriaceous, about 6-7 inches long, dark green, somewhat rough on the upper surface, covered beneath with thick ferruginous or white shaggy filt; *pinnæ* alternate, remote, short, pinnatifid ; upper ones sessile, lowermost opposite, smaller, shortly petioled ; *segments* ovate, rounded. *Stipites* aggregate, flexuose, black-purple, shining, clothed with fugacious shag. *Caudex* creeping, densely surrounded by linear-acute, margined scales.

On hills between Spectakel and Komaggas, Namaqualand. (Rev. H. Whitehead, July, 1856.) *v. s.*

130. *Notholæna inæqualis.* Kze. *Frond* ovate-oblong, bluntly acuminate, coriaceous, stiff, hairy on the upper surface, clothed with thick rufous shag at the underside, 2-*pinnate* at base, simple above, confluent at the apex ; *pinnæ* opposite or alternate, remote, patent, unequally sided ; lower ones stalked, almost 3-angular-oblong, subfalcate obtuse ; *pinnules* sinuate, the lowermost bent downwards, inciso-pinnatifid, elongated ; *sori* concealed under the shag. *Stipes* and the stout *rachises* flexuose, ebenous, hairy. *Rhizome* horizontal, densely scaly. Kze. Suppl. to Schkuhr. Filic., p. 146, tab. 64, fig. 1.

In the fissures of rocks in the Magalisberg. (Zeyher.) *v. s.*

XXXIX. PTEROPSIS. DESV. (1 Species.)

131. *Pteropsis angustifolia.* Desv. *Fronds* fascicled, linear-lanceolate, erect, simple, perfectly entire, coriaceous, smooth, tapering towards the base into a short *stipes ; sori* marginal. *Rhizome* round, covered with linear ferruginous scales. *Pteris angustifolia.* Sw.

Between rocks on the mountains near Genadendal. (Rev. C. R. Kölbing.) *v. s.*

XI. ACROSTICHACEÆ. Presl.

XL. STENOCHLÆNA. J. SMITH. (1 Species.)

* 132. *Stenochlæna Meyeriana.* Nob. *Fronds* oblong, lanceolate ; *sterile frond* pinnate, *pinnæ* alternate, lanceolate, acuminate, smooth, glossy, very veiny, twice and irregularly serrate ; *ribs* furrowed on the upper side ; *fertile frond* 2-pinnate ; *pinnæ* alternate, *pinnules* linear, sub-recurved at the apex, rather obtuse ; *partial rachises* slender, flexuose. *Caudex* bent, angular, rough, climbing. *Lomaria Meyeriana.* Kze. Linnæa, vol. 10, p. 509.

Climbing up large trees in damp ravines near the coast of Natal. (Drege, Plant, Gueinzius.) *v. s.*

H

XLI. OLFERSIA. RADDI. (2 Species.)

133. *Olfersia angustata.* Presl. *Frond* oblong, blunt, smooth, tapering down into a long *stipes*; *fertile one* longer and narrower. *Caudex* creeping, clothed with broad fulvous scales. *Acrostichum angustatum.* Schr. Schlecht. Adumb., p. 14, tab. 5.

In clefts of rocks on the east side of Table Mountain, at Hottentot's Holland, Caledon, Swellendam, George, &c. *v. v.* and *s.*

134. *Olfersia conformis.* Presl. *Frond* oblong, acute, glabrous on the upper, paler and slightly scaly on the under surface, tapering down into a stalk, entire; *fertile one* somewhat longer. *Caudex* creeping, paleaceous. *Acrostichum conforme.* Sw.

On the face of rocks on Table Mountain, at Caledon, Swellendam, in Albany, &c. *v. s.*

XLII. ACROSTICHUM. LIN. (1 Species.)

135. *Acrostichum inæquale.* Willd. *Frond* pinnate, coriaceous, smooth; *pinnæ* alternate, lanceolate-oblong, quite entire, unequally wedge-shaped at base; all of them blunt, terminated by a hard short point. Willd. Enum. Plant, vol. 5, p. 117.

In marshy soil near the Natal coast. (Dr. F Krauss, Plant.) *v. s.*

XII. HYMENOPHYLLEÆ. ENDL.

XLIII. HYMENOPHYLLUM. SM. (2 Species.)

136. *Hymenophyllum tunbridgense.* Sw. *Fronds* pinnate, small, tender, quite smooth; *pinnæ* distichous, pinnatifid; *segments* linear, truncate, entire or 2-fid, and as well as the supra-axillary, solitary, compressed *involucres*, spinuloso-serrate; the *valves* semi-orbicular; *rachis* winged above. *Stipes* filiform procumbent. Hook, Spec. Filic., vol. 1, p. 95. Schkuhr's Filic., tab. 135. d.

In shady, moist places between rocks on Table Mountain, at Hottentot's Holland, &c. *v. v.* and *s.*

137. *Hymenophyllum rarum.* R. Br. *Fronds* pinnate, flaccid, decompound, linear oblong; *pinnæ* pinnatifidly incised; *segments* entire, obtuse, erect; *involucres* rhomboid, wedge-shaped at their lower half, the upper forming two semicircular entire compressed valves. *Stipes* slender. Hook. Spec.

Filic., vol. 1, p. 101. R. Br. Prodrom, Flor. Nov. Holland. p. 159. *H. fumarioides.* Bory. Schlecht, p. 56.

In the same localities with the former, also in Blockhousekloof, Graham's Town. (Dr. Atherstone.) *v. s.*

XLIV. TRICHOMANES. LIN. (3 Species.)

138. *Trichomanes Filicula.* Bory. *Fronds* pinnate, smooth, opaque, ovate-lanceolate; *pinnæ* 2-3-fid; *segments* linear, blunt, retuse, entire; *involucres* solitary, supra-axillary, cylindrical 2-lipped, tapering at the base, immersed or winged at the sides. *Stipes* short, compressed, margined at its upper portion; *caudex* creeping, clothed with dense black down. Hook. Spec. Filic., vol. 1, p. 124. *Trichomanes melanotrichum.* Schlecht. Adumb., p. 56. *Hymenophyllum alatum.* Schkuhr. Icon. Filic., tab., 135. b.

On the trunks of old forest trees, near Genadendal, Plettenberg's Bay, Graham's Town, &c.; also in Kaffraria. *v. s.*

139. *Trichomanes pyxidiferum.* Lin. *Frond* 2-3-pinnatifid oblong-ovate, pellucid, membranaceous, not margined, somewhat glossy; *segments* linear, smooth, entire or emarginate at the apex; *involucres* solitary, axillary, immersed, sub-cylindrical; *receptacles* very long, filiform, much exserted. *Stipes* winged above or rarely naked. Hook. Sp. Filic., vol. 1, p. 124.

On trees at Natal. (Plant.)

140. *Trichomanes rigidum.* Sw. *Frond* 2-pinnate, ovate, acuminate, rigid; *pinnules* linear-lanceolate, cuneate, sub-2-pinnatifid; the ultimate *segments* sub-acute, simple or 2-fid; *rachis* wingless, or very narrowly margined; *involucres* supra-axillary, sub-urceolato cylindrical, free; the mouth entire. Hook. Spec. Filic., vol. 1, p. 133.

Between fissures of rocks in shady places at Natal. (Drege.)

XIII. SCHIZAEACEÆ. MART.

XLV. SCHIZÆA. SM. (2 Species.)

141. *Schizæa pectinata.* Sm. *Fronds* cæspitose, simple, filiform, channelled, stiff, leafless, smooth, bearing on their summit pectinate spikes, composed of fifteen one-sided pairs of appendages bearing the fructification. Schkuhr. Filic., tab. 136.

In sandy soil on the Cape flats, on the summit of Table Mountain, and in many more places within the colony. *v. v.* and *s.*

142. *Schizæa tenella.* Kaulf. *Fronds* simple, linear, slender, filiform, compressed, terminated by sub-erect spikes, containing eight pairs of fruit-bearing appendages. Kaulf. Enum.
Filic., p. 50, tab. 1, f. 7.

Between rocks on the mountains of Hottentot's Holland. (Chamisso, Zeyher); in similar places near Genadendal. (Rev. C. R.
Kölbing.) *v. s.*

XLVI. ANEMIA. SW. (1 Species.)

143. *Anemia Dregeana.* Kze. *Sterile fronds* pinnate,
linear-oblong, membranaceous, *pinnæ* nearly sessile, obliquely-
ovate, blunt, somewhat auricled, wedge-shaped at base,
slightly notched at the margin, smooth and glossy above,
strigose along the veins below; *fertile frond* 3-partite, 2 of
its partitions fruit-bearing, 3-pinnate; the third sterile one
pinnate. *Stipes* and *rachises* hairy; *caudex* creeping, shaggy.
Kze. Linnæa, vol. 10, p. 493. Suppl. to Schkuhr., tab. 20.
Hook. Icon. Plant, vol. 3, tab. 236.

In moist shady places amongst rocks in the forests of Natal.
(Drege, Gueinzius.) *v. s.*

XLVII. MOHRIA. SW. (1 Species.)

144. *Mohria thurifraga.* Sw. *Fronds* 2-pinnate, coriaceous, covered beneath with chaffy scales; *pinnæ* alternate,
stalked; *pinnules* ovate; the upper fruit-bearing ones crenate;
the barren ones deeply incised. *Caudex* creeping, paleaceous.
Adiantum coffrorum. Thbg.

Common on the mountains of the Cape Colony, Kaffraria, and
Natal. *v. v.* and *s.*
This fern, when bruised, is fragrant, and smells of *Benzoin* or
Olibanum. In some parts of the colony, the dry fronds are pulverised, and with fat made into an ointment, which is cooling and
serviceable in burns and scalds. The vernacular name of this
plant is *Brand-boschjes.*

XIV. OSMUNDACEÆ. R. BR.

XLVIII. OSMUNDA. SW. (1 Species.)

145. *Osmunda regalis.* Lin. *Fronds* 2-pinnate, smooth;
pinnæ stalked, alternate, oblong-ovate, many-yoked; *pinnules*
shortly petioled, unequally sided, and more or less auricled at
base, oblong, slightly notched, blunt; *fertile panicle* 2-pinnate,

placed at the extremity of the frond. Schkuhr. Icon. Filic., tab. 145.

On a cataract between the Omzamcaba and Omzamvoobo Rivers Natal. (Drege.)

Var. *Spectabilis*. Kze. *Sterile pinnules* elongated, thicker, obliquely truncate and inciso-crenate at base. *Osmunda spectabilis*. Willd. Spec. Plantar, vol. 5, p. 98.

In shady places near rivulets, in the mountains of Hottentot's Holland, Swellendam, Tulbagh, Uitenhage, &c. (Eckl. & Zeyh.), at Natal. (Drege.) *v. s*

XLIX. TODEA. WILLD. (1 Species.)

146. *Todea africana*. Willd. *Fronds* 2-pinnate, oblong, erect, smooth, coriaceous 5-6-feet high; *pinnæ* opposite, shortly petioled, oblong-lanceolate, many-yoked, patent, the upper and lower ones being smaller by degrees; *pinnules* alternate, linear-lanceolate, cohering at base, blunt, crenate-serrate. *Stipes* quadrangular, smooth. *Osmunda barbara*. Thb. Schkuhr. Icon. Filic., tab. 147.

In shady localities near rivulets, common all over the Cape colony and Natal. *v. v.* and *s.*

XV. MARATTIACEÆ. Sw.

L. MARATTIA. SW. (1 Species.)

147. *Marattia salicifolia*. Schrad. *Fronds* 2-pinnate, subcoriaceous; *pinnæ* oblong-lanceolate, alternate or opposite, stalked, patent, erect, acuminated; *pinnules* subsessile, lanceolate, cuneate at base, sharp pointed, acutely inflexo serrate, the terminal larger one often pinnatifid or lobed; *partial rachises* margined or winged in the upper portion, smooth. *Synangia* elliptical, remote from the edge and from one another. *Caudex* short, creeping, paleaceous. Schlecht. Adumb. p. 11. Kunze Linnæa, vol. 10, p. 488. Suppl. to Schkuhr. Icon., p. 79, tab. 38.

In the forests of the Tzitsikamma and Natal. (Drege, Gueinzius, &c.) *v. s.*

XVI. OPHIOGLOSSEÆ. R. Br.

LI. OPHIOGLOSSUM. LIN. (4 Species.)

148. *Ophioglossum nudicaule*. Lin. fil. *Frond* sessile, elliptical or lanceolate-ovate, sheathing, mucronate, reticulated,

placed near the middle of the *scape*. *Scape* short, slender 3-4-inches high, terminated by the linear, acuminated spike which bears the fructification ; *rhizome* fibrous. *O lusitanicum.* Thbg. Flor. Cap *O capense*. Schlecht Adumb. p. 9. tab. 1, fig. 2. Kunze Suppl. to Schkuhr. Filic., p. 59, tab. 29, fig. 3.

On grassy hills and at ditches near the Olifant's River (Mundt), at Gamka River and between the Bushmen's and Koega Rivers, (Eckl. & Zeyher.) *v. s.*

149. *Ophioglossum Bergianum*. Schlecht. *Scape* slender, 1½-2 inches high, naked ; *radical leaves* linear, narrow ; *spike* cylindrical, pointed; *rhizome* fascicled. Schlecht. Adumb., p. 10. Hook. Icon. Plant, vol. 3, tab. 263.

Amongst grasses at the base of Lion's Mountain. (Bergius Harvey, W. C. Faure); in turf near Kuil's River (June, 1845, Pappe.) *v. v.* and *s.*

150. *Ophioglossum reticulatum*. Lin. *Spike* arising from the stem; *frond* cordate-ovate, acute, loosely reticulated. Willd. Enum. Plant, p. 60.

Between grasses near the Umlaas River, Natal. (Dr. Krauss.)

151. *Ophioglossum costatum*. R. Br. *Spike* arising from the stem ; *frond* lanceolate-oblong, one-nerved, reticulated. R. Br. Prodr. Flor. Nov. Holland., p. 163.

Found somewhere in the colony by Capt. Carmichael ; special locality unknown. (Tulbagh ?)

XVII. LYCOPODIACEÆ. D. C.

LIII. LYCOPODIUM. LIN.. (9 Species.)

152. *Lycopodium carolinianum*. Lin. *Leaves* lanceolate, sub-falcate, acuminate, one-sided ; *stalks* erect, elongated, bearing one solitary cylindrical *spike* ; *bracts* auricled, sub-cordate, patent, pointed. *Stem* creeping, branchy. *L. repens*. Schlecht, p. 5, tab. 14.

In wet sandy soil on the Lion's Mountain (Rev. Hesse); in Attaquaskloof, Swellendam (Mundt.); at Hottentot's Holland, and Montagu's Pass (Eckl. & Zeyher.) *v. s.*

153. *Lycopodium cernuum*. Lin. *Leaves* awl-shaped, scattered, curved ; *terminal spikes* sessile, nodding ; *bracts* ovate,

acuminate-subulate, appressed, membranaceous; serrato-ciliate. *Stem* very branchy. Schlecht. Adumb., p. 5.

Near the hot springs of the Goudine (Mundt), near Klip River, Swellendam, and at Natal. (Dr. Krauss.) *v. s.*

154. *Lycopodium pygmæum.* Kaulf. Annual. *Leaves* scattered, sessile, ovate or ovate-lanceolate, squarrose; *spikes* terminal, oblong, sessile, solitary; *bracts* ovate, acuminated. *Stem* erect, simple, or rarely branched. Kaulf. Enum., Filic., p. 9. Schlecht. Adumb., p. 6., tab. 3.

Between grasses on the Lion's Rump, in the mountains of Hottentot's Holland, and in Grootvadersbosch, Swellendam. *v. v.* and *s.*

155. *Lycopodium gnidioides.* Sw. *Leaves* sessile, subcoriaceous, imbricated, oblong-obtuse, quite entire; *spikes* long, hexagonal, confluent; *bracts* ovate, leaflike, slightly acuminated. *Stem* dichotomous, leafy. Schlecht. Adumb., p. 7, tab. 2.

Upon the trunks of forest trees in the division of George (Bergius., Mundt.); in Blockhouse Kloof, near Graham's Town (Dr. Atherstone); at Natal (Gueinzius.) *v. s.*

Var. *pinifolia.* *Leaves* densely imbricated, coriaceous, decurrent, glossy; *spikes* two inches long, sessile, standing in pairs; *branches* dichotomous, fastigiate, curved at the apex; *bracts* keeled. *Stem* erect, 10-12 inches high. *Lycopodium pinifolium.* Kaulf. Enum., p. 7.

In the fissures of rocks on the summit of Table Mountain (Bergius., Chamisso, Zeyher, etc.) *v. v.* and *s.*

156. *Lycopodium clavatum.* Lin. *Leaves* nerveless, squarrose, incurved, hair-pointed; *spikes* in pairs, cylindrical, stalked; their *bracts* or scales ovate-acuminate, eroso-dentate. *Stem* creeping, long; *branches* ascending. Willd. Enum. Plant., vol. 5, p. 16. Schkuhr. Icon. Filic., tab. 162.

In damp, shady places on the mountains of Hottentot's Holland, and near Bethel, Kaffraria (Zeyher) *v. s.*

157. *Lycopodium verticillatum.* Lin. *Leaves* whorled, linear-lanceolate, acuminate, patent, quite entire, smooth. *Stem* dichotomous or twice 2-partite; *capsules* axillary. Willd. Sp. Plant., vol. 5, p. 48.

In shady localities in Makazan's country, Natal. (Plant.)

158. *Lycopodium rupestre.* Lin. *Leaves* scattered, imbricated, linear-lanceolate, ciliate, hair-pointed at the apex; *spikes* solitary, sessile, terminal, erect, quadrangular; *scales* keeled, 2-lobed at base; *capsules* kidney-shaped. *Stem* creeping, branchy. Willd. Enum. Plant., vol. 5, p. 30. Schkuhr. Icon. Filic., tab. 165.

Between rocks on the banks of the Omzamcaba River, Natal. (Drege. Plant) *v. s.*

159. *Lycopodium setaceum.* Hamilt. *Leaves* whorled, linear, bristly at top, curved; *capsules* axillary, reniform. *Stem* slender, dichotomously branched, creeping. Kze. Linnæa., vol. 18, p. 113

Parasitical on trees in the forests of Natal, between the Omfondi and Togela rivers. (Gueinzius.) *v. s.*

160. *Lycopodium Kraussianum.* Kze. *Leaves* remote, oblong, acuminated, obliquely cordate and aurialcd at base, scabrid, margined, ciliated; *stipules* sub-erect lanceolate-ovate, falcate, rounded at base. *Stem* creeping, branchy; *branches* rather erect, dichotomous. Kze. Linnæa., vol. 18, p. 114.

In the forests of the Tzitsikamma (Dr. Krauss.), near Chakaa's Kraal, Natal (Gueinzius.) *v s.*

LIV. PSILOTUM. SW. (1 Species.)

161. *Psilotum triquetrum.* Sw. *Stem* angular, smooth, dichotomously branched about its middle; *branches* 3-cornered, acuminate, fructiferous; *leaves* sessile, alternate, remote, acute, very remote; those subtending the fruit deeply 2-partite; *spores* kidney-shaped. *Bernhardia dichotoma.* Willd. Schkuhr., Icon. Filic., tab. 165, b. Hook. genera Filic.. tab. 87.

Parasitical on trees in the forests of Natal. (Gueinzius.) *v. s.*

APPENDIX.

1. *Aspidium* (Polystichum?) *stramineum*. Kaulf. *Fronds* 2-pinnate; *pinnæ* oblong-trapeziform, mucronate, serrate, auricled at base, rather hairy below; *sori* scattered, placed near the margin; *rachis* and *stipes* very scaly. *K. Sprengel*, in Linn. Syst. Veget., vol. 4, p. 105.

2. *Aspidium* (Lastrea?) *oppositum*. Kaulf. *Fronds* 3-pinnate or supra-decompound, lower *pinnæ* opposite, 2-pinnatifid, smooth; their *pinnules* one-sided, oblong-lanceolate, decurrent, confluent at base; tertiary *inferior pinnæ* ovate-oblong, entire; *terminal ones* rather acute, sub-dentate. *Sori* solitary; *rachis* sparingly scaly. *Sprengel.* l. c., p. 108.

3. *Asplenium flexuosum*. Schrad. *Fronds* pinnate; *pinnæ* ovate-lanceolate, acute, pinnatifid; *segments* lanceolate-cuneate, truncate, 2-dentate at the apex; *lower ones* deeper incised; *uppermost* confluent; *rachis* flexuose, glabrous. *Schlecht.* Adumb., p. 29. (*A. discolor. Nob. ?*)

Locality not recorded. (Rev. Mr. Hesse.)

4. *Pteris cuspidata*. Thbg. *Fronds* pinnate, smooth; *pinnæ* alternate on very short stalks, lanceolate, cuspidate, serrate, straight-veined. *Stipes* half-round, doubly channelled, glabrous, 12 inches high. Thbg. Flor. Cap., p. 732.

5. *Pteris tabularis*. Thbg. *Fronds* pinnate, glabrous; *pinnæ* alternate, sessile, approximate, lanceolate, veiny; *lower ones* short; *terminal pinnæ* 3-5 fid. *Stipes* half-round, channelled, smooth. *Caudex* clothed with long ferruginous scales. Thbg. Flor. Cap., p. 732.

In moist places on Table Mountain. (Thunberg.)

6. *Pteris* (Allosorus?) *involuta*. Sw. *Fronds* 2-pinnate, oblong-lanceolate; *pinnæ* opposite, oblong, short; *pinnules* alternate, adnate, subcordate-ovate, blunt; *terminal one* 3-lobed or hastate, all of them entire, subinvolute, glabrous. *Fructification* marginal, continuous. *Stipes* round, black-purple, glossy, sparingly palcaceous. Schlecht. Adumb., p. 46.

I

7. *Onychium capense.* Kaulf. This Fern had been mistaken for a South African plant by former botanists. It is, in fact, a native of Japan, and described as *Trichomanes japonicum* by Thunberg. *Onychium japonicum.* Kze.

8. *Dicksonia anthriscifolia.* Kaulf. *Fronds* 3-pinnate, ample spreading ; *pinnæ* ovate-oblong, pinnatifid nearly to the costa ; *segments* oval-oblong, obtuse, dentate, soriferous in the axils of the teeth ; *rachis* glabrous ; *costa* and *veins* slightly hairy. Hook. Spec. Filic., vol. 1, p. 79, tab. 27 B. Kze. Linnæa., vol. 10, p. 545. *Cheilanthes anthriscifolia* (Willd?) *Lonchitis anthriscifolia.* Bory. (Perhaps identical with *Hypolepis anthriscifolia.* Presl.)

Locality unknown. (Bergius.)

9. *Adiantum thalictroides.* Willd. *Fronds* 3-4-pinnate ; *upper pinnules* stalked, semi-orbicular, cuneate-subtruncate, slightly lobed ; *lobes* emarginate, soriferous; *involucres* kidney-shaped. *Stipes* roundish, smooth, black-purple, glossy. Schlecht. Adumb., p. 53. (Probably a variety of *A. æthiopicum.* Lin.)

On the north side of Table Mountain. (Bergius.)

10. *Adiantum rotundatum.* Kze. *Fronds* pinnate, linear-lanceolate, smooth ; *pinnæ* alternate, stalked, approximate, transversely-oblong, subfalcate, blunt; *terminal ones* small, obovate, truncate at base ; *upper edge* and apex inciso-lobate; *lobes* obtuse, toothed at the top ; *fertile ones* incised ; *involucres* large, reniform; the base of the glabrous *stipes* and the *rachis* chaffy. Hook. Spec. Filic., vol. 2, p. 53, Kze. Linnæa, vol. 10, p. 528.

Locality unknown.

11. *Polypodium argentatum.* Jacq. *Frond* 2-pinnatifid, smooth, silvery at the underside; *pinnæ* alternate, lanceolate, pinnate at the base ; *segments* lance-shaped, subdentate, elongated. *Sori* clustered in the middle of the disk. *Sprengel.* Lin. System Vegetab., vol. 4, p. 56.

12. *Polypodium tomentosum.* Thouars. *Fronds* 2-pinnatifid and, as well as the *stipes*, shaggy ; *pinnæ* alternate, lanceolate ; *lobes* oval, blunt, subcrenate. *Sori* in one single row on each side of the midrib. Spreng. l. c., p. 59. (Could this be *Polypodium Bergianum.* Schlecht?)

13. *Vittaria* (*Tænitis?*) *acrostichoides*. Hook. and Grev., *Fronds* stipitate, coriaceous, lanceolate, blunt; *fertile ones* linear. *Sori* submarginal. Hook. and Grev. Icon. Filic., tab. 186. Kunze Linn., vol. 10, p. 528. (*Pteropsis angustifolia*. Desv.?)

Found somewhere in the colony; locality however, unknown. (Rev. Mr. Thom, Caledon?)

14. *Hymenophyllum flabellatum*. Labil. *Fronds* flaccid, curved, ovate or oblong, acuminate, pinnate; *pinnæ* sharp-pointed, pinnatifid; the *lower segments* subflabellate, all of them blunt or emarginate. *Involucres* terminal, nearly orbicular; *valves* entire. *Stipes* round, smooth. Hook. Spec. Filic., vol. 1, p. 111. Kaulfuss in Linnæa., vol. 6, p. 187.

15. *Lycopodium ambiguum*. Schrad. *Leaves* arranged in 6 or 8 rows, scattered, linear-lanceolate, subfalcate, acute, quite entire, imbricated, patent. *Stems* simple, ascending from the base. Schlecht. Adumb., p. 8.

Habitat not known. (Rev. Mr. Hesse.)

16. *Lycopodium depressum*. Sw. *Stem* branchy; *branches* very short; *leaves* in a double row, alternate, ovate, acute, obsoletely toothed, patent; *stipules* leaflike, ciliated. *Spikes* sessile, leafy, oblong. Schlecht. Adumb., p. 8. Spreng. Lin. Syst. Veget. vol. 4, p. 17.

In conclusion, we have to notice a very singular plant, which, for some time, had been mistaken for a Fern. We allude to the *Lomaria eriopus* of Kunze., mentioned in the Linnæa., vol. 13, p. 152, and vol. 18, p. 116. It does not belong, however, to the Filical tribe, but to the natural order of *Cycadeæ*, and has been named by Mr. Moore in honour of the late Dr. Stanger, Surveyor-General of Natal. Cf. Hooker's Jour. of Bot., and Kew Gard. Miscellany, v. 5, p. 228.

Stangeria paradoxa. T. Moore. (l. c.) *Stem* simple, erect, 6-8 inches high, without scars. *Frond* single, pinnate, coriaceous. *Stipes* stiff, smooth, 2 feet long, sprinkled with numerous minute dots, and clothed with white shag at its lower extremity. *Pinnæ* opposite, sessile, lanceolate, marginate, very veiny, obtuse, unequal at base and decurrent on the inferior side; *lowermost pinnæ* subpetiolate, patent, all of them slightly waved, reflexed, and obsoletely toothed at the edges; *midrib* stout, rigid, prominent on both surfaces; *veins* divergent, parallel, forked once or twice near the costa. *Rachis* doubly channelled at the upper extremity.

Flowers unisexual, without either calyx or corolla, and collected in stalked, terminal, resiniferous cones; *peduncle* round, furrowed, spirally twisted, tomentose. *Male cone* 3½ inches long and two inches thick, formed of numerous imbricated, rigid scales which bear on their lower or inner side innumerable, irregularly grouped *anthers* or one-celled pollen-cells which are longitudinally split. *Scales* broad, 3-angular, connate and appressed at base, blunt, serrato-crenate at the margin, smooth on the inner, densely clothed with thick fulvous felt on the outer surface.

Female cone oblong-ovate, broad, 3 inches long, 4 inches in circumference. *Scales* like those of the male plant, but larger, concave within, saccate, and perforated on each side of the base by a small roundish aperture or sinus, which is destined for the insertion of the ovules. Ripe fruit hitherto unknown.*

* The description of the female cone was drawn from an immature specimen. " I find it impossible," says Mr. Plant (who sent it from Natal) " to preserve the female cones if suffered to reach a larger size on the plant. The process of ripening goes on till the whole falls to pieces."

INDEX.

SAUL SOLOMON AND CO., STEAM PRINTING OFFICE, CAPE TOWN.

www.ingramcontent.com/pod-product-compliance
Lightning Source LLC
Chambersburg PA
CBHW030837270326
41928CB00007B/1092